ENGLISH-SPEAKING CARIBBEAN IMMIGRANTS

Transnational Identities

Edited by

Lear Matthews

University Press of America,® Inc.
Lanham · Boulder · New York · Toronto · Plymouth, UK

Copyright © 2014 by
University Press of America,® Inc.
4501 Forbes Boulevard
Suite 200
Lanham, Maryland 20706
UPA Acquisitions Department (301) 459-3366

10 Thornbury Road
Plymouth PL6 7PP
United Kingdom

All rights reserved
Printed in the United States of America
British Library Cataloging in Publication Information Available

Library of Congress Control Number: 2013945221
ISBN: 978-0-7618-6202-4 (clothbound : alk. paper)
eISBN: 978-0-7618-6203-1

Cover image, interior design, and author photograph
by Ashton Franklin

∞™ The paper used in this publication meets the minimum
requirements of American National Standard for Information
Sciences—Permanence of Paper for Printed Library Materials,
ANSI Z39.48-1992

Dedication

This book is dedicated to the English-speaking Caribbean Immigrant population whose hopes and dreams must be realized, with feet in two worlds. To my brother Pat Matthews, whose perseverance and strength shine beneath the darkness of lost sight, despite his inability to see the beauty of either world. In memory of my brother Clem, whose world view inspired me to write.

Contents

Foreword   vii

Acknowledgements   ix

Introduction   xi

1. Transnationalism: Trends and Practices among English Speaking Caribbean Immigrants   Lear Matthews   1

2. Migratory Patterns and Experiences of Anglophone Caribbean Women   Mary Spooner   17

3. Migration and Occupational Change   Lear Matthews   33

4. Transnational Parenting in the African Caribbean Community   Christiana Best-Cummings   53

5. Transnational Migration: The Elderly and Healthcare   Joyce Hamilton-Henry and Beverley Russell   73

6. Caribbean Immigrant Families: Transnational Identity   Annette Mahoney and Lear Matthews   95

7. Hometown Associations: Needs and Challenges   Lear Matthews   113

8. English-Speaking Caribbean Immigrant Students: Providing Culturally Competent Educational Services   Lear Matthews and Rosalind October-Edun   137

9. Indo and Afro-Guyanese Immigrants in New York City: An Analysis of Selected Transnational Experiences   Desmond Roberts   167

Notes on Contributors   199

Index   203

Foreword

In a growing interconnected global society, with spiraling migratory streams worldwide, it becomes increasingly difficult for researchers and students of immigration to deal with new and previously unarticulated questions which emanated from transnationalism. This book highlights a diverse range of issues relating to the transnational experiences of English Speaking Caribbean Immigrants in the United States. Few students of international migration envisioned the changes in migration trends, policies and events that have shaped the immigration process at the onset of the 21st Century. Informed by their experiences as educators, researchers and community advocates, the chapter contributors focus on the successes made and challenges that confront this population as they sustain connections and identities with their sending societies. At the core of these presentations is the exploration of the "lived experiences" of Caribbean immigrants and the institutions through which they bridge nation-states, while maintaining a transnational life style. Drawing from empirical data and theoretical assumptions on the topic, the intent is to continue the tradition of international migration scholars who recognize the centrality of the impact of contemporary migration on the lives of people and institutions, thus providing a lens for understanding current and future transnational relationships. Possible solutions and intervention strategies to emerging problems are also presented. Ultimately, analyses of the various topics were informed by my experience in research and teaching in the Caribbean and US, and ongoing interaction within a transnational environment.

Lear Matthews
New York
February 2013

Acknowledgements

The seeds of this book were planted over many years of observing and experiencing the bi-cultural context of living in two worlds. Once I decided to launch the project and grasped the realization of the challenge of documenting the multidimensional relationships of a prominent immigrant population, I invited contribution of scholars and practitioners who represent a cross-section of the subject matter. I extend my gratitude to the writers who have contributed to this book. Despite personal and professional commitments, they embarked upon the task with enthusiasm and unwavering perseverance. Each scholar was particularly excited to be part of researching and documenting experiences and relationships with which they could identify. Indeed, they found the idea of "stepping back" and objectively examining aspects of a culture some of them may have lived as both intriguing and motivating.

Special thanks to Aubrey Bonnet, Michael Parris, and John Maxwell for their generosity, time and effort in critically reviewing the chapters. I am also grateful to Juliet Carol Powdar, for her expert editing, Ashton Franklin, for his guidance in the technical dimensions of this project, including type-setting and designing the cover, Justin Giordano who provided critical legal advice and Jennifer Pyne, an efficient proof reader. Finally, I am forever indebted to my family: Monica, Dion, Malindi and Nicola for their patience and encouragement.

Introduction

> "You can never go home again, but the truth is,
> You can never leave home, so it's alright"
> —*Maya Angelou*

This book highlights important but insufficiently documented dimensions of the experience of English-speaking Caribbean immigrants in the United States. It focuses on successes and challenges of socio-cultural adaptation, as many of these immigrants cope with new realities of what might be perceived as living in two worlds. The central theme, post-migration transnational connections and identity, is informed by new research on the topic (Healy and Link, 2012; Acosta and de la Cruz, 2011; Orozco, 2010; Bonnet, 2010; Bacon, 2008; Portes and Rumbaut, 2006; Mills, 2005; Goulbourne, 2002; Levitt and Jaworsky, 2007).

The world in which immigrants live has changed dramatically. At the same time that globalization has facilitated the dispersion of families around the world, communication has become cheaper and more accessible. Long-distance phone calls, international airfare, the Internet and cell phones have facilitated ties to their homelands. In recent years, studies on transnationalism have emerged to describe the ties and relationships that span across sending and receiving societies (Tilly, 2007; Mills, 2005; Orozco, 2003; Glick-Schiller et al. 1992; Levitt and Jaworsky, 2007; Portes, 2006; Vertovec, 2001)

The socio-cultural ties that link immigrants to the home country and the native-born population influence how they structure their lives, socialize their children, worship, and express their political views (Levitt, 2001). These ties practically define their life space. No longer is it fashionable for immigration scholars to promote the argument that it is necessary for immigrants to abandon their customs, language, values, homeland practices and identities in order to achieve socioeconomic progress (Levitt and Glick Schiller, 2004).

For many immigrants, the bicultural experience creates the opportunity to maximize the acquisition of various resources that enhance life chances in the new society, while retaining vital connections with the country of origin. For others, however, creating opportunities sometimes occur at the expense of losing connections with the home country, depending on factors such as age, occupational skills, human capital, immigration status and identification with the immigrant community. Whether the decision to migrate is voluntary or driven by unconventional socio-political circumstances, can also impact the extent of sustained links with the home country.

A significant aspect of the transnational lifestyle of today's immigrants that requires further exploration is the ongoing linkage with the home country that is increasingly facilitated by the attributes of modernity such as the internet, globalizatio, and efficiency in transporting remittances. Since the late 1990's, there has been a surge in organized Diaspora activities among English-speaking Caribbean immigrants, particularly through social networking, and collective remittances, essentially sustaining an ardent bridge between countries of origin and the adopted country. Turner (1991) notes that due to global structural shifts and technological advances, "it is now more likely that people will maintain connections in two or more locations over extended periods of time . . . " (p. 407).

A series of policies since the mid-1960 has resulted in a realignment in the thinking about the immigrant experience. The gist of these policies is informed by the perception of, and response to immigration in North America, as well as extraneous events that appear to change the status quo in American society. Few social analysts envisioned the trends, issues and experiences of newly arrived immigrants in the first decade of the 21st century following the passage of the 1965 U.S. Immigration and Naturalization Act. With its emphasis on family reunification, the Immigration and Naturalization Act removed the national origins quota system, resulting in an increased flow of immigrants from the Caribbean and Latin America, Africa and Asia.

The connection between sending countries and the US as host country has intensified as a result of the family-sponsoring system, in which host relatives and those awaiting sponsorship to the United States became engaged in an extended process of planning, travel and unrelenting communication across nations. However, by 1986, the Immigration Reform and Control Act of 1986 (IRCA) modified the flow of immigrants through border enforcement, legalization and employment sanctions. As a result, the relationship between immigrants and their adopted society was not only carefully monitored but also redefined.

By 1996, the Illegal Immigration Reform and Immigrant Responsibility Act further reframed the immigration rules, resulting in a noticeable transformation of the newcomers' reality. This law instituted drastic changes in policies affecting admission, deportation and entitlements for legal permanent residents (LPR's). Controls were established on the granting of visas and limitations on social service benefits were further restricted.

More recently, perspectives on immigration status and patriotism have been significantly altered after the World Trade Center tragedy of September 2001. Overarching policies regarding homeland security have changed relations between native-born and immigrant populations since the World Trade Center act of terrorism. This has resulted in an unprecedented broadly defined response to the war on terrorism. Further, the debate regarding undocumented immigrants, the reluctance of US lawmakers to move forward with comprehensive immigration reform, the increase in the number of deportees, Secure Communities Programs, and more restrictive proposals highlight the need to examine the effects on transmigration. What has generally been a topic of some national importance has become a simmering social issue churned by politics, economics and sentiments relating to ethnocentric ideals.

Concomitantly, cultural globalzation, which emphasizes increased cross-cultural contacts and interaction among diverse populations and institutions throughout the world, has only partially begun to explain the links between immigrants' adopted home and their country of birth. Ongoing exchange of goods and services, as well as reciprocation of ideas, ideals, cultural styles and humanitarian causes through various forms of communication, continues to enhance the transnational process. Foner (1997) asserts that cultural practices are kept alive by "strong immigrant communities and institutions, dense ethnic networks and continued transnational ties to the sending society" (p. 963). Thus, the transnational lifestyle that emerges features a "paradox of distance and closeness" involving opportunities and challenges (Orozco, 2008). Within this context, maintaining actual or symbolic transnational attachments to the home country serves as a catalyst in the interpersonal and social adaptation process.

English speaking Caribbean immigrants are among the burgeoning numbers of people comprising the most recent wave of new global citizens in North America. They have become part of an expanding 'West Indian Diaspora', primarily represented by Afro-Caribbean and Indo-Caribbean people. Since the early 1990's, there has been exponential growth in the population of Caribbean people throughout the United States (US Department of Census, 2005). However, because of the English-speaking Caribbean population's familiarity with the language and customs of the native-born English speakers, especially African-Americans, their identities have often not been sufficiently distinct from this group to enable researchers to study and understand them. Thus, a legitimate and recurring question lingers-who are the English-speaking Caribbean immigrants and what are their experiences as transnationals?

The English-speaking Caribbean countries are part of the former British West Indies. They include the independent countries of Jamaica, Guyana, Barbados, Trinidad and Tobago, Grenada, St. Lucia, St. Vincent, Dominica, Antigua, St. Kitts-Nevis, Belize and The Bahamas, as well as the small British colonial territories of Anguilla, British Virgin Islands, Montserrat, Cayman, and the Turks and Caicos Islands.

The people from these nations share common cultural characteristics, including language, closely related history and pattern of social and political evolution. They also account for the largest number of immigrants from the non-Hispanic Caribbean. Some of these countries, in particular Jamaica, Guyana, and Trinidad and Tobago, are among the top sending sources of the newest immigrants in the United States (New York City Department of City Planning, 2010). Not only are these sending countries geographically larger than the other countries in the Anglophone Caribbean, but immigrants from these countries are among those that are numerically well represented in the migrant labor force and communities throughout the United States.

The dynamics of transnational migration within the context of contemporary American society are shaped by a confluence of historical trends, perceptions, misconceptions, empirical knowledge about immigrant populations, political ideology and expressed preferences of both new comers and the host society. The themes of the chapters in this book are framed by these considerations, in addition to the realities of globalization and its implications for transnational identity. The lived experiences of this author and other chapter contributors as immigrants to the US also inform the discourse about immigrant experience thereby making a profound contribution to the transmigration literature.

The intent is to fill the current information gap on this topic so that educators, human service professionals, social scientists, students across disciplines, and policy makers can better understand the context of the English-speaking population's transnational experiences. Central to the presentations in this book is the cultural context within which transformations in Caribbean immigrants' lives occur, manifested through transnational practices, the influence of modernity, economic and political realities, modifications in family constellations, and coping with the stress of migration. This is not to say that the issues and structures described represent the prototype for the Caribbean immigrant experience. However, we hope that the conceptualizations, discussion and conclusions set the stage for continued analysis of the topic.

Chapter I examines the framework for understanding transnational migration, as presented in the literature and the ways in which trends and practices reflect the experience of English-speaking Caribbean immigrants. The experience of Anglophone Caribbean women is the focus of Chapter II. Often considered pioneers among immigrant groups to the United States, these women have been central to the economic, domestic and emotional support spheres at home and abroad. Their role as parents, including socialization agents and as purveyors of connectedness with the home country is explored. The cultural traditions, compromises and challenges resulting from changing gender roles and rewards that characterize their experience are critically examined, with notable implications for immigrant women in general. Chapter III focuses on an often under reported, but significant aspect of the transnational experience, i.e. the incongruence created when newly arrived professional immigrants accept employment that is not commensurate with their training and education. Professionals, including medical doctors, engineers, teachers, and high level government officials have been known to settle for menial jobs they would not accept in their home country. Forced to emigrate because of changing global conditions or the desire to reap better returns for their investment in their education and training, these professionals are often required to make adjustments in personal characteristics/values, and even demeanor, as well as professional habits. A hidden aspect of this experience, i.e. the stress of altered socio-economic status along with their adaptive strategies, is explored in this chapter.

In Chapter IV, the author explores the phenomenon of transnational parenting in the African Caribbean community that is identified as invoking sympathy for children and criticism of mothers who migrate leaving youngsters behind. However, it gives a voice to the African Caribbean mothers who experience transnational parenting firsthand and illuminates their experiences.

Chapter V examines the experience of elder Caribbean immigrants as they attempt to cope with healthcare and wellness issues within the context of transnationalism. Often representing a neglected dimension of transnational migration, the measure of prosperity or despair among the elderly is ostensibly determined by the availability of healthcare and other resources within and outside the Diaspora.

Chapter VI focuses on the unique challenges faced by Caribbean immigrant families within a cultural context that demands a merging of a dominant, often unfamiliar culture with their own. The role of transnational communities and the function of family/kinship networks in identity formation are explored. The cultural stressors of 'translocation' with regard to these families and the impact on gender roles are also examined.

The data for Chapter VII were collected for a presentation on the topic, Hometown Associations (HTAs), at the Ninth Caribbean and International Social Work Educators Conference in Martinique. The chapter initially outlines the merits of Hometown Associations that have become increasingly instrumental in sustaining transnational connections in the Caribbean Diaspora. The development and integration functions of these organizations have been plagued by engagement barriers and delivery difficulties. The author argues for a more prominent role of 'helping professionals' such as social workers in rendering HTAs more effective and sustainable. This topic is particularly significant in light of the emerging interest of Caribbean governments in Diaspora Development Projects.

In Chapter VIII, the author utilizes qualitative methods to gain insight into the experiences of teachers and related staff from New York City Public Schools that serve large numbers of Caribbean immigrant students of African and East Indian heritage. The chapter examines the policies and procedures that schools enact to ensure a smooth transition, and the level of cultural competence brought to bear in their work with these children. The study is informed by theoretical formulations of empowerment-based practice, including the strength perspective and NASW (National Association of Social Workers) standards for cultural competence. Chapter IX presents a perspective on the migratory experience of immigrants from one of the major English Caribbean sending countries. The author notes that the pre- and post-independence social and economic conditions in the home country, "fell neatly into a serendipitous immigration spiral to developed countries such as the United States . . . the migration story continues, leading to an ongoing relationship between these Guyanese immigrants and their homeland".

The chapters presented in this book purport to identify essential dimensions of Caribbean immigrants' attempt to reconcile their transitional experiences, encapsulated by elements of two different social contexts. In the pursuit of a 'better life', key indicators of this existential duality include the interpersonal and sociological adaptations these newcomers are required to make in a 21st century international arena vastly different from the experience of the "old immigration" of the 19th century.

Post-migration life experiences among transnationals of various immigration statuses (i.e. documented and undocumented) in a number of areas are not sufficiently understood. Likewise, some of the consequencesof globalization and economic crises increasingly forge immigrants to have 'feet in two worlds'. Meaningful conclusions about how immigrants make the transition successfully while maintaining cultural 'roots' can be drawn from the topics discussed.

The book presents both an academic and applied approach. The thrust is not only on trends, theories and policies pertaining to the issues addressed, but includes possible solutions to problems these immigrants, change agents and policy analysts confront. Scholars of international migration emphasize the importance of verifiable evidence to inform this emerging discussion (Goulbourne, 2002; Levitt and Glick Schiller, 2004). This book attempts to answer that call. The topics presented are empirically validated and theoretically informed. Some of the prevailing assumptions and responses of both sending and receiving societies are captured and unraveled.

Drawing from the conceptualization and conclusions of studies on the topic, and more significantly, the voices and expressions of immigrants themselves, the chapters identify and examine a range of critical issues and situations that define the English Caribbean transnational experience. Possible solutions to emerging concerns, as well as intervention strategies, are also presented.

Social scientists, graduate and undergraduate students interested in international migration, could benefit from the themes as a basis for further research on challenges faced by immigrants, as well as their accomplishments through collective effort. Hopefully, the ideas and strategies put forward will contribute to the on-going cumulative inquiry of the topic and could help policy decision makers to maintain a global vision. Educators and human service professionals working with immigrants will be able to draw from these presentations as part of the knowledge-base for effective planning, teaching and intervention. We hope that the book would also be a reliable source of information for the casual reader who wants to know more about the subject of Transnationalism.

Bibliography

Anjelou, M. (2005). *The Sun Magazine.* Issue 356. Chapel Hill, NC. August.

Bacon, D. (2008). *Illegal Peple: How Globalization Creates Migration and Criminalizes Immigrants.* Boston, Beacon Press.

Basch, L.G., N.G. Schiller and C. Blanc-Szanton (1994). *Nations Unbound: Transnational Projects, Post Colonial Predicaments, and De-Territorialized Nation States.* Langhorne, PA: Gordon & Breach.

Bonnett, A. W. (2011). Wendell Bell, "The Democratic Revolution in the West Indies: Some Reflections On the Past, Present, and Future": *Futures,* Volume 43, Issue 6, August

Caribbean Media Enterprise (2005). Collaboration of Caribbean Media & Social Science Project. Symposium on Strengthening Caribbean American Media, Queens, NY.

Crowder, K. and Tedrow, L. (2001). West Indian and Residential Landscape. In N. Foner's *Island in the City: West Indian Migration to New York.* Berkeley: University of California Press, pp 81-114.

Foner, N. (1997). "The Immigrant Family: Cultural Legacies and Cultural Changes." *International Migration Review* Volume 31, Number 4. (Winter).

Goulbourne, H. (2002). *Caribbean Transnational Experiences.* Kingston, Jamaica : Arawak Publications.

Healy, L and R. J. Link (2012). *Handbook of International Social Work: Human Rights, Development, and the Global Profession.* New York: Oxford University Press.

Kasinitz, P. (1993). *Caribbean New York: Black Immigrants and the Politics of Race.* New York: Cornell University Press.

Levitt (2001). "Transnational Migration: Taking stock and Future Directions." Global Networks 1, 3: 195-216.

Levitt, P. and N. Jaworsky (2007). "Transnational Migration Studies: Past Developments and Future Trends." *Annual Review of Sociology.* Vol 33: 129-158. August.

Levitt, P. and N. Glick Schiller (2004). "Conceptualizing Simultaneity: A Transnational Social Field Perspective on Society." *International Migration Review,* 38 (145): 595-629, Fall.

Mills, B.H. (2005). "The Transnational Community as an Agent for Caribbean Development." *Southern Geographer,* Vol. 45, Issue 2.

Murphy, J. (2010). The Immigrant March: New York's Homelands. *City Limits.*

Orozco, M. (2003). "Remitting Back Home and Supporting the Homeland: The Guyanese Community in the U.S." Washington, DC: U.S. *Agency for International Development.*

Tilly, C. (2007). "Trust Networks in Transnational Migration." *Sociological Forum.* Vol. 22, No. 1.

Trotz, A. (2006). "Rethinking Caribbean Transnational Connections: Conceptual Itineraries." *Global Networks.* Vol. 6. Issue 1.

Turner, J. (1991). "Migrants and Their Therapists: A Trans-Context Approach." *Family Process.* Vol. 30 (December).

United States Department of Census, Census Bureau (2010).

United States Department of Census, Census Bureau (2000).

Valdez, R.S. (2006). "Transnationality – A New Phase of Migration." *New York Liberty Star,* Friday, May 12.

Vertovec S. (2009). *Transnationalism.* New York: Routledge Publishing Company.

Chapter One

Transnationalism: Trends and Practices among English-Speaking Caribbean Immigrants

Lear Matthews

INTRODUCTION

Transnational migration has long been a major feature of Caribbean life. The rapidly globalizing world and the implementation of more stringent immigration policies and practices following the World Trade Center tragedy in 2001 have further influenced the level and nature of transactions conducted by Caribbean immigrants across national boundaries. Reciprocal transnational ties between countries of settlement and homelands usually extend beyond the private sphere of the family and friends and are being sustained through new forms of communication technology and by frequent movement to and from primary countries of residence. This chapter focuses on the trends and practices of English-Speaking Caribbean Immigrants as transnationals.

Transnationalism, viewed as connections and interactions that link people and institutions across nation-states, has emerged as a concept to describe new identities and communities in a global world (Vertovec, 2009). Kasinitz (1992) notes that long-term transmigration of Caribbean people has greatly impacted their societies. As a result of resource depletion, isolation, population changes, and restricted opportunities, they have used migration "as a survival strategy whenever they were free to do so. In much of the Anglophone Caribbean, migration has become a normal and expected part of the adult life cycle, a virtual rite of passage" (p. 20).

Increases in communication and mobility of financial and human capital have made it possible for immigrants to be grounded in two different countries at once. With the emergence of transnational migration studies, the focus of international migration has largely shifted from examining immigrant integration in receiving nations to exploring their transnational behaviors. As Levitt and Glick Schiller

(2004) observe, even when 'remaining ethnic' became more fashionable, it was believed that sustained contacts with the home country would decrease. That was not to be.

Today's Immigrants as Transnationals

Scholars of international migration have increasingly recognized that immigrants maintain ties with their countries of origin in ways and means not practiced in earlier times (Levitt and Jaworsky, 2007; Vertovec, 2009; Sorensen, 2007; Foner, 2001). In the early 1960's, the word "transnational" was widely used by students of economic processes to refer to the establishment of corporate structures with organizational bases to more than one state (Martinelli, 1982).

In a separate intellectual tradition, several generations of scholars have been using the adjective, "transnational", to signal an abatement of national boundaries and development of ideas or political institutions that span national borders. Transnational migration in the United States has been shaped by its critique of the unilinear assimilationist paradigms of classic migration theory and research. Basch, Schiller and Blanc-Szanton (1994) suggest that the emergence of "transnationalism" as a key field of study in the international migration arena only began in the latter part of the 1980's. They note that scholars of transnational culture speak in the vocabulary of postmodernism and make reference to hybridity, hyperspace, displacement, disjuncture, centering and Diaspora. Further, transnational migration and movements are informed by the conditions of global capitalism (Hondagneu-Sotelo, 2012).

The constant, yet unevenly distributed flow of capital and labor across borders and between nations are not solely an economic process, but it also affects social identities and cultural relations across ethnicity, gender and race. Scholars have turned to the notion of transnationalism to conceptualize what many see as new immigrants' identities and communities (Kivisto, 2001). In the United States, several researchers have viewed immigrants as persons who have uprooted themselves, leaving behind home and country and face the painful process of incorporation into a different society and culture (Basch et. al., 1994). It is now recognized that "some migrants and their descendants remain strongly influenced by their continuing ties to their homeland or by social networks that stretch across national borders" (Levitt and Glick Schiller, 2004). Many maintain ties to their country of origin, at the same time becoming integrated into the country that receives them.

Immigrant incorporation and enduring transnational practices are not antithetical, but simultaneous processes that mutually inform each other (Levitt and Glick Schiller, 2004; Morawska, 2011).

The process of transnationalism involves groups of people who are connected in some significant ways to maintain close links across the boundaries of nation-states. It may include residing in, or holding citizenship in two societies simultaneously. This situation may be caused by voluntary migration, move across borders due to natural disasters or civil unrest which results in "streams of refugees and asylum seekers who maintain close and living links with their homeland" (Goulbourne, 2002, p. 6).

An important dimension of this relationship is the role of "trust networks", which define expected responsibilities and obligations among immigrants and relatives in the home country. Tilly (2007) posits that these networks have a key role in the "organization, maintenance, and transformation of long-distance migration stream . . . within them, remittance flows reinforce commitments among all participants in the stream" (p. 5).

Transnational migration, then, is the process by which immigrants forge and sustain simultaneous multi-stranded social relations that link together their societies of origin and settlement. In so doing, they "create transnational communities at different stages of development retaining ties to their communities of origin and establish new communities as they migrate in search of work" (Bacon, 2008, p. 252). The term "transnational" is also used to signal the fluidity with which ideas, objects, capital and people now move across boundaries. In identifying a new process of migration, scholars emphasize the ongoing ways in which current-day immigrants construct and reconstitute their simultaneous embeddedness in more than one society (Glick Schiller, Basch, Szanton and Blanc, 1994).

Caribbean Immigrants: Who are They?

Caribbean peoples have been immigrating to the United States since the early 19th century and by the beginning of the 20th century, their numbers had begun to increase substantially (Ueda, 2011), making them one of the largest foreign-born groups residing in states such as New York, New Jersey and Florida. Caribbean and West Indian are terms that are used interchangeably in reference to a group of people from an archipelago of islands which stretch from the tip of Florida to the coast of South America. This definition usually includes some people from outside the region, including Guyana in South America and segments of the population in Panama, Costa Rica and Belize, where ethnic enclaves of predominantly English-speaking people reside.

There is considerable cultural and ethnic heterogeneity among Caribbean peoples. However, most share the common legacy of European colonialism, African and East Indian ancestry. These shared common experiences work in tandem to shape what may be described as a unique Caribbean culture, a culture that extends far beyond the distinct speech patterns, food and music. Vestiges of colonialism is still evident in many of the social and political institutions within the region – the structures of educational and legal systems, and possibly in the migratory practices of Caribbean peoples (Mahoney, 2004).

Transnational Experiences: Patterns and Challenges

Transnational migration is a central part of the English Caribbean immigrants' social life and political economy. They have immigrated to the United States, Canada and other countries in the region. Specifically, Caribbean people of African descent have been among "the most mobile members of the African Diaspora within the Caribbean and the Americas" (Goulbourne, 2002, p.8). Their numbers have increased significantly post 1965, subsequent to changes in the U.S. immigration legislation that abolished national-origins quotas and changed the preference system, prioritizing admission based on family reunification and job skills (e.g. the Hart Celler Act of 1965 and the Immigration Reform and Control Act of 1986). More than 1 million "West Indians" have been granted legal immigrant status, with over 600,000 of these arriving between 1981 and 1996 (U.S. Immigration and Naturalization Service cited by Crowder and Tedrow, 2001).

Notwithstanding the various levels of success of Caribbean states in responding to the fundamental needs of the people and transition from a legacy of colonialism, national development has been quite challenging. Bilateral agreements supporting local development in English Caribbean territories have been dependent on institutions such as the World Bank and the International Monetary Fund (IMF) to buttress their economies. They have also relied on pledges (sometimes unfulfilled) from foreign governments, individuals and philanthropic organizations to mitigate the after-effects of natural disasters and restoration of infrastructure.

Unfortunately, the structural adjustment that the lending institutions were purportedly designed to enhance has been constricted by reciprocal non-negotiable demands on these developing nations. The intended debt relief appeared to render them worse off at the end of the relief period. Notwithstanding the gallant efforts and activities of CARICOM (Caribbean Common Market), and NGO's (Non-Governmental Organizations), unemployment rates have fluctuated, healthcare services and higher education opportunities have been compromised by a shortage of human capital and other vital resources, and there has been an erosion of confidence in the criminal justice system (Matthews, 2006).

Trends and Practices

The above mentioned conditions have resulted in increased out-migration, especially to the United States, a trend evidenced by the fact that the immigrant population of countries such as Jamaica and Guyana represents nearly half of their respective total population (NYC Department of City Planning, 2010). This in turn has led to heightened levels of transnational activities. Concomitantly, Sewpaul (2008) notes that the transnational lifestyle among English Caribbean people places them "in specific locations in the global divide both spatially and ideologically, often occupying simultaneous spaces in the North and South, if not physically via migration, but ideologically and symbolically with cultural diffusion engendered by the predominance of Western media" (p. 17). Similarly, the emergence of transnational communities in the 21st century is viewed as the most significant "strategic political and economic resource" for the Caribbean region (Nurse, 2004, p.108).

Each year, thousands of English Caribbean nationals continue to immigrate to the United States of America for a variety of reasons. Many come to reunite with family members already in the United States, but a majority, like millions before them, come to improve their economic and educational opportunities for themselves and their family. Nevertheless, Matthews (2012) argues that not all immigrants migrate intentionally in search of 'a better life'. Rather, some may do so out of curiosity about life outside of their own place of birth and either visit periodically or only seek permanency of residence in the recipient country in deference to family members who have decided on planned settlement.

Basch et.al (1994) view transnationalism as the practice that enables immigrants to maintain multiple social relations across national boundaries, binding immigrants in the countries of settlement and non-migrants in their countries of origin. These social relations range from the individual to collective ties including familial, economic, organizational, political, and religious connections. The experiences of English Caribbean immigrants are indeed characterized by such relations.

It is generally believed that English-Speaking Caribbean immigrants have fared relatively well in the United States. Their success has been variously associated with such factors as high levels of English competency, strong work ethic and aspirations and valuable entrepreneurial histories. For example, an examination of income and poverty rates gives a picture of the socioeconomic levels among this population. In New York City, the median household income among Jamaican immigrants is $50,973 and the poverty rate is 10.0%. For Guyanese immigrants, the median household income is $54,772 with a poverty rate of 10.0% while among immigrants from Trinidad and Tobago, the median household income is $45,976 with a poverty rate at 13.2% (U.S. Census Bureau, 2009).

Transnational practices among this population are framed by three interfacing conditions: (a) the challenges caused by the social and personal consequences of underdevelopment, (b) the hope of sustaining a Caribbean Diaspora's identity, and (c) the desire to 'give back' to communities of origin. Transnational connections, the vehicle for realizing such activities, are upheld by frequent travel between the United States and the Caribbean, enhanced by geographic proximity, widespread use of internet technology, sending of remittances; sustaining cultural links, and maintaining property ownership in the home country. Negi and Furman (2010) observe that "Globalization has altered the lives of people forever . . . more and more people are living transnational lives" (p. 4).

Apart from continuing strong ties with the home country through the above-stated mechanisms, many immigrants tend to have an unmitigated sense of awareness and knowledge of social and political changes therein. This is reinforced by varying degrees of emotional attachments. Portes and Rumbaut (2006) note that transnational activities "bridge the gap between past and present through periodic visits back home and the maintenance of active ties with family, friends and colleagues there" (p. 26). Continuous identification with the home country, reinforced by immigrant community networks, provide a persistent grounding in the culture of origin and by extension, emotional connectedness. English speaking Caribbean immigrants have been variously described as having a positive work ethic, traveling between the U.S. and the Caribbean and investing resources in both locations (Caribbean Media Enterprise, 2005).

The extent to which these immigrants internalize the cultural and political values of the society of destination, while compromising those customs and beliefs of the home country, are crucial to their identity in what Lehmann (1998) refers to as "diasporic communities" and to the attainment of migratory goals and individual objectives. Re-establishing residence in a technologically advanced nation is one way of compensating for the felt deprivation of essential resources, and the desire to ensure a promising future for immigrants and their children. Portes (2001) posits that immigration potentially offers the opportunity to experience the lifestyle to which they have been exposed primarily through the media, but lack the resources at home to attain it.

Despite this, many immigrants tend not to completely sever ties with the home country, but maintain a transnational lifestyle that is partly characterized by the ambivalence of living in two worlds. This compromised status appears to conform to the immigrant experience. In this regard, Turner (1991) notes that it is difficult to avoid the tensions created by the demands of this lifestyle, while Orozco (2006) views the transnational lifestyle that emerges as a "paradox of distance and closeness" involving opportunities and challenges.

Undoubtedly, large-scale loss of human capital, including essential skills and the "brain drain" in various sectors of the sending country occurs because of emigration. However, as Putnum (1994) notes, following migration "social capital as features of social life– networks, norms and trust, enable participants to act together more effectively to pursue shared objectives" (p. 2). Remittances, as well as private and commercial investments by immigrants who acquired varied levels of economic success and gain occupational expertise in the host country, invariably help to sustain key social institutions in the home country. These include educational institutions, community centers, road building and other infrastructural developments, sport centers, and political networks.

Notwithstanding their contributions to the success of sectors in American society, these people also actively support the growth of the communities they left and ostensibly, the development of their country of origin. In writing about this connection in relation to Guyanese immigrants, Karran (2012) argues that the Caribbean Diaspora readily identifies with the home country and constantly demonstrates its preparedness to contribute to national development. Under the theme Revitalizing the Diaspora, Rebuilding Jamaica, the Jamaican Diaspora's Northeast USA Advisory Board launched a project designed to organize the Jamaican Diaspora to contribute to long-term nation building (Caribbean Life, 2012).

A sort of "transnational fusion" occurs as immigrants learn to live in two places at once, a phenomenon that has become critical to the organization of personal and social life space. This example of biculturalism has advantages and disadvantages. According to Basch et al. (1994), transnationalism emphasizes the process whereby "many immigrants build social fields that cross geographic, cultural and political borders. An essential element of this is the multiplicity of involvements that transmigrants sustain in both home and host societies". (p. 6). They note further that Caribbean immigrants tend to merge political and economic practices of the US with cultural traditions and practices brought from the home country as they adjust to their adopted home (Basch, 2012). This hybridization or merging of transnational ties and identities cross-continentally results in a plethora of opportunities, risks and challenges.

Relocation inevitably transforms individual lives, households and communities. In order to decrease cultural dissonance between customs people bring and those to which they are introduced, immigrants often modify their behavior through compromises in social and personal life experiences, while doing their best to preserve the familiar where possible. For example, some immigrants inevitably relinquish hometown prestige, privilege (achieved or ascribed) and proprietorship as they resettle in the new society. Some adults are relegated from professional to menial occupations, while children and adolescents are torn away from kin, friends and familiar places. Some of these shifts occur with much trepidation and emotional strain, but also represent inevitable economic and personal sacrifice - the cost of 'making it' in the new society.

Whatever form these transformations take, they incrementally or radically modify habits relating to family obligation, social and interpersonal relationships, work and overall aspirations. While some celebrate an anticipated new and prosperous life, others express cautionary optimism about their future. Yet others either belittle their homeland as backward and unsophisticated, or mourn its loss. In her discussion of the stages of migration, Sluzki (1997) refers to the phenomenon of "splitting", where immigrants either denigrate or glorify their adopted home as a way of coping.

Regardless of the stage of resettlement or level of adaptation to the country of destination, Caribbean immigrants regularly return in large numbers to the home country to visit kin, sustain real estate or celebrate important cultural events. These include going home for Christmas, carnival and Independence celebrations, to spend winter and to conduct business. Maintaining professional practices in both the United States and the Caribbean is also prevalent (Holder, 2004).

It is not uncommon for governments in the English Caribbean to offer repatriation incentives and attempt to recruit those in the Caribbean Diaspora interested in contributing to the development of the home country. For example, in 2012 the Government of Guyana, in collaboration with the International Organization for Migration (IOM), "in its efforts to promote social and economic development through migration, embarked on the Guyana Diaspora (GUYD) Project to engage the Guyanese Diaspora by documenting skills, resources, interests and plans of those willing to support the country's development" (GUYD Project, 2012, p.1). Although such efforts to recruit expatriates have been attempted for many years, its success has been minimal. This appears to be so due to a lack of confidence and trust in the governments in the region. Instead, individuals and organizations in the Diaspora prefer to make their hometown contributions independent of government involvement (Karran, 2010; Matthews, 2011).

While some return permanently to their homeland after retirement, others dream of doing so. Increasing numbers of Caribbean immigrants appear to favor returning to their home country from the United States after retirement, particularly in light of the world economic crisis. As one such returnee stated, "This country (U.S.) is too expensive to live in. I cannot make it on Social Security. I plan to return home where I can live a more comfortable life". Notwithstanding the reality of late life stage financial hardships that may cause despair, the decision to return permanently to the country of origin may create a dilemma for some who have grown accustomed to life in North America, dimensions which can hardly be duplicated in the Caribbean.

Sending incorrigible adolescents back to the home country to counter behavioral problems or to be socialized in what may be viewed as a more structured educational environment has been a practice. Confidence in the home country's educational system, swayed by the belief in the remnants of a more traditional, disciplined former British curriculum, may have accounted for this practice that is less prevalent today. This may be due to emigration-generated depletion of skilled teachers and changes in institutional disciplinary measures in the home country. Such practices, according to Turner (1991) lead to "the emergence of a trans-context lifestyle ... family members move in a circular, connecting and reconnecting pattern between two places, bridging geographic locations and distinctive meaning systems" (p. 408). The returning of the deceased immigrants' remains for burial in the home country is also symbolic of this trans-attachment. Connections are further sustained when immigrants return to attend funerals, weddings and family, village and school reunions.

Another stark example of sustained connectedness is found among professional immigrants, who are generally able to vacillate between two countries, contributing to the development of their respective fields in their home country (Portes and Rumbaut, 2006). Other examples of efforts to maintain linkages and emotional attachment to countries of origin include the display of unwavering support for overseas-based or visiting entertainers and athletes. Nowhere is this more explicitly demonstrated than at the Annual Penn Relays, held at the University of Pennsylvania in the US, where throngs of flag waving Caribbean immigrants turn out to encourage and support hundreds of their hometown athletes.

The above-mentioned transnational exchanges result in social and emotional attachments to the homeland, serving to keep alive the flames of ethnic, political, regional, and indigenous hometown consciousness. Furthermore, partly due to inter-territorial proximity, the continuous social network of Caribbean immigrants decreases the disjuncture with communities of origin that is often experienced by immigrants over time, as evidenced by earlier waves of European immigrants to the United States. In this regard, what may be uncharacteristic of the 21st century immigrant is "a uniform assimilation process that different groups undergo in the course of several generations" (Portes, 2006, p. 23).

Holder (2004) made the seemingly paradoxical suggestion that persistent ties of English Caribbean immigrants to the homelands ultimately shape their assimilation into American society. Their transnational status is further solidified by the capacity in some cases, to hold dual citizenship. More than 80 % of sending countries allows dual-citizenship status (Renshon, 2005) and English-speaking Caribbeans are among those who are increasingly choosing to become American citizens. While citizenship through naturalization allows them to more actively participate in the fabric of American social institutions, including the political process, the effect on their continued social and economic attachment to the country of origin is largely unknown. DeParle (2010) gives some insight into this when he notes that, "transnationalism is a comfort, but also a concern for those who think it impedes integration" (p. 4).

What is clear, however, is that aspects of the home culture are perpetuated in the United States by events, activities and continued practices that provide much more than the images and memories of the homeland, and beyond just a nostalgic re-creation of the past. Such activities include: Annual West Indian Day Parades, National Days of celebration in the Park, access to, and consumption of nostalgic goods, i.e. products indigenous to the Caribbean, participation in social events and folk festivals that feature elements of the home culture (art, theater, folklore, music and dance, poetry, comedy, and intellectual discourse), and organizing charitable and cultural organizations such as Home Town Associations (HTAs).

According to Orozco (2006) who found an increasing number of such organizations among Caribbean immigrants, those who participate in HTAs "are as much involved with their families both in the U.S. and abroad the longer they have been in the country. They are U.S. citizens, but also visit the home country more often and help the family back home . . . these members mix their commitments to both homes, signifying a transnational membership" (p. 8). The work of HTAs is not only important for local infrastructure development, but help to mitigate natural disasters therein.

HTAs include 'give-back' philanthropic organizations that have become essential as a funding source for a vast number of community-based initiatives in the immigrants' home country, represented by village, town, parish, school or church. Not only does this demonstrate the success of the Diaspora, but the participatory enthusiasm in these activities and events at the international level appear to be increasing among first and second generation immigrants. As Foner (2001) observes, "transnational connections may foster a complex cross-fertilization process as immigrants bring new notions to their home communities at the same time as they continue to be influenced by values and practices there" (p. 964).

With legal permanent residency (LPR) status or naturalized citizenship in the United States, many of these immigrants may consider themselves 'settled' on American soil but still remain involved at various levels of commitment with the home country. The social psychology regarding conceptions of ethnic identity, patriotism, citizenship and nationality, as put forward by Renshon (2005), draws attention to this phenomenon. Becoming a permanent resident or a naturalized American citizen does not necessarily mean defining oneself as 'American'.

According to Levitt and Glick Schiller (2004), identifying oneself by using a bi-national label "would ultimately reflect ethnic pride within a multicultural United States rather than enduring relations to an ancestral land". However, beyond such an argument, identification as Caribbean-American or West Indian American may be less symbolic than significantly representing the essence of a transnational existence. Fletcher (2010) argues that immigrants enter the host nation "with a racial consciousness that is shaped by the ideologies, histories and experiences from the home country (and) perceptions of the racial hierarchy in the target country" (p. 1)

In order to fully understand the dynamics of resettlement, it is important to have a notion regarding pre-migratory ethnic relations. In Guyana and Trinidad and Tobago, colonialism and subsequent racial politics planted the seeds of ethnic divide between those of Indian ancestry and those of African ancestry. A cogent argument can be made that upon resettling in the US, the political tension between these groups has been defused by voluntary residential segregation and preoccupation of each group with its respective personal and social development within the context of the American stratification system and paternalistic orientation, thus decreasing the incidence of vying for power between the two groups. In this regard, it is worthy to note that while African-Caribbean immigrants are generally dispersed residentially, East Indians are more likely to settle in their own ethnic enclaves, such as Richmond Hill, New York. In addition, each group tends to support its own Hometown Associations, and by extension, communities in the home country, with little interaction across organizations (Matthews, 2011).

The genesis of this continued ethnic separation in the recipient society is influenced by engrained cultural and political factors. It must be noted however, that symbolic collaboration between the two groups in the U.S. during the home country's Independence Celebration for example, has increased over the years.

An examination of the expectations and cultural identity issues in the United States where these immigrants are considered, by American standards, 'people of color' and therefore part of a 'minority group' by virtue of their phenotype (physical appearance), reveals an important dimension of their transnational stature. Coming from post colonial societies where indigenous (Caribbean-born) people are the visible managers of the state, life under a system that does not reflect similar ethnic visibility require significant adjustment for some but may evoke consternation in others. Consequently, these immigrants of color, unlike the 'old immigrants' of European ancestry, may be reluctant to relinquish their national identity to assimilate fully into the American mainstream.

It is important to note that the 'post-racial American society' expected by some and touted by others, after the election of the first African-American president, remains elusive. Machinations in the politics, economics, religion and sentiments regarding various socio-cultural issues, including immigration contribute to this elusiveness.

The politics of transnationalism is clearly evident by the noticeable increase in deportations under the Obama administration (almost 400,000 in 2011). A significant number of these deportees are Caribbean immigrants. It has been reported that the justification for this increase centers on the desire of democrats to demonstrate that they are strong on immigration (Hong, 2010). Walking a political tightrope and in an effort to counterbalance such draconian policies, in July 2012, the Federal Government announced the Deferred Action for Childhood Arrivals for thousands of immigrant youth who were brought to the United States by undocumented parents or other relatives (USCIS, 2012). The effect of this policy, that would enhance the stability of immigrant families, including those from the English Caribbean, applies to immigrants 30 years of age and under, who came to the US before they were 16 and who met other criteria.

The fact that many contemporary (post-1965) immigrants do not fully assimilate into the American social structure, as noted by Portes (2006), can be viewed as a function of a deliberate or subconscious desire to retain key aspects of their culture. They expect a better life economically, but may have varying ideals, strategies and interpretations of how this is achieved. Many seek to attain the proverbial 'American dream' of unspecified, self-defined accomplishments. However, in some instances, efforts to improve their standard of living are stymied by their inability to adequately access the system, coming from a less fast-paced society, as well as the existence of structural barriers such as racism and xenophobic stereotyping based on their 'foreignness'.

This is perpetuated by the notion of "otherness based on cultural incompatibility" which, in an era of a potential resurgence of nativism, appears to define the relationship between immigrants and native-born Americans (Fletcher, 2010). Some immigrants may underestimate the impact of the various forms of discrimination, racism, marginalization, exclusion and injustice, since they tend to believe that personal economic gain is worth the sacrifice of acquiescing to such improprieties.

Notwithstanding the social and economic location of Caribbean immigrants, there is a general belief that they are at increased risk for encountering various types of structural barriers due to their racial and cultural characteristics. As Crowder and Tedrow (2001) noted, Caribbean immigrants face the prospect of assimilating into the country's most stigmatized groups. They suggested further that in response, there is a strong motivation among Caribbean immigrants to maintain their ethnic distinctiveness.

Transnational existence is characterized by rewards and accomplishments as well as by interpersonal and social stresses in the effort to acquire new cultural meaning. In the process, Caribbean immigrants are not insulated from the disparaging stereotypes associated with their ethnic/racial characteristics and anti-immigrant sentiments that pervade parts of American society.

CONCLUSION

Transnationalism as a sustained movement of people across borders has become a force to be reckoned with in the 21st century, summarily defined by the changing nature of labor demands, amorphous immigration policies, political rhetoric, cultural assumptions and ethnocentric beliefs. This chapter has highlighted important trends and practices of Caribbean immigrants in the United States, within the context of their transnational experiences. They participate in a field of reciprocal relationships and practices in a life space that spans the Caribbean and North America.

The American experience, despite its undisputed benefits and vast opportunities, is likely to take its toll on the well-being of a vast number of immigrants. The phenomenon of people understanding themselves as transnationals may further complicate the picture. As Turner (1991) observes, it is important "to question how the differential experience of having two rather than one place to call home affects emotions, constructions of reality, and descriptions of self." (p. 408). Equally important is examining the ways in which American attitudes can create barriers for immigrants, making their 'otherness' more pronounced and thus problematizing working relations. Often, the challenge of this bi-cultural existence is to sustain a balance between two worlds. In this process, regardless of how post-migration success is measured, the life chances of many immigrants may be grounded in hometown heritages. The personal and social adjustment needs and intervention strategies to effectively address such concerns among the increasing number of immigrants to North America require further research.

Bibliography

Bacon, D. (2008). *Illegal People: How Globalization Creates Migration and Criminalizes Immigrants.* Boston: Beacon Press.

Basch, L, G., N.G. Schiller and V. Blanc-Szanton (1994). *Nations Abound: Transnational Projects, Post Colonial Predicaments and De-territorialized Nation States.* Longhorn, PA: Gordon and Breach.

Bonnett, A.W. (2009). "The West Indian Diaspora in the USA: Remittances and Development of the Homeland." In *Wadabagel: Journal of the Caribbean and its Diaspora.* 12.001, 6-32.

Caribbean Life (2012). Jamaica Diaspora Northeast USA Conference. http//Caribbeanlifenews.com/stories/2010/10/2010_10_08_nicole_clarke _jamaica_diaspora... Retrieved 10/24/2012.

Caribbean Media Enterprise (2005). Collaboration of Caribbean Media and Social Science Project. Strengthening Caribbean-American Media Symposium: Queens, New York.

Crowder, K. and L. Tedrow (2001). "West Indians and the Residual Landscape of New York." In N. Foner, (Ed), *Islands in the City: West Indian Migration to New York. Berkeley:* University of California Press, pp. 81–114.

DeParle, J. (2010). "Global Migration: A World Ever More on the Move." *The New York Times.* June, 25th.

Fletcher, B. (2010). *Race, Racism, Xenophobia and Migration.* Speech to World Social Forum on Migration. *The Black Commentator.* www.BlackCommentator.com

Foner, N. (2001). "Introduction: West Indian Migration to New York." *In, Islands in the City: West Indian Migration in New York.* Berkeley: University of California Press. P. 1–21.

———, "Transnationalism Then and Now: New York Immigrants Today and at the Turn of the Twenty-First Century." In Cordero-Guzman, Smith and Grosfoguel (eds) *Transnationalization and Race in a Changing New York.* Philadelphia: Temple University Press.

Glick Schiller, N.G., L. Basch, and V. Blanc-Szanton (1994). "From Immigrant to Transmigrant: Theorizing Transnational Migration."

Anthropological Quarterly, Volume 68, Number 1, pp. 48–63.
Goulbourne, H. (2002). *Caribbean Transnational Experiences.* Kingston, Jamaica: Arawak Publications.
GUYD Project (2012). "Guyana Diaspora Project: Let's Build Guyana Together." *IOM Development Fund*: Developing Capacities in Migration Management.
Ho, C. (1999). "Caribbean Transnationalism as a Gendered Process." *Latin American Perspectives* 26, no. 5: p 34–54.
Holder, C.B. (2004). "West Indies: Antigua, Bahamas, Barbados, Grenada, Guadeloupe, Guyana, Martinique, St. Kitts, and Trinidad." *The New Americans: A Guide to Immigration since 1965.* Edited by Mary Waters & Reed Ueda, with Helen B. Marrow. Cambridge: Harvard University Press.
Hondagneu-Sotelo, P. (2012). "Transnational Motherhood." *NNIRR's Network News.* Retrieved 10/30/12.
Hong, C.W. (2010). "Immigrant Issues in the United States: Reform and Advocacy". Talk Delivered at SUNY, Empire State College, Metropolitan Center, New York: Fall.
Kasinitz, P. (1992). *Caribbean New York: Black Immigrants and the politics of Race.* Ithaca and London: Cornell University Press.
Karran, B. (2012). "The Guyanese Diaspora in the United States as a factor in National Development." Retrieved 9/30/12.
Kivisto, P. (2001). "Theorizing Transnational Migration: A Critical Review of Current Efforts." *Ethnic and Racial Studies.* 24 (4) 549-578.
Lehmann, S. (1998). "In Search of a Mother Tongue: Locating Home in Diaspora." *MELUS.* Volume 23, Issue 4.
Levitt, P. and N. Jaworsky (2007). "Transnational Migration Studies: Past Developments and Future Trends." *Annual Review of Sociology.* Vo. 33: 129–158. August.
Levitt. P. and Glick Schiller (2004). "Conceptualizing Simultaneity: A Transnational Social Field Perspective on Society". *International Migration Review:* 38(145):595–629,Fall.
Mahoney, A. (2004). *The Health and Well-Being of Caribbean Immigrants in the United States.* New York: The Haworth Press.
Martinelli, A. (1982). "The Political and Social Impact of Transnational Corporations." In H. Makler, A. Martinelli and N. Smelser (eds.) *The New International Economy.* International Sociological Association. Sage.
Matthews, M. (2012). "A Word With Mark— Folklorist, Actor, Poet, Dramatist, Cultural Communicator." Guyana Cultural Association Workshop held at the HQ Lounge, Brooklyn, New York: October 25th.
Matthews, L. (2011). "Hometown Association among English Speaking Caribbean Immigrants: Implications for Social Work Practice." Tenth Biennial Caribbean and International Social Work Educators Conference. Martinique, July 11–16.
———, (2006*).* "Social Violence in the Caribbean: The Case of Guyana and Jamaica." *Caribbean Journal of Social Work.* Volume 6/7.
———, L. and A. Mahoney (2005). "Facilitating a Smooth Transitional Process for Immigrant Caribbean Children: The Role of Teachers, Social Workers and Related Professional Staff." *Journal of Ethnic and Cultural Diversity in Social Work.* Vol. 14, No. 2/3.
Morawska, E. (2011). "Diasporas' Representations of their Homeland: Exploring the Polymorph." *Ethnic and Racial Studies* 34 (6) 1029-48.
Negi, J.N. and R. Furman (2010). *Transnational Social Work Practice.* New

York: Columbia University Press.
New York City Department of City Planning (2010). Population Division Report.
Orozco, M. (2006). "Diasporas, Philanthropy, and Hometown Associations: The Central American Experience." *(draft)* (Washington DC: Inter-American dialogue.
Portes, A. & R.G. Rumbaut (2006). *Immigrant America: A Portrait.* (3rd Edition). Los Angeles: University of California Press.
———, and R.G. Rumbaut (2001). *Legacies: The Story of The Immigrant Second Generation.* Berkeley and New York: University of California Press.
Putnum, R. (1994). "Tuning in, Tuning Out: The Strange Disappearance of Social Capital in America." *American Political Science Association Online.*
Renshon, S.A. (2005). The 50% American: Immigration and National *Identity in an Age of Terror.* Washington, DC: Georgetown University Press.
Sewpaul, V. (2008). "Social Work Education in the Era of Globalization." *Caribbean Journal of Social Work.* Vol. 7 & 7, December, pp 16–35.
Sluzki (1997). "Migration and Family Conflict". *Family Process,* 18:379–390.
Sorensen, N. (2007). "Living Across Worlds: Diaspora, Development and Transnational Engagement." Switzerland: *International Organization for Migration.*
Tilly, C. (2007). "Trust Networks in Transnational Migration." *Sociological Forum.* Vol. 22, No. 1.
Turner, Jean (1991). "Migrants and Their Therapists: A Trans-Context Approach." *Family Process.* Vol. 30 (December).
USCIS About Deferred Action for Childhood Arrivals. Consideration of Deferred Action for Childhood Arrivals. Retrieved 8/29/12.
Ueda, R. (2011). *A Companion to American Immigration.* New York: John Wiley and Sons.
Vertovec, S. (2009). *Transnationalism.* New York: Routledge Publishing Company.

Chapter Two

Migratory Patterns and Experiences of Anglophone Caribbean Women

Mary Spooner

> "As a woman I have no country. As a woman my country is the whole world." —Virginia Woolf

Pressured by the need to provide for their households, Anglophone Caribbean women seek opportunities for economic advancement wherever their services are needed in the global economy. Neither the regulation of labor within Caribbean states nor by countries such as the United States, Canada, and the United Kingdom, has halted Caribbean women's efforts to escape the "hard scrabble" life in their countries of origin. Even today, Caribbean women's migration in search of work is said to resemble that of their enslaved ancestors (Watkins-Owens 2001). Women travel widely across the globe and undertake a range of jobs through which they contribute to the economic development of their adopted homelands and their own social and economic advancement.

Although in recent times migration appears to be more spontaneous and voluntary in nature than the forced movement, which occurred during slavery, scholars argue that migration is seldom spontaneous or desired (Chang, 2000; Sassen, 1988). Nor is it always a response to the "push" and "pull" of social and economic conditions. According to Chang (2000), "migration from the Third World into the United States doesn't just happen in response to a set of factors but is carefully orchestrated – that is, desired, planned, compelled, managed, accelerated, slowed, and periodically stopped – by direct actions of US interests, including the government as state and as employer, private employers, and corporations" (pp. 3-4). In fact, Chang (2000) cites the claim made in the 1994 Declaration on Immigrants and the Environment, the National Network for Immigrant and Refugee Rights that, "First World imperialism and development policy in the Third World have resulted in resource depletion, debt, and poverty for many people in these nations. The extraction of resources by the United States and other First World nations forces many people in the Third World to migrate to follow their countries' wealth" (cf. Chang, 2000, pp 2-3).

Despite the politics of transnational migration, Anglophone Caribbean women have for decades managed to advance themselves and sustain their families. It is important to highlight women's efforts because despite an extended history of female migration, the literature remains scant on the details of the gender differentials in migration patterns and the role of migrant women in the U.S. economy (George, 2005). Not until the work of Gabaccia (1992) and Pessar (1999) did it become clear that the majority of immigrants to the United States were not traditional lone male sojourners seeking ways to support their families and to facilitate family reunification in the U.S.

The Anglophone Caribbean, which this chapter references, comprises colonies and independent states located in the Caribbean Sea, stretching from the Bahamas in the North to Trinidad in the South and also includes Guyana on the South American mainland. In discussing the experiences of women from this region, it is evident that they are not a homogeneous group and for immigration purposes, women were classified in different categories. Generally, women were classified as documented or undocumented immigrants. Being classified as documented means that women entered the U.S. with the proper records and identification and being classified as undocumented means that they entered without such documentation. These status differences are instrumental to the integration of women into American society. They also create commonalities between Anglophone Caribbean women and women of other immigrant groups whose achievements are then subsumed within the study of migrants as a homogeneous group (Hondagneu-Sotelo, 2003, Pessar, 1999). This chapter provides insight into the migratory patterns and life experiences of Anglophone Caribbean women who entered the U.S. as documented immigrants. It discusses the challenges that early groups of women and more recent immigrants encounter in employment, education, and health sectors as well as their role in transmitting remittances that benefit families and their countries of origin.

MIGRATION PATTERNS

Caribbean immigrants made their way to the U.S. in three waves (Kasinitz, 1992; Crowder & Tedrow, 2001). The first wave with the largest numbers arrived during the influx of the 1920s through 1932, and comprised primarily male blue-collar workers. Caribbean women were, according to (Watkins-Owen, 2001), " . . . numerically significant in the first wave of immigration from the Caribbean. Barely visible in the historical literature on U.S. immigration of this period, African Caribbean women's experiences and perspectives are critical to understanding the larger story of Caribbean migration and the black Diaspora in the twentieth century" (p. 48).

By 1930, the population of foreign-born Blacks in the US, a significant portion of whom were of West Indian origin, comprised 1.5% of the total Black population (Crowder & Tedrow,2001). The second wave arrived between the latter part of the 1930s and 1965, and the third wave arrived in the post-1965 era. According to scholars, (Kasinitz, 1992; Marshall, 1982; Zhou, 2002), the second wave of immigrants to the U.S. comprised primarily persons joining family members who migrated during the first migration wave. The population also included students, many of whom remained in the U.S. after their studies ended.

The third wave of Caribbean immigrants to the U.S. comprised a heterogeneous and economically diverse group of individuals seeking economic opportunities but with increasing numbers in search of opportunities for higher education. This group increased the foreign-born black population from 125,000 in 1960 to 816,000 in 1980. By 2005, the foreign-born black population was estimated at 2.8 million of which two-thirds were born in the Caribbean or Latin America. A third of this population comprised persons of Jamaican nationality; the largest proportion of the Anglophone population (Kent, 2002).

The upswing in Caribbean migration to the United States was helped greatly by the passage of the Hart-Cellar Immigration Act of 1965 (Kasinitz 1992). By the 1990s, more than half of the 9.1 million immigrants entering the U.S. were women (Zhou 2002). Caribbean women were part of the female-led global influx of new immigrants whose numbers steadily increased from 1985 to 2000 (Marshall 1982; Kasinitz, 1992). The United Nations Population Division estimates that with the exception of Montserrat, Jamaica, St. Kitts and Nevis, and Trinidad and Tobago, all of the Anglophone Caribbean states experienced a steady increase in out-migration over the decade from 1990 to 2000.

According to the United Nations Population Division (2002) data, the number of migrants relative to the population of the islands remained high from 1990 through 2000. The island of Anguilla, for example, experienced the highest rate of out-migration relative to its population (27.97 percent in 1990 compared to 35.61 percent in 2000). Outmigration from Antigua and Barbuda was also high (19.18 percent in 1990 compared to 24.47 percent in 2000). Jamaica and Trinidad and Tobago experienced the lowest migration rates of all the islands, which is perhaps reflective of the greater lack of economic opportunities in the smaller island states.

Caribbean women comprised almost half of the population of Caribbean migrants among the international migrant population from 1960 to 2000. In 1960, Caribbean migrants comprised 45.3 percent of that population, in 1980, 46.5 percent and in 2000, the migrant population increased to 48.9 percent (Zlotnik, 2005). Many Anglophone Caribbean women either migrated permanently or joined the group of transnational migrants traveling to and from the U.S. trading in cheap goods with low economic value but of high social utility in the informal sector (Ramirez, Dominguez, & Morais, 2005). Table 1 (see addendum) shows migration rates that were higher among women than men in all Caribbean countries except Dominica, Montserrat, and St. Kitts and Nevis at the point of mid-year estimates across the time period - 2000-2005 and 2010. The numbers migrating trended upwards among both female and male migrants with the exception of Montserrat and Trinidad and Tobago that experienced a decrease in migration.

Anglophone Caribbean women migrating in the third wave differed from those of non-English speaking Caribbean countries such as Haiti, the Dominican Republic, and Cuba (Kasinitz, 1992). They were likely to be better educated than non-English speaking women and to have been heads of their households in their countries of origin. Therefore, Anglophone women migrated to the U.S. more frequently as household heads seeking to improve their socio-economic status rather than as companions to migrant workers or in search of asylum or to escape wars and persecution (Sunshine, 1998; Ho, 1993). According to Vernez (1999), "First, the intent to work in the United States is a primary reason for many women to migrate in the first place – not only for single, but for married women as well, often as part of a strategy to improve their families' well-being." (p. 4).

Caribbean Women in the U.S. Workforce

Migration patterns emerged in direct response to the growing need for women to fill service positions that dovetailed with their domestic roles. The demands of the U.S. economy for labor provided work for Caribbean women and the opportunity to secure their residence in the U.S. Caribbean women comprised the second largest proportion of women engaged in domestic work and represented 14% of this class of workers (Foner, 1987). According to Kasinitz (1992), as more middle and upper-middle class American women joined the U.S. labor force, their need for childcare increased and Caribbean women gained the benefit of resident status in the U.S. "Increased numbers of middle- and upper-middle class women working outside of the home during child-bearing years has been made possible in part by the importation of English-speaking Caribbean childcare workers, and it is noteworthy that U.S. immigration policy encourages household employment as one of the few available legal routes to a green card." (p. 105)

The dynamic role that Anglophone Caribbean women played in the U.S. economy reflected the varied life experiences in their home countries and their reasons for migrating to the U.S. According to Vernez (1999), immigrant women " . . . come with varied human capital endowment and socio-demographic characteristics." (p. 29). Because of women's skills as household heads, many women were able to find work quickly and this was particularly important because of their commitments to persons who financed their travel to the U.S. and the need to provide economic support for family members left behind (Palmer, 1983).

The attributes that Anglophone Caribbean immigrants displayed in the labor force — strong work ethic, ability to speak English, and readiness to assimilate into American society — earned them the controversial label of "model minority". Women also found that they often received preference in hiring by non-Black employers who found them to be a more industrious group with better attitudes on the job than native-born blacks (Waters, 1999; Kent, 2007). These positive aspects of Caribbean immigrant experiences and successes should not overshadow the challenges that Anglophone Caribbean immigrants encountered in the workplace. Although Anglophone Caribbean immigrants seemed to experience selective favoritism in the workplace over native counterparts and African Americans, they had similar outcomes to internal migrant African Americans (Model 2008). According to Model (2008), Caribbean migrants took more than a decade to gain similar footing in the U.S. economy as African Americans.

Gender and race discrimination played a key role in keeping women out of the workplace. Caribbean women in the early years of migration, in particular, found that their male folk gained preference in better paying jobs in business and the professions. Many highly skilled Anglophone Caribbean women were often forced to work in hourly-paid jobs, such as live-in domestics, while they attended school to prepare for the American labor force before they could regain their occupational status.

Legal migration status, even today, guarantees Anglophone Caribbean women neither the parity nor the level of job security that U.S. citizens experience. According to the New York Post, "Hundreds of teachers recruited by New York City from Jamaica, Trinidad and other Caribbean countries a decade ago say city officials have not followed through on promises to help them obtain U.S. citizenship. The teachers were recruited in 2001 when the city faced a teacher shortage. Some say they are now worried about possible deportation." (Associated Press; New York Post on the Web. June 29, 2011). Thus, as long as women remain in a status less than that of full citizenship even though jobs provide the opportunity for economic engagement, there is less guarantee of stability. It should not be surprising that women continue to look to the homeland for social, cultural, and emotional support and connectedness. This is especially so for women who are household heads and migrate as a survival strategy leaving their children and spouses behind.

Since Anglophone Caribbean women are not a homogeneous group, each individual's achievement within the U.S. economy is dependent to a great extent on individual attributes, reasons for migrating, immigrant status and utility of their skills to the economy. According to Batalova, Fix & Creticos (2008), with migration comes a sharp drop in occupational status and recovery of such status is dependent on several factors; knowledge of English, a U.S. education degree, employment in the United States prior to permanent settlement, the employment visa categories under which a migrant entered the U.S., and the country from which one migrates.

Within the U.S. economy, some Anglophone Caribbean women experienced upward social mobility through job placement while others experienced the reverse. The migration of better educated and skilled Anglophone Caribbean women, especially those in search of higher education, since the third migration wave, has enabled many women to acquire better paying jobs in the U.S. economy. Their skills and knowledge have also enabled the U.S. economy to reap optimal benefits from a workforce that is equipped to enhance productivity without the costs of extensive training. However, although many women now migrate to the United States in search of an education and use this opportunity as a stepping-stone to establishing residency, many still enter the United States as domestic workers.

Despite their evident progress in the workplace, Caribbean women have not been exempt from racial discrimination. In fact, they have developed strategies for coping with racism in the workplace by using their communities as points of reference. In a study of two generations of West Indians, Bobb & Clarke (2001) found that first generation study participants treated racism more as an inconvenience that could be avoided than a major problem. A foreign reference point enabled Caribbean migrants to disassociate from, and not personalize experiences of racism buffered by negative experiences (Bobb & Clarke, 2001). Further, by engaging with an immigrant social network, migrants were able to better deal with racism when it was encountered and identification with West Indian ethnicity also caused others to treat them differently than they would treat African Americans. Bobb & Clarke (2001) found that because second generation study participants did not identify as strongly with the West Indian society as the first generation, they were less likely to overlook or ignore racism than first generation study participants.

The Role of Women's Remittances in the Transnational Migration Process

Although neo-classical Marxists associate the impact of migration with the reproduction of class and spatial inequalities conducive to capitalistic endeavors, the significance of migrant remittances to Caribbean states cannot be overstated. The benefits of economic growth and development consistent with spatial relocation of labor were not factors considered by strict neo-classical theorists in developing migration models until the 1950s and 1960s (Todaro, 1969; Djajic, 1986, Taylor, 1999). However, by the late 1960s, historical-structuralist and dependency theorists introduced perspectives of migration as a catalyst of a "brain drain" that robs the developing countries of their brightest and best workers. More importantly, migrant remittances to home countries were blamed for fueling high levels of "conspicuous consumption" and inflation without strong migrant investments.

Despite the negative perspectives of the role of remittances, migrant women not only boost the Caribbean economy but also class formation (Basch, 2001). Amidst the growing stress placed on Caribbean economies, many families rely on the cash, food and goods they receive from abroad to maintain their standards of living (Terry & Wilson, 2005). According to O'Neil (2003), "We do know that the countries of Latin America and the Caribbean contribute half of the US foreign-born population and receive almost one-third of the world's remittances. The Inter-American Development Bank estimates over three-quarters of remittances to Latin America and the Caribbean originate in the United States." In the case of Jamaica, for example, remittances from the United States accounted for 13.6 percent of total remittances as a percentage of GDP (International Monetary Fund, Balance of Payments Yearbook 2002; Migration Information Source; World Bank, World Development Indicators 2002).

Without gender specific data, however, it is impossible to establish with certainty exactly how much Anglophone Caribbean women contribute to the stream of remittances that makes its way back to the Anglophone Caribbean from the U.S. However, because the level of remittances is consistent with the sender's role in the household before migrating and the purpose for which they migrated, it is reasonable to assume that many Anglophone Caribbean women make significant contributions to the flow of remittances to Caribbean states (Yinger, 2007). According to Palmer (1983), although immigrant women face hard times in the US, they are forced to send remittances back home because, "They need the money not only for their financial independence in this country, but also to satisfy accrued debts and obligations in their native land" (p. 6). Caribbean women having also perfected the art of "making ends meet" meet through pooling their economic resources and drawing on their social networks are also likely to find means of economic survival that allows them to remit large sums of money and goods overseas (Gussler, 1975; Palmer, 1983).

The ability of governments to effectively track and quantify migrant remittances has been hampered by the complexity of the negotiations and transactions between migrants and their household members who remain in the sending countries of origin. Women's contributions, for example, include not only hard currency but also items such as food and household goods. The importance of this form of support to families and households in the sending countries was the subject of Crawford-Brown's work. In her seminal publication, Who will Save our Children: The Plight of the Jamaican Child in the 1990s, Crawford-Brown (1999) discusses the efforts of Caribbean women to provide for the needs of their children left in the home countries. Using the concept of "barrel children", she highlights the sacrifices made by women to gather food items and goods and ship them in barrels to those caring for children left behind. Yet, the full commercial value of the contents of these barrels are never likely to be captured at the ports of entry by government records.

Education

Education represents one of the surest ways to achieve the American dream. Immigrants generally comprise a significant proportion of the U.S. college population. In 2007, among college graduates in the U.S. labor force, 15 percent were immigrants. Among the population of 41.8 million workers ages 25 years and older, 15.4 percent were immigrants with a college education (Migration Policy Institute, 2008).

First and second-generation Caribbean migrants to the U.S. showed strong commitment to education as a means of social mobility. According to Bobb & Clarke (2001), many Caribbean women came to the U.S. by way of domestic employment but later returned to school to make or advance their careers. "A well-known and common scheme – for women at least – was to enter the country under a visa that allowed them to start work as babysitters or housekeepers (employers in these niches typically filed the necessary papers under exceptions to the usual immigration laws), and then to go to school to learn the skills that would permit a career change" (p 219).

Women's advancement has since the early waves of migration been tied to education. In the American education system, many women found themselves at a disadvantage because the system either totally devalued foreign educational qualifications or rated them lower than their true worth. In other instances, immigrants were required to take the U.S. General Education Diploma (GED) even if the GED represented a lower level of educational attainment than is common in the home countries. In seeking entry to American colleges, women who did not meet the requirements of residency did not qualify for lower tuition rates. This increased the cost of education significantly and placed higher education out of reach of many poor immigrant women. In applying to higher educational institutions, women were required to retake classes because their educational qualifications gained abroad did not receive the appropriate level of credits. These significant roadblocks in the American education system forced many professional immigrant women into low paying service jobs despite their ambitions to advance academically.

Yet, because Caribbean migrants considered education to be a privilege and not a right, many were willing to make the sacrifice to return to school Bobb & Clarke (2001). The decision to return to school was not always a smooth process. Many women experienced challenges advancing in the classroom because the approach to learning differs in the U.S from their home countries. According to Alfred (2002), the early learning and socialization of women from Anglophone Caribbean states was based on indigenous or informal learning within the family and community more than on institutional knowledge in the academic setting. Additionally, Alfred argues that because Caribbean women were taught to accept and respect teachers, they did not perform well in U.S. classrooms that rated knowledge based on the outspoken response of students. To be successful in the classroom, therefore, Caribbean women had to find ways "to renegotiate their identity, language, and their conceptualization of voice in order to participate in American cultural systems." (p. 3)

Women's Health and Wellbeing

Racialized social structures in the U.S. might well determine the adaptation of Caribbean women to a healthy life in the U.S. (Williams, Neighbors, & Jackson, 2003). Since advancement in American society is determined by socio-structural factors and discrimination along lines of race, gender, and socio-economic status, immigrants are exposed to many disparities in day-to-day living. Disparities in access to and utilization of healthcare based on race is a major challenge for immigrant populations. According to Williams et. al. (2003), " . . . the subjective experience of racial bias may be a neglected determinant of health and a contributor to racial disparities in health" (pp 206). Many Anglophone Caribbean women, like other ethnic minority groups, are likely to have less access to quality healthcare because as low-income earners they are more likely to have no insurance or be under-insured than their native-born Black counterparts. The discrepancy is exacerbated by immigrant status since immigrant women might not immediately qualify for healthcare through benefits like Medicaid and Medicare that are available to native-born Blacks. It is often several years before immigrants qualify for some publicly funded programs.

Passage of welfare reform in the US in 1996 pressured many immigrant women to seek work but it did not necessarily improve access to health insurance and thus healthcare as many women found themselves employed in jobs without health benefits (Kaestner & Kaushal, 2007). According to Kaestner & Kaushal (2007), the proportion of low-educated, single mothers who were born outside the U.S. and delayed or failed to seek medical care because of exorbitant cost increased between 6.5 percent and 10 percent. Visits to health professionals by single, low-income women also fell by nine percent.

For Anglophone Caribbean women with a greater pool of resources as a result of better economic status, access to healthcare is more predictable. Yet these women of all social and economic means tend to engage with the healthcare system in much the same way by blending traditional health treatments with more modern western medicines. Herbal remedies are often tried at the first sign of illness before consultation with a medical professional. The decision to resort to traditional herbs enables women to avoid the high cost of prescription drugs and saves time spent in emergency rooms where those with no primary care physicians routinely seek healthcare.

The health and wellbeing of Anglophone Caribbean women is inextricably linked with their religious beliefs and faith. Anglophone Caribbean women draw heavily on the spiritual aspects of their faiths in order to cope with illness of any magnitude. Taylor et. al., (2007) found significantly higher levels of religiosity and participation in non-organizational religious activities among Caribbean women relative to their male counterparts. Women were quick to pray and lay hands on the sick to invoke improvement in health. Many also turn to local priests and spiritual healers at the first sign of an illness (McEachern & Kenny, 2002).

Anglophone Caribbean women were at increased risk for psychiatric disorders. Williams (2003) found an association between increased risks for psychiatric disorders and minority status and this risk was particularly high among Black Caribbean immigrants. Caribbean Black women exhibited lower odds than African American women for 12-month and lifetime psychiatric disorders. Despite the lower odds of psychiatric disorders for Caribbean women, however, they are still prone to mental illness due to the added burden of caring for other family members.

Mental health risks also appear to vary by immigration history, and generation status. According to Williams (2007), "First-generation Caribbean Blacks had lower rates of psychiatric disorders compared with second or third-generation Caribbean Blacks, and, compared with first-generation Caribbean Blacks, third-generation Caribbean Blacks had markedly elevated rates of psychiatric disorders." In many instances, mental illness, which goes untreated because of cultural taboo, can be debilitating for women and their families. High societal stress and poor chances of social mobility combined with race raise the odds of psychiatric disorder among black Caribbean immigrants (Williams, 2003). Nadeem (2007) also found that Caribbean immigrant women were so strongly affected by the stigma of mental illness within their communities that they were reluctant to seek mental health treatment. Black Caribbean immigrant women who became depressed were six times as likely as U.S.-born white women to identify stigma-related issues as the reason for not seeking mental health treatment. Compared with U.S.-born white women, the odds of mental illness were 45 percent higher among immigrant Caribbean women while African women had odds that were 39 percent higher and Latinas 26 percent higher.

Anglophone Caribbean women experience significant disparity in other areas of healthcare. In the case of cervical cancer, for example, Caribbean women exhibit higher rates of cervical cancer mortality rates than U.S.-born women. Fewer Caribbean women were also being screened for cancers. In the case of the Human papillomavirus (HPV), for example, Ragin, et al. (2009) found a higher prevalence of cervical HPV infections together with multiple high-risk infections was present among Caribbean and US-Black women than among U.S.-White women. Researchers suggest that these findings are likely to elevate the incidence and prevalence of cervical cancer in these populations (Ragin, et.al, 2009).

Women's Role in Social Networking

Upon migrating to the U.S., Anglophone Caribbean women in the first and second waves encountered myriad problems that created hardships in adjusting to life in the American society. Despite the assets that they brought with them to the U.S., the early years were particularly difficult. Cities such as New York became home to clusters of Caribbean women who lived alongside African Americans and other black immigrants based on their social networks. In some cases, women lived in the vicinities close to the white neighborhoods so that they could get to and from their work as domestic servants easily (Watkins-Owen, 2001).

Issues of gender, economic status and skin color were ever present. The economic advancement of women was often stifled because men were more highly favored than women to fill the more lucrative opportunities in business and the professions. Women's advancement was also frequently hampered by discrimination associated with skin tone. According to Watkins-Owen (2001), women of lighter skin tones who were mostly of privileged economic status, were favored over those with darker skin tones on the job market. Discrimination in the U.S. housing market also meant that women were often forced to occupy substandard housing and it took some time before they could become homeowners.

Despite these challenges, women utilized their social networks through families and friends, churches and social associations, to navigate their adapted space. Informal social groups were also created to leverage resources such as childcare and through informal savings groups women were able to build assets and invest in real estate or other ventures (Watkins-Owen, 2001). Women also formed several voluntary social welfare organizations that played a strategic role in promoting charitable work, particularly among immigrants in the U.S., and among those in need in the home countries. According to (Watkins-Owen, 2001), "Such affiliations promoted social class standing and status, served as sites of socialization for children, and provided places to meet appropriate marriage partners from one's home community. On the other hand, women's work in these associations also reflected collective consciousness and opposition to colonial and racial oppression." (p. 44)

Anglophone Caribbean women failed to develop the same type of political capital as their men. Contrary to the narrow focus on charitable work by Caribbean women's associations, Caribbean men's associations engaged in and became part of the political structures particularly in cities like New York. According to (Palmer, 1983), even when legal status was not an issue, many Afro-Caribbean women have not fully engaged in U.S. society. One major reason is that women did not perceive a relationship to or understanding of the power structures of U.S. politics and political machinery. In many instances, women were so busy working multiple jobs and caring for children and other family members that they are unable to find the time for political and social engagement.

CONCLUSION

Not all Anglophone Caribbean women entered the U.S. for the long-term. Many women who entered the U.S. in the early waves of migration did so with the goal of returning to the country of origin when they felt economically secure (Kasinitz & Waters, 2006). The challenges they encountered upon arrival in the U.S. made the decision to return to the home countries plausible. Nonetheless, the longer they remained, the more difficult it was for them to leave.

With frequent travel and modern technologies, however, subsequent populations of migrants have more options. Most are now able to connect in real time with relatives in the home countries. Close ties with their home countries also decrease the need for Caribbean women to become fully engaged in the social and political life of the U.S. Thus, many women subsist in the U.S. with only fragile, tangential arrangements in the U.S. society. In many cases, the networks that support women were limited to family members, as well as churches, social groups and organizations comprising persons from their countries of origin.

Nonetheless, Anglophone Caribbean women have made significant contributions at a global level with a multiplier effect that is both social and economic. Their contributions to Caribbean economies can be measured by remittances to their home countries that enable these economies to bolster their balance of payments. At the societal level, paving the way for family members to migrate and find opportunities for advancement in education and the job market has led to social mobility among generations of Caribbean families. Caribbean women have also worked tirelessly in the private and public sectors of the United States economy under challenging circumstances. Many children of Anglophone Caribbean women were now poised, with the benefits of higher education, to continue the legacy of contribution well into the future. In this regard, although women's contributions may initially be undercounted and undervalued, the multiplier effect of those contributions to global advancement remains far-reaching and reformative in its impact.

Bibliography

Alfred, M. (2002). "Women's Learning and Development Across Borders: Insights from Anglophone Caribbea Immigrant Women in the United States." *43rd Annual Meeting of the Adult Education Research Conference* (pp. 7695-7801). Raleigh NC: Adult and Community College Education.

Associated Press; New York Post on the Web. June 29. (2011, 6 29). *New York Post*. Retrieved 8 11, 2011, from New York City Teachers from Caribbean Seek Immigration Help: http://www.nypost.com/p/news/local/nyc_teachers_from_caribbean_seek_Wpi6aLCtDeES0gOFnoFC5J

Basch, L. (2001). "Transnational Social Relations and the Politics of National Identity: An Eastern Caribbean Case Study". In N. Foner, *Islands in the City: West Indian Migration to New York* (pp. 117-141). CA: University of California Press.

Batalova, J., Fix, M., Creticos, P.A. (2008). "Uneven Progress: The Uneven Pathways of Skilled Immigrants in the United States". *Migration Policy Institute*.

Best-Cummings, C., & Gildner, M. (2004). "Caribbean Women's Migratory Journey: An Explanation of their Decision-making Process." *Journal of Immigrant and Refugee Services*, 2 (3/4), 83-101.

Bobb, V. F., & Clarke, A. Y. (2001). "Experiencing Success: Structuring the Perception of Opportunities for West Indians." In N. Foner, & N. Foner (Ed.), *Islands in the City: West Indian Migration to New York* (pp. 216-236). LA, CA: University of California Press.

Borjas, G. (1999). *Heaven's Door: Immigration Policy and the American Economy*. Princeton NJ: Princeton University Press.

Borjas, G., & Hilton, L. (1996). "Immigration and the Welfare State: Immigrant Participation in Means-tested Entitlement Programs." *Quarterly Journal of Economics*, 575-604.

Chamberlain, M. (2006). *Family Love in the Diaspora: Migration and the Anglo-Caribbean Experience*. New Brunswick: Transaction Publishers.

Chang, G. (2000). *Disposable Domestics: Immigrant Women Workers in the Global Economy*. Cambridge MA: South End Press.

Crawford-Brown, C. (1999). *Who will Save our Children: The Plight of the Jamaican Child in the 1990s*. Kingston: Canoe Press University of the West Indies.

Crowder, K., & Tedrow, L. (2001). "West Indians and the Residential Landscape of New York." In N. Foner, *Islands in the City: West Indian Migration to New York*. Berkeley: University of California Press.

De Haas, H. (2010). "Migration and Development". *International Migration Review*, Spring 2010, 227-264.

——, (2007). Turning the Tide? Why Development Will Not Stop Migration. *Development and Change*, 38 (5), 819-841.

Djajic, S. (1986). "International Migration, Remittances and Welfare in a Dependent Economy." *Journal of Development Economics*, 21, 229-234.

Farley, R., & Allen, W. (1989). *The Color Line and the Quality of Life in America*. NY: Oxford University Press.

Foner, N. (2001). *Islands in the City: West Indian Migration to New York*. NY:

University of California Press.
——, (2001). *New Immigrants in New York.* NY: Columbia University Press.
Forde, D. (2002). *Caribbean Americans in New York City 1895-1975.* Charleston, SC: Arcadia Publishing.
Frank, A. (1969). *Capitalism and Underdevelopment in Latin America.* New York: Monthly Review Press.
——, (1966). *The Development of Underdevelopment. Monthly Review* .
George, S. (2005). *When Women Come First: Gender and Class in Transnational Migration.* Los Angeles, CA: University of California Press.
Gussler, J. (1980). "Adaptive Strategies and Social Networks of Women in St. Kitts." In E. Bourguignon, *A World of Women: Anthropological Studies of Women in the Societies of the World* (pp. 185-209). NY: Praeger.
Kasinitz, P. (1992). *Black Immigrants and the Politics of Race.* NY: Cornell University Press.
Kaushal, N., & Kaestner, R. (2007). "Welfare Reform and Health of Immigrant Women and their Children." *Journal of Immigrant Health, 9,* 61-74.
Kent, M. (2007). *Immigration and America's Black Population.* Washington DC: Population Reference Bureau.
Macisco, J. J., & Pryor, E. (1963). "A Reappraisal of Ravenstein's Laws of Migration: A Review of Selected Studies of Internal Migration in the United States." *The American Catholic Sociological Review , 24* (3), 211-221.
Marshall, D. (1982). "The History of Caribbean Migrations: The Case of the West Indies." *Caribbean Review , 11,* 451-467.
Martinez Pizarro, J., & Villa, M. (2005). "International Migration in Latin America and the Caribbean: A Summary View of Trends and Patterns." *United Nations Expert Group Meeting on International Migration and Development.* UN Population Division, Department of Economic and Social Affairs.
McEachern, A., & Kenny, M. (2002). "A Comparison of Family Environment Characterisitcs among White (Non-Hispanics), Hispanic, and African Caribbean Groups." *Journal of Multicultural Counseling and Developmennt , 30* (1), 40-58.
Model, S. (2008). *West Indian Immigrants: A Black Success Story?* NY: Russell Sage Foundation.
Nadeem, E., Lange, J., Edge, D., Fongwa, M., Belin, T., & Miranda, J. (2007). "Does Stigma Keep Poor Young Immigrant and U.S.-Born Black and Latina Women from Seeking Mental Health Care?" *Psychiatric Services* , 1547-1554.
O'Neil, K. (2003). *Remittances from the United States in Context.* Retrieved May 15, 2010, from http://www.migrationinformation.org/feature/display.cfm?ID=138.
Palmer, A. (1983). *Afro-Caribbean Women in the United States: Images and Reality.* pp. 2-14.
Quinlan, R. (2005). "Kinship, Gender and Migration from a Rural Caribbean Community". *Migration Letters , 2* (1), 2-12.
Ragin, C., Watt, A., Markovic, N., Bunker, C., Edwards, R., Eckstein, S., et al. (2009). "Comparisons of High-risk Cervical HPV Infections in Caribbean and U.S. Populations". *Infect Agent Cancer , 4* (Suppl 1), S9.
Ramirez, C., Dominguez, M., & Morais, J. (2005). *Crossing Borders: Remittances, Gender and Development.*
Ravenstein, E. G. (1889). "The Laws of Migration". *Journal of the Royal*

Statistical Society , 241-305.
Rogers, R. (2006). *Afro-Caribbean Immigrants and the Politics of Incorporation: Ethnicity, Exception or Exit.* Cambridge MA: Cambridge University Press.
Safa, H. (1995). *The Myth of the Male Breadwinner: Women and Industrialization in the Caribbean.* Boulder CO: Westview Press.
Salmon, M., Yan, J., Hewitt, H., & Guisinger, V. (2007). "Managed Migration: The Caribbean Approach to Addressing Nursing Services Capacity". *Health Services Research* , 42 (3 Pt 2), 1354-1372.
Stark, O., & Bloom, D. (1985). "The New Economics of Labor Migration". *The American Economic Review* , 75 (2), 173-178.
Sunshine, C., & Warner, K. W. (1998). *Caribbean Connections: Moving North.* Washington DC: Network of Educators on the Americas.
Taylor, R., Chatters, L., & Jackson, J. (2007). Religious Participation among Older Black Caribbeans in the United States," *The Journals of Gerontology: Social Sciences* , 62 (4), S238-S250.
Taylor, J. (1999). The New Economics of Labour Migration and the Role of Remittances in the Migration Process. *International Migration* , 37 (1), 63-88.
Terry, D., & Wilson, S. (2005). *Beyond Small Change: Making Migrant Remittances Count.* Washington DC: Inter-American Development Bank.
In E. Thomas-Hope, *Regional and International Migration in the Caribbean and its Impacts on Sustainable Development* (pp. 53-67). Port-of-Spain: Trinidad and Tobago: Economic Commission on Latin America and the Caribbean.
Todaro, M. (1969). "A Model of Labor Migration and Urban Unemployment in Less-Developed Countries." *American Economic Review* , 59, 138-148.
Vernez, G. (1999). *Immigrant Women in the U.S. Workforce. Who Struggles? Who Succeeds?* New York: Lexington Books.
Waters, M. (1999). *Black Identities: West Indian Immigrant Dreams and American Realities.* Cambridge MA: Harvard University Press.
Waters, M. (1999). *Black Identities: West Indian Immigrant Dreams and American Realities.* NY: Russell Sage Foundation.
Watkins-Owens, I. (2001). "Early Twentieth-Century Caribbean Women: Migration and Social Networks in New York City." In N. Foner, *Islands in the City: West Indian Migration to New York* (pp. 25-51). LA, CA: University of California Press.
——, (1996). *Blood Relations: Caribbean Immigrants and the Harlem Community: 1900-1930.* Bloomington IN: Indiana University Press.
Williams, D., Neighbors, H., & Jackson, J. (2003). "Racial/Ethnic Discrimination and Health: Findings from Community Studies." *American Journal of Public Health* , 93, 200-208.
Yinger, N. (2007, February). *The Feminization of Migration: Limits of the Data.* Retrieved June 15, 2011, from http://www.prb.org/Articles/2007/FeminizationofMigrationLimitsofData.aspx
Zhou, M. (2002). "Contemporary Female Immigration to the United States: A Demographic Profile." *Women Immigrants in the United States.* Washington DC: Woodrow Wilson International Center for Scholars.
Zlotnik, H. (2005). *Global Dimensions of Female Migration.* Washington DC: Migration Policy Institute.

Chapter Three

Migration and Occupational Change[1]

Lear Matthews

INTRODUCTION

A Caribbean immigrant leaves his community and job as an Assistant Commissioner of Police to find more educational opportunities and a 'comfortable life' in the United States. It is unlikely that he would find employment of the same stature, so he becomes a Security Guard and also accepts a part-time job as a Handyman to support his family that he left in the Caribbean. A middle-aged woman, who worked as a Senior Government Official migrated to the United States and three months after her arrival is employed as a Home Attendant and part-time Clerical Aide.

Although many newly arrived immigrants appear to make crisis-free adjustment, such involuntary transformation of vocation, i.e. taking a job not commensurate with one's educational and occupational level, has been common among them (Portes, 2006; Holder, 1998; Lamb, 2006). Not only is this experience prevalent among those entering with professional training, but the phenomenon appears to be associated with the link between stress and immigration (Sher and Vilens, 2010; Sluzki 1979; Dressler, 1985).

In this chapter, the author contends that there is a relationship between adaptation to a new environment and employment status determined by compromising changes in occupation, particularly among professional immigrants. Immigrants, from the former School Principal and Medical Doctor, to the Taxi Driver and Nurse's Aide, have relinquished pre-migration benefits such as occupational status, community recognition and prestige. This chapter focuses on the impact of occupational change on social adjustment among English Caribbean immigrants, implications for transnational conduct, and the effects on their mental health.

Occupational Background and Adjustment

The occupational background of international immigrants to the United States determines to a considerable degree how well they will be incorporated into the workplace. By 1940, of 25,345 English-speaking Caribbean immigrants with a reported occupation, only 898 or 3.5 percent were in the professional category (US Sixteenth Census, 1943). Since then, major changes have occurred in the representation of migrating professionals such as teachers, doctors, civil servants, and managers. Between 1990 and 1994, of the 28,000 immigrants (primarily from Jamaica, Guyana, and Trinidad & Tobago) settling in New York, one of the largest ports of entry for this population, approximately 42 percent were in the professional group (NY City Department of City Planning 1996). While some arrived under the temporary "H-1B" or Work Visa Program, others may have overstayed their Non-immigrant Visa.

By 2000, approximately 38% of the immigrants from these countries were considered professionals and this figure steadily increased by 2009 (New York City Department of City Planning, 2004; Salvo, 2011). The perennial concern of sending nations has been the "brain drain", which include large numbers of professional immigrants to North America (Caribbean Life, 2006). An International Monetary Fund study (Jamaica Gleaner, 2006), reported that more than 80% of the graduates from Caribbean countries, including doctors, nurses, pilots, teachers, and engineers, were leaving to settle and work in the United States, Canada and Europe. Although high-skilled immigrants are recruited in comparable professions for which they have been trained in the home country, many end up doing other, unrelated jobs (Lamb, 2006).

Generally entering with a strong work ethic, those with experience as laborers and service workers tend to integrate into the job market much easier than professionals do (Singh, 2001). Consequently, a more drastic change in occupation is higher within the professional group, often resulting in a downward shift in social status that for many is the basis for psychological distress and other problems of adaptation. The decision to make such a shift, though strategic and economically driven, often results in forced modification of various aspects of their lives. This generally requires a resiliency that enables them to overcome an array of structural obstacles and psychological barriers to successfully navigate the new environment, often utilizing their professional expertise to do so, as noted by Portes (2006). For some, transnational ties may become a catalyst to counter the strain of occupational change. Such ties are generally forged through political participation and economic investment or involvement in cultural events reminiscent of the home country. Portes (2006) found that foreign professionals usually enter the U.S. legally and "are not destined to the bottom of the rungs of the American labor market... they do not come to escape poverty but to improve their careers and life chances, seldom accepting menial jobs in the United States" (p. 25). However, little is known about the growing numbers of those who do not fit this model because of immigration status or other circumstances relating to interpersonal, structural or cross-cultural factors.

Concerned about occupational dissonance of foreign professionals, the New York City Immigration Council sought to develop a strategy to increase the employment opportunities of entering professional immigrants (Lamb, 2006). Kendall Stewart, Chairperson of the Immigration Council, argues that the problem is exacerbated by the unwillingness of employers in the United States to negotiate the immigrants' educational credentials, and the inability of entering professionals to effectively access the North American workplace system (Lamb, 2006). It is important to note that with the economic crisis, some native born professionals are likely to have a similar experience.

Literature Review

Studies of international migration and transnationalism have emphasized economic and political factors (Foner, 2001; Basch, Schiller and Szanton-Blanc, 1994). However, though immigration has become a sensitive issue in foreign and domestic policy, the psychological/health dimension, which is intimately linked to adaptation to the new environment, has not been given wide attention. Neither is there any clear understanding of the consequences of occupational change among immigrants following their arrival in the United States (Chiswick 1998). Three explanations, namely human capital, assimilation, and cultural and structural pluralism, provide a basis for understanding how immigrants merge occupationally into American society.

The human capital perspective posits that the flow of labor across national boundaries is beneficial to both the host and sending societies. While immigrants bring needed skills to the host society, this also contributes to the "brain drain" in the country of origin. Emphasis is placed on the direct relationship between immigrants' work-related skills and success in the larger economy. According to Powers and Seltzer, 1998) the presumptions of the assimilation model are that many immigrants 'enter at the bottom' of the labor market and gradually ascend as they are acculturated. Portes and Rumbaut (2006) posit that "professional immigrants are among the most rapidly assimilated. Reasons include their occupational success and absence of strong ethnic networks to reinforce the culture of origin" (p. 26).

Emerging from these perspectives is the question of personal and social costs of immigration, including the change in occupational status and the ambivalence it creates. Not only does the immigrant have to mourn the loss of kin and community, but he/she also sacrifices an occupation for which there may have been long-term commitment, while entering a host society which invariably restricts access to the status/honor system (Misir 1997).

Structural explanations suggest that newly arrived immigrants, regardless of pre-migration occupational status, become vulnerable to low wages and low status periphery jobs offering little opportunity for promotion (Doeringer and Piore 1971; Tolbert et al. 1980). Among such immigrants are those who "enter the country illegally or have not managed to meet the high accreditation requirements of their respective fields" (Portes, 2006, p. 27). In her research on English-speaking Caribbean immigrants, Brice-Baker (1996) found that the available jobs such as domestic work are far below many immigrants' training, and educational background. The impact of such workplace shifts can result in negative emotional outcomes or promote creative coping strategies. Holder (1998) argues that those immigrants with a professional background have been discriminately excluded from high-paying jobs and "some either exaggerated the importance of their work or outright lied about it to friends and family" (p. 39). The consolation in accepting secondary employment is that it allows immigrants to provide for their families without the worry of lacking American experience/certification soon after their arrival. Alternatively, "well-educated immigrants turn to entrepreneurial pursuits" (Foner, 2013, p.12), while others become frustrated by the necessity of accepting 'any job' in an environment where they are already experiencing cultural dissonance.

Resettlement is a transitional life crisis since it causes disruptions in the efforts to satisfy basic human needs and improve life circumstances (Hulewat 1996; Sontag 1998). Indeed, the receiving society promises attractive features such as better employment opportunities, advanced education and social services. But "almost every migration story is a psychodrama of a family, its aspirations and frustrations, its separations and reunions, its traditions and compromises" (Sontag 1998: 1). This often includes having to discard certain customs and rituals that were essential to their sustenance in the home country.

Amidst this transition are opportunities to reconfigure their life space with the demands in the new culture in order to return to the task of satisfying basic needs. A stark reality, however, is that adaptation to novel environmental situations that includes occupational changes often follows a 'bumpy line' (Gans 1996), making the regaining of occupational or community status either unreachable or arduous. There are those who endure the hardship of simultaneously holding two or three jobs in areas other than their profession or training while internalizing the emotional effects of personal sacrifices. A dilemma for many Caribbean immigrants is the potential erosion of previously earned occupational status in a new social setting where they no longer control resources such as land and community access. They may also have to contend with unfamiliar institutional barriers.

The manifestation of professional competence acquired in the home country is frequently muffled by a compromising change in occupation following migration. Some immigrants define their personal worth by their vocation and it is not uncommon for the working immigrant to be in conflict with 'self' and begin to question the decision to emigrate (Ramadar 2006). Waters found that low skilled and working class first generation West Indians "are able to separate their own self-worth from their work" (1997: 4).

However, this does not seem to hold true for the entering professionals, many of whom tend to be status conscious and for whom occupational and personal fulfillment is not only attained by satisfactory performance of one's profession, but can also symbolize self-definition. Other experiences that have an impact on self-perception are ethnic discrimination and anti-immigrant sentiment, both within the occupational arena and wider society. Gopaul-McNicol and Brice-Baker (1997) refer to racism as a risk factor for the development of anxiety among Caribbean immigrants, while Poussaint and Alexander (2000) view racism as a mental health problem for African Americans, a group into which many Caribbean immigrants have been categorized due to phenotypic similarity and minority status.

As persons of color, Caribbean immigrants are subjected to inequalities and discrimination based on race, ethnicity and their immigrant status, particularly in light of the apparent resurgence in nativism in the United States (Matthews, 2006). This is indeed an added burden for those who are already troubled by change in occupation. In some instances, abandoning one's career for a low-status job or retraining in a new career path produces a necessary alternative and causes new anxieties. In the quest to improve their life situation in their adopted home, immigrants face many challenges including those related to cultural, social and psychological issues (Sher and Vilens, 2010). Kasinitz (1993) posits that in general, Caribbean immigrants enter a social system that is more economically advanced than the country of origin, and because of their ethnicity (primarily Afro and Indo-Caribbean), tend to join the ranks of America's most oppressed groups. Consequently, their efforts to reestablish occupational and other life-sustaining social activities are largely defined by their social/ethnic categorization in the new society.

In an effort to reestablish a career, the immigrant's hope is to resume personal and occupational development. Notwithstanding adjustment difficulties, professional growth and the capacity to adapt to the new environment have been demonstrated among immigrants. Increasing numbers of Caribbean college graduates and entrepreneurs have integrated into a wide cross-section of society in the United Sates. In addition, the trend among English Caribbean immigrants of considering education and professional training as essential is reflected in their socioeconomic characteristics. For example, in New York City, 38% percent of the total immigrant population (383,835) from Jamaica, Guyana and Trinidad and Tobago are college graduates (U.S. Census Bureau, 2009).

Those who are successfully integrated into the job market have done so in a wide area of occupations including teaching, human services, entrepreneurship, and healthcare (Singh, 2001). To underscore the attempt to adjust socially and psychologically, Maingot (1985) contends that English-speaking Caribbean immigrants demonstrate "aggressive compensatory behavior frequently associated with entrepreneurship and drive" (p. 28).

However, racism and discrimination have also accompanied these successes, as revealed in an occupational environment lawsuit filed in New York City by a group of English-speaking Caribbean immigrants against a leading brokerage firm. The suit charged that immigrants were constantly harassed and ridiculed by supervisors (Barrett, 2000).

In his study of English-speaking Caribbean immigrants, Nwadiora (1995) reported that 65 percent of his sample experienced work-related stress. During the first few years of their arrival, immigrants are at risk of alienation and psychological stress as they attempt to cope with physical, biological, climatic and cultural changes while integrating pre-migration and migration experiences. Social and psychological outcomes of migration can be exacerbated by downward occupational adjustment and diminished social status (Alba 1997; Ramadar 2006). This 'crisis of loss' is also the fate of entering nonprofessionals, for whom menial service employment in the United States represents occupational and upward social mobility (Holder 1998). These immigrants also have problems of adjustment. Migration may improve social standing, but certain factors such as documentation status, age, traditionalism, circumstance of departure and host society accommodation do impact on the strides of achievement in the United States. In this regard, Lewis (1990) notes: "On the one hand they are welcomed to low-status jobs nobody else wants; on the other, they are pilloried for taking away jobs from the local working class." This contradiction is unequivocally played out in the controversial immigration debate regarding undocumented immigrants. The United States House of Representatives and the Senate have struggled to pass a comprehensive bill that would perhaps strike a balance between restrictive and liberal immigration procedures, much of which center around employment (Hulse and Johnston, 2006).

Finally, Naditch and Morrissey (1976) point to other significant stress-related problems such as role conflicts and loss of control over life circumstances. Entering professional immigrants who experience a downward shift in social/occupational status are likely to have carried out their occupational, family provider and protector roles with varying degrees of success before migrating. As such, feelings of self-fulfillment from vocational competence and self-actualizing abilities were already in motion. After migration, anxiety and optimism tend to predominate (Sluzki, 1979). Anxiety or depression may be caused by dissatisfaction with a new occupation and inability to fully affirm the provider role, while optimism rests upon aspirations that may or may not be realized. This study attempts to add to the literature by investigating the extent to which adjustment problems and mental health issues emanate from occupational change.

Conceptual Framework

This study draws from the concepts of social capital, cultural capital, and social identity (Campbell, Cornish, & McLean, 2004) as conceptual tools for exploring the impact of changing one's occupation and social environment due to migration. Social capital involves community participation through activities such as employment and volunteer work for community building. Cultural capital, which may include academic qualifications and training, comprises "a set of social practices and skills that are cultivated during a person's development and demonstrate his or her membership of a particular social grouping or class" (Campbell, et. al, 2004, p. 317). Social identity provides the grounding required for membership to a particular social grouping, which for the purposes of this study may include other immigrants and members of the host society. The immigrant's loss of personal resources, such as employment held in the home country does not only impact social and community spheres of life, but is often accompanied by compromises and emotional difficulties. It is imperative that the immigrant finds sustainable alternatives and productive activities for "making a living" in the adopted country.

Method

This is an exploratory study using two approaches. The first data set of this study was a survey conducted to collect information from Caribbean immigrants about the type of occupational change they made and to identify adjustment issues in making the change. Adult immigrants with pre-migration, professional occupational backgrounds were selected since it has been problematic for this group to occupationally integrate into American society. The researcher identified and visited institutions such as schools, churches and social clubs frequented by English-speaking Caribbean immigrants to explain his research interest and the voluntary nature of the project. Two trained research assistants, knowledgeable on both American and Anglophone Caribbean culture, assisted him. After follow-up phone calls to those who were willing to participate, a 15-item self-administered questionnaire was mailed to each participant.

The subjects were instructed to complete the questionnaire to the best of their ability and mail it to the researcher. Fifty-two (52) questionnaires were sent out and 35 were returned completed. This accounted for a response rate of 67% percent. The questionnaire data were reviewed and grouped into categories by themes. There were certain patterns that emerged from the data that clearly identified similar and dissimilar experiences among participants.

The second set of data was gathered from formal interviews conducted with English speaking Caribbean clients at the Bedford Stuyvesant Community Mental Health Center in New York City to determine the impact of occupational change on mental health. The goal of this aspect of the research was to explore the link between occupational change and mental health. The cases were selected from a group of ten recipients of service whose presenting problem included change of occupation as a psychosocial stressor. Due to confidentiality concerns, the interviews were conducted over a period of six months by this writer, a trained clinical social worker who is also familiar with Caribbean culture. Authorization to conduct the study was granted by the Clinic Director and subjects were made aware of the use of the shared information exclusively for the purpose of research. Data from the interviews were used to verify some of the issues that emerged from the questionnaires.

FINDINGS

Occupational Change and Adjustment Problems

Most of the respondents resided in the United Sates for five years or more. Fourteen (14) of them reported that they were in management posts in the Caribbean, 12 were teachers and nine of them described their profession as "technical" or medical. When asked what changes they had made in their occupation after migrating to the United States, 70% (24) of the respondents reported that they changed to a non-professional job. The post-migration employment included home attendants (10), factory workers (4), hotel workers (2), security guards (7), hospital lab assistant (1), file clerks (2), and receptionists (2). Four former teachers and three former managers continued in a similar profession.

However, many of the teachers taught at a grade-level far below their training, and individuals who had less managerial skills were supervising the immigrant managers. Most of the respondents, 72% (25) reported frustration and disappointment in their post-migration occupation, while 29% (10) stated that they were satisfied with their employment situation and one reported that the job experience was "humbling". Among those who experienced frustration, regret or disappointment, the most frequently reported reasons were job conditions, unfamiliar procedures and cultural differences. An interesting finding is that those who retained a lower level professional job in the United States reported that job conditions (as compared to those in the home country) ranked as the primary reason for satisfaction with their occupation. Their American work experience in that field seemed to be more rewarding.

Table 3.1
CHARASTERISTICS OF OCCUPATIONAL CHANGE

PRE-MIGRATORY POSITION	NO. OF PERSONS	%
Management	14	40
Teaching	12	34
Technical/Medical	9	25
TOTAL	35	100
POST-MIGRATORY POSITION	NO. OF PERSONS	%
Home Attendant	10	28
Factory Worker	4	11
Hotel Worker	2	6
Security Guard	7	20
File Clerk	4	11
Hospital Lab Assistant	1	3
Continued Similar Position	7	20
TOTAL	35	99

When asked about the way in which they dealt with negative feelings regarding the change in occupation, 81% of respondents (28) stated that they talked to a friend or co-worker. Only one respondent reported talking to a family member openly about the problem. Fifty-nine percent (59%) of respondents (20) felt that the change in occupation had little or no effect on their personal relationships, while 18% of respondents (5) thought that serious relational difficulties resulted from occupational change. However, none of the respondents from this survey group sought professional help.

One of the researcher's interests was to find out what changes in the immigrants' lifestyle occurred and to what extent these were related to occupational change. The reported changes in lifestyle were grouped into four categories: cultural, interpersonal, work-related and social status. Those lifestyle changes related to cultural differences appeared to be characteristic of the general immigrant population and included "living in an apartment", "food habits", "adapting to discriminatory issues", "changed customs", and "increased fiscal responsibility". There was no indication that cultural dissonance had any bearing on the shift in occupation. Conversely, interpersonal relationships were affected by occupational change.

The majority of those respondents who were forced to accept non-professional jobs, 77% (26), identified interpersonal problems as manifestations of their changed lifestyles. Other responses included "socialize less", "fractured family", "impersonal treatment", "changes in relationships", "teenage rebellion", "isolation from family", "living in other people's houses", "assuming leadership role in family", and "changed to an aggressive person". Many respondents, 66% (23) also reported being "saddened" when they learned that they had to start over. These findings highlight the potential effects of occupational change on interpersonal relations, and require strategies of adaptation that include a reexamination of the normal adult roles in employment, including the impact of occupational change on gender roles among immigrants.

Work-related problems as a lifestyle issue had some relationship to occupational change. All of the respondents, who changed from a professional to non-professional job after migrating experienced job-related lifestyle changes and adjustment problems. The concerns centered around extended working hours, the need to have more than one job, lack of freedom and mobility, accepting low level jobs, working unfamiliar shifts, and job insecurity. One immigrant who worked as a home attendant reported resentment at having to conform to the rules/regulations of the employer's household . . . I "was not treated as a person".

Finally, although many immigrants reportedly enjoy a better standard of living and have taken opportunities that facilitate upward mobility in the United States, for some, adjustment in social status was identified as a function of occupational change. Those respondents who reported being frustrated over their changed occupation tended to express concern about a decline in social status. One respondent reported, "My status has changed from upper middle class . . . to a very humbling position in this new society." Another stated, "For immigrants to survive in this country they should be prepared and be ready to forego the status they enjoyed in their native land." While a third one reported having to adjust to "a lower standard of living." There is a tendency to assume that immigrants' acceptance of any job in the United States or other developed country means an automatic conduit to improved social standing.

Eighteen percent of respondents (6) reported that they were not aware of the employment changes they had to make in the United States, while 40% (14) stated that they knew they had to make adjustments in occupation, albeit not as radical. Many, 74% of respondents (25) felt that immigrants must be prepared to take jobs below their education or skills level, seeing this process as a means to an end. However, there was much variation in the suggestions about how this could be accomplished. One respondent stated that immigrants should try to get rid of their accent as a way of communicating with co-workers. Another reported that it was important to maintain your work ethic (i.e. behavior, dress, dependability). There was a general understanding that occupational demands are much different from those in the Caribbean. In this regard, one respondent referred to the difficulty in acquiring a position equivalent to that held in the Caribbean, the need to be qualified to hold such a position and the realization that racial/ethnic discrimination exists.

Occupational Change And Mental Health

The anecdotal responses and discussion that follow are based on clinic interviews.

Ms. M., age 47, a senior history teacher in one of the most renowned high schools in her Caribbean hometown, was well respected and highly competent. She resided with her cousin, her only close host relative in the United States. Ms. M. tried unsuccessfully to gain employment in her field. Eventually, with the responsibility of providing for her family in the Caribbean and embarrassment at her extended dependence on her cousin, she reluctantly accepted a job as a Housekeeper. After months of trying to cope on her own, she was seen at the clinic for depressive symptoms.

Ms. M.'s experience typifies the frustrations often faced by immigrants who find themselves unhinged from their accustomed means of productive activity, self-sufficiency and occupational status. Adequate satisfaction of a number of her basic needs was being thwarted, seemingly precipitated by change in employment and other stressors. She had also become dependent on someone who did not have as much formal education, was not a member of her immediate family, and who was living in a more stable situation than she was. This created in Ms. M. a sense of alienation and a negative self-image—prime ingredients for further stress.

Ms. M.'s ambivalence about living in the United States became apparent when she began to question her decision to relocate, which was based on the need to provide for her family because "things were getting hard in that place [home country]". It is believed that the decision to emigrate is often forged by "rational economic choice"

(Massey et al. 1993) devoid of anticipated social and psychological difficulties, namely alteration in occupation, status and interpersonal relationships. Ms. M., unprepared as she was for this morass of stress producing situations, was potentially at risk for physical and emotional problems. She envisioned little opportunity for self-actualization.

Mr. H. was a high-ranking government official and former political party candidate in the Caribbean. At 55 years of age, with an advanced degree and married with three adult children, he arrived in New York City on a visitor's visa with his wife. They resided with her niece in a two-bedroom apartment for six months. Mr. H. had intended to return to his home country at the expiration of the visa, but after some discussion on the matter with host relatives, decided to remain in the United States. He did not take to the United States the personal effects that he would have needed had he initially planned to migrate on a permanent basis.

He began looking for a job in his field by networking with friends, sending out resumes and following up on contacts he had made on previous home country-related official visits to the United States. After several promising interviews and no positive outcomes, he became frustrated, much of which was manifested by angry outbursts and periodic bouts of anxiety. His wife, an ex-senior bank official in the home country, was able to find a part-time job as a Home Attendant. Drained of the paltry resources and feeling a growing sense of imposition on the host relative, Mr. H. developed a stomach malady, while his wife became clinically depressed. As Sluzki (1997) observes, as a result of the stress related to looking for a stable job, and slow familiarization with the new social environment, an anxious depression tends to emerge among some immigrants.

The case of Mr. and Ms. H. reveals some interesting aspects of the problems relating to occupational change and how it may affect mental health. Although there are no accurate figures of immigrants who overstay their visas, this situation is not uncommon. A man who wielded much influence and prestige and a man of considerable pride, he was determined not to accept a non-professional job, preferring to work in his field. Self-actualization for him was determined by his ability to retain his self-worth through continued practice of his chosen occupation.

Mr. H's behavior may seem irrational, considering his undocumented immigration status. He was accustomed to being independent, owned a luxurious home in the Caribbean, and made important business/professional decisions that influenced public policy. In his new environment, the family resided in a cluttered apartment, rubbing shoulders with individuals considered of lower social class status. Consequently, these events and transformations caused consternation and psychological distress.

After about six months, Mr. H. was caught in what he described as a "no win situation". He thought of returning to his home country, but felt that it would be embarrassing to face the community, whom he felt would see him as a failure. Once he decided to reside permanently in the United States, he began making alternate arrangements for his assets in the Caribbean, the long distance administration of which was difficult to manage, and created additional emotional strain. Mr. H. entered therapy, but discontinued after a short time. He was optimistic about an interview for a teaching position at a prestigious university, but was not hired, and attributed this to his 'age'. Shortly thereafter, he relocated to another state and attempted to find a middle management job in industry in the hope that he would be sponsored for permanent residency. That too did not materialize and he returned to New York.

Despondent, Mr. H. eventually accepted a paid position assisting a friend who had a small business located in one of the Caribbean immigrant communities. Still frustrated by his inability to find employment that would measure up to his skills and knowledge, he decided to join a community based ethnic organization. In this regard, Misir (1997) notes that immigrants' decision to join Hometown Associations appears to be typically linked to an attempt to cope with alienation, reduce stress, improve self-image and regain lost social standing.

Portes and Rumbaut (2006) noted that it is not uncommon to find professional immigrants in the United States illegally. In their discussion of risk factors causing anxiety, Gopaul-McNicol and Brice-Baker (1997) note that it could be traumatic for Caribbean immigrants who enjoyed certain benefits and privileges because of their social class, lighter skin color, or occupational status to arrive in the United States and "be relegated to the lowest rung of society" (p. 90).

Holder (1998) highlights the experience and behaviors associated with changed social status among professional and privileged Caribbean female immigrants who had to cope with the psychological and physical stress they encountered in domestic or other menial employment. Some of them demanded respect and courtesy "in an apparent attempt to maintain their sense of self-worth and to diminish the social distance between themselves and their employers" (Holder, p. 56).

For both social adaptation and therapeutic reasons, it is important to identify and adequately assess the needs of those immigrants who are unable to emotionally disconnect from or adequately compensate for past occupational and community status. Helping them through advocacy and resource identification to establish a support network through community organizations could serve as a conduit to effective occupational and personal adjustment. Sometimes the shame and guilt is so intense that even family members are not an effective source of comfort.

Ms. S., age 42, migrated to the United States with her teenage son, who was referred for mental health treatment. She is a trained teacher and prior to her migration served as a High School Principal. A documented resident, she works as a nurse's aide. During the initial period of her arrival in the United States, she worked as a teacher's aide for two months, until she quit because: I just could not deal with those kids . . . it was different at home (in the Caribbean) . . . we did not have this discipline problem. She stated that working as a nurse's aide is hard work, but it paid the bills, although it was an unwilling compromise in occupation.

Ms. S. took her son, who had a history of mental health problems, to the clinic on a regular basis. After missing several appointments she complained to the Clinic Director that she had difficulty communicating with the Social Worker and requested one of Caribbean background that she believed would understand her situation better and understands her culture. Upon investigating the complaint, it was found that there were a number of problematic issues related to cultural difference, self-image and change in occupational status. When the assigned worker saw Ms. S. and her son, she was told that her son's case would be terminated if he missed future appointments. Ms. S. insisted that she tried her best to keep appointments and distressingly bemoaned: "My work schedule makes it difficult for us to get here . . . I know it is important, but not only would I be losing $80 for the day taken to come here, I could also lose my job." She later reported to the Clinic Administrator that she felt scolded and belittled by an individual (social worker) whose position at the clinic reminded her of persons she had supervised in the Caribbean. Furthermore, she thought that very little effort was made to empathize with her situation. This experience evoked in Ms. S. feelings of frustration, aggravation, and helplessness. She referred to her profession as an educator, reminisced about her lifestyle in the Caribbean and made contrasts with her occupation and status as an immigrant struggling to survive.

Immigrants grappling with issues of self-esteem and painful adjustment may engage an adaptive defense against the trauma of migration (Sher and Vilens, 2010; Sluzki, 1979). Ms. S. and others who experience a change in occupation and social standing consider that which was left behind, i.e. career, community recognition in country of birth, as the ideal to be glorified. At the same time they disparage the initial post-migration experience that involves doing jobs that are far below their education and skill level, while being deprived of community recognition and a lifestyle to which they had grown accustomed.

As part of her treatment plan, Ms. S. was encouraged to join the Caribbean ex-Teachers Association, one of several burgeoning Hometown Associations, as a way of networking with others from her culture, and to help alleviate the stress she was experiencing. These organizations promote heritage activities. Nostalgic recreations of the past, though symbolic, generally have a therapeutic effect on the adaptation of immigrants to a new and different social environment. The immigrants' association with community organizations, whose activities can potentially fulfill filiation needs and rebuild positive self-image, may be crucial to their social identity. Recognition of the interdependent relationship between the immigrant and the community is crucial in helping to alleviate adjustment problems.

Compromising occupational change and the issues relating to it do not only affect newly arrived immigrants. Such an experience may be temporary, and may be overcome when immigrants attain a better footing in the United States. Contrastingly, occupational compromise could develop into a lingering discomfort that, in turn, affects interpersonal relations.

Mr. and Mrs. K., who were high salaried civil servants in the Caribbean, lived comfortably in an urban community there. After arriving in the U.S., they resided with relatives for approximately six months in an overcrowded apartment located in a section of the city which had a large Caribbean population. Their two children, ages 6 and 14, were placed in public school and were adjusting well.

Mr. K., a skilled civil engineer, found a part time job within a few weeks, but Mrs. K. was unable to find a job for several months. Among the reasons for not being hired were: No American experience; we are looking for a younger person; we cannot use these credentials, you will have to take a test; you need a State driver's license. This frustrated Mrs. K. whose contribution to the household expenses was essential, and as a result of conflict with the host relative, the K. family moved to their own apartment earlier than they were prepared to. However, Mrs. K. began to complain about living in this lower class neighborhood . . . I don't even feel safe in the neighborhood. She was initially resistant to taking just any job, but eventually accepted employment as a Home Attendant since the family's resources were diminishing and they wanted to avoid any further dependence on their host relatives.

A remarkable consequence of immigration to the United States is the equalizing effect with regard to occupation, income and status.

This is exemplified when immigrants of different social positions in the Caribbean find themselves juxtaposed in the same community of residence and work setting, holding similar job titles and sharing the same public, mass transportation in the United States. Much to her dislike, Mrs. K. had to contend with that situation. Among those who have had to surrender their pre-migratory occupational status, feelings of embarrassment manifested by avoidance behavior and denial have been reported (personal communication).

Mrs. K. expressed joy at having migrated to the United States, but resented where she lived and what she had to do for a living. The family was referred for therapy, due to marital conflict and allegations of child abuse. Frustrations relating to occupational change and household conditions were presenting problems. During the initial phase of adjustment, there is usually a strong dependence on host relatives for basic resources. However, migration unintentionally disrupts the spatial arrangement of family/household constellations. Extended family members, who have never lived together, find themselves in intimate interaction, expecting to quickly adjust to one another, and to respect unfamiliar boundaries. This situation can strengthen ties and mutual support, but can also produce anxiety and tension, especially if there are role diminishment and feelings of occupational displacement.

Within four years, the K. family was able to accumulate enough money and other resources to purchase a house. For Mr. and Mrs. K., moving into their own home in the suburbs, even though there was occupational dissonance, compensated for what they had lost in the Caribbean (professional status and residency in a middle class neighborhood), but they also had an opportunity to begin their journey toward what they defined as the 'American dream'.

Mrs. K. stated anxiously that she looked forward to the day when she could "measure up" to her friends, who also had their own homes. In this regard, it is likely that immigrants such as Mrs. K would realize that dream of accomplishment. In doing so, they would have a sense of regaining the status they had to relinquish. To this point, Powers and Seltzer (1998) posit that there is evidence to conclude that "geographic mobility may permit a redefinition of gender relations and improvement in women's status as they move to areas where a wider spectrum of social and economic opportunities are open to them" (p.27).

The final case is a 38 year old physician, who left her home country on a medical visa and remained in the United States after the successful completion of her treatment. She was also a political activist, who had some disfavor with the local home country government. Aware of the dilemma of her inability to gain meaningful employment due to her undocumented status, she avoided socializing with others from her home country, accepting a job as a Nursing Assistant. Although in constant communication with her family in the home country by phone and via the Internet, she did not reveal to them the nature of her employment, fearing that the consequence of such news would be devastating.

Discussion

The data provided an understanding of the effects of occupational change on immigrants' adjustment. The study did reveal the existence of negative experiences among immigrants who once held professional jobs in their country of origin. Clear themes emerged from the sample, including frequent problematic outcomes such as work-related issues, decrease in social status (compared to social standing in home country), and difficulties with interpersonal relationships. Giving up one's professional identity, cultivated through many years of training and education, and modifying certain customs and beliefs are within the realm of migratory sacrifices.

The findings support the literature by confirming that migration is a transitional crisis, characterized by stress and anxiety, at times exacerbated by occupational compromises. Structural issues such as institutional racism, ageism (many professional immigrants tend to be middle-aged), and the inability to negotiate the American workplace, may result in prolonged occupational and social adaptation difficulties. The inevitability of occupational change among professional immigrants encompasses issues relating to integrity, self-esteem and job security. In assessing work-related problems and the impact on adjustment, it is essential that advocates push for immigrants' rights and help professionals become aware of the ethical and social justice implications when occupational changes occur.

Change in occupation of entering professionals is common among English-speaking Caribbean immigrants. Indeed, immigrants benefit from educational and employment opportunities in the United States and this may compensate for some of what they have lost in the transition. Despite the argument that "foreign professionals have generally done very well occupationally and economically" (Portes and Rumbaut, 2006, p.27), this study reveals that occupational change is stress producing. Although many 'new Americans' appear to have the will and host relatives' support to help them make employment changes, there are hidden dimensions of structural barriers and acculturative stress, and the tendency to mask the pain, frustration, and compromise.

This experience is not limited to the undocumented and to those who did not plan their migration carefully. As Maingot (1985) observes, migration is not always accompanied by stress and other psychological afflictions, but the inevitability of emotional and physical distress stemming from occupation and status change must be acknowledged and addressed. This study builds on the theoretical models of international migration by providing empirical data and raises key questions pertaining to a significant aspect of adaptation to a new society.

CONCLUSION

With the large number of entering professional immigrants in the United States, it is important to understand the dilemma they often face and the effects on their social adaptation and mental health. The unintended consequences of migration are generally underestimated but do influence the nature of adjustment to the new host society. Acknowledging the problems encountered by skilled professional immigrants, the New York City Council's Immigration Committee committed to assist immigrant professionals adapt to the job market and advise them about available options (Lamb, 2006).

The intensity of the immigration debate, including human capital issues, demonstrates the social, political and economic significance of immigrants to the US workforce at all levels of employment. Recognizing the shortage of scientists and engineers, proponents of the proposed Immigration Bill seek to promote the admission of professionals (Nextgov Newsletter 2013). This would increase the granting of work visas to selected groups. This study highlighted the activities of those professional immigrants whose transition has been challenging. The consequential dilemma of occupational change is evident and so is the relationship between human capital of immigrants and their transnational experiences.

As Lamb (2006) proposed, institutions, including those in higher education, must assume an empowering role in providing academic upgrading and training of newly arrived professional immigrants, helping them navigate the American employment opportunity structure. This privilege should not be afforded exclusively to those holding H1B (Employment) visas. Educators and other helping professionals can enhance the immigrants' coping capacity and knowledge of civil, political, and legal systems. Not only would this help in the adjustment process, but it would make appropriate employment more feasible and accessible to immigrants, paying attention to professional identity and occupational functioning. With such a design, their contribution to national development and civil society in general, both as skilled professionals and taxpayers, would be immeasurable.

NOTES

1. Information for this chapter was drawn from a study conducted by the author on the topic: "Occupational Change among Caribbean Immigrants: Implications for Adjustment and Mental Health".

Bibliography

Alba, R. (1997). "Rethinking Assimilation Theory for a New Era of Immigrant." *International Migration Review* 31, No. 4: 826-834.

Barrett, D. (2000). "Wall Street Giant Hit With Race-Bias Suit." *The New York Post*, Saturday, September 30th.

Basch, L, G., N.G. Schiller and V. Blanc-Szanton (1994). *Nations Abound: Transnational Projects, Post Colonial Predicaments and De-territorialized Nation States*. Longhorn, PA: Gordon and Breach.

Brice-Baker, J. (1996). "Jamaican Families". In *Ethnicity and Family Therapy*. Edited by M. McGoldrick, J. Giordano, and J.K. Pierce. NY: Guilford Press.

Campbell, C, F. Cornish, and C. Mclean (2004). "Social Capital, Participation & Perpetuation of Health Inadequacies: Obstacles to African-Caribbean Participation in 'Partnership' to Improve Mental Health" *Ethnicity & Health*, Vol. 9, No. 4, November, 313-335.

Caribbean Life (2006). "Leaders Face Reality Check: Brain Drain", *CSME Dominate Agenda*. New York, July, 11th.

Chiswick, B.R. (1986). "Is the New Immigrant Less Skilled than the Old?" *Journal of Labor Economics*, Volume 4, No. 2: 168-192.

Deoringer, P.B. and M.J. Piore (1971). *Internal Labor Market and Manpower Analysis*. Cambridge, MA: Lexington.

Dressler, W.W. (1985). "Stress and Sorcery In Three Social Groups." *International Journal of Psychiatry*, 31, no. 4: 275-281.

Foner. N. (2013) One Out of Three: Immigrant New York in the 21st Century. New York: Columbia Univ. Press.

Gans, H. (1996). "Comment: Ethnic Invention and Acculturation – A Bumpy-Line Approach." In *Taking Sides: Clashing Views on Race and Ethnicity*, edited by R.C. Monk, 2nd edition. Guilford, CT: Dushkin Publishing Group.

Gopaul-McNicol, S. and J. Brice-Baker (1997). "Caribbean Americans." In S. Friedman (Ed.) *Cultural Issues in the Treatment of Anxiety*. NY: The Guilford Press.

Holder, C. (1998). "The West Indian Economic Adjustment in New York City, 1900 to 1952." *WADABAEI* (A Journal of the Caribbean and its Diaspora), Volume 1, no. 1, p. 39.

Hulewat, P. (1996). "Resettlement: A Cultural and Psychological Crisis". *Social Work*, 41, no.2: 129-135.

Hulse, C. and D. Johnston (2006). "Border Fight Divides G.O.P. As President and Senate Differ with White House." *The New York Times*, May 26th.

Jamaica Gleaner (2006). Major Brain Drain – IMF says Caribbean has lost 70 percent of Workforce. Washington (CMC), February 20th.

Kasinitz, P. (1993). *Caribbean New York: Black Immigrants and the Politics of Race*. New York: Cornell University Press.

Lamb, D. (2006). "Immigration Committee Tackles Problems Facing Skilled Professional Immigrants." *Caribbean Life*, May, 16.

Lewis, G. (1990). "Foreward". *In Search of a Better Life: Perspective on*

Migration From The Caribbean, Edited by R. Palmer, New York: Praeger.

Maingot, A.P. (1985). "The Stress Factors In Migration, A Dissenting View." *Migration Today*, 13, no. 5: 26-29.

Massey, D.S., et al. (1993). "Theories of International Migration: A Review And Appraisal." *Population and* Development Review, no. 3: 431-466.

Matthews, L. (2002). "Occupational Change among Caribbean Immigrants: Implications for Adjustment and Mental Health". *Caribbean Journal of Social Work,* Volume 1, March.

——, (2006). "The Immigration Debate: All about Politics, Economics, And Resurgence of Nativism." *Caribbean Impact.* April, 1st. Social Work, Volume 1, March.

Misir, P. (1997). "Toward an Understanding of Division in Community Organization." *Caribbean Journal*, 17.

Naditch, M.P. and R.F. Morrissey (1976). "Role Stress, Personality, and Psychopathology in a Group of Immigrant Adolescents." *Journal of American Psychology,* 85:113-118.

New York City Department of City Planning Publication (2004).

New York City Department of City Planning Publication (2000).

New York City Department of City Planning Publication (1996).

NextGov. Newsletter (2013). "Democrat's Dilemma on High-skilled Immigration reform." http://www.nextgov.com/cio-briefing/2013/03/democrats-dilema-h . Retrieved 3/4/13.

Nwadiora, E. (1995). "Alienation and Stress among Black Immigrants: An Exploratory Study." *The Western Journal of Black Studies* 19, no. 1.

Portes, A. and R. Rumbaut (2006). *Immigrant Life in America: A Portrait.* Los Angeles: University of California Press, pp 25, 27.

Poussaint, A. and A. Alexander (2000). *Lay my Burden Down*. New York: Beacon Press.

Powers, M. G. and W. Seltzer (1998). "Occupational Status and Mobility among Undocumented Immigrants by Gender." *International Migration Review* 32, no. 1: 21-48.

Ramadar, F. (2006). *Caribbean East Indians in New York City, 1950-2000: Social Adjustment in a Core Global City. New York:* Caribbean Diaspora University Press.

Salvo, J. (2011). "The Demographic Highlights of a Changing New York." Presentation for Empire State College. NYC Planning: Department of City Planning, City of New York. November 10th.

Sher, L. and A. Vilens (2010). "Immigration and Mental Health: Stress, Psychiatric Disorders and Suicidal Behavior among Immigrants and Refugees. New York". *Nova Science Publishers*.

Singh, T. (2001). Senior Research Consultant, New York City Department of City Planning: Personal Communication, p 25.

Sluzki, C.E. (1979). "Migration and Family Conflict." *Family Process*, no.18: 379-390.

Sontag, D. (1998):1. "A Mexican Town that Transcends all Borders." *The New York Times,* July, 21st.

Tolbert, C., P.M. Horan, and E.M. Beck (1980). "The Structure of Economic Segmentation." A Dual Economy Approach. *American Journal of Sociology* 85: 1095-1116.

U.S. Sixteenth Census, (1940). Population Characteristics of Non-White Populations by Race. Washington, D.C.

Waters, M. (1997). "Race and Migration: The Case of West Indians". *EPIC CENTER (Newsletter of the International Center for Migration,* Ethnicity, and Citizenship) 11, nos. 1-2:4.

Vergel, G. (2009) "Shedding Light on the Lives of Black Migrants to New York." *In Focus*. Faculty and Research. New York: Fordham University.

Chapter Four

Transnational Parenting in the African Caribbean Community

Christiana Best-Cummings

INTRODUCTION

Transnational parenting or "mothering from a distance" (Hondagneu-Sotelo, & Avila, 1997; Salazar-Parrenas, R. 2009) is a phenomenon that invokes a variety of strong emotions. Many people are understandably sympathetic towards children who are separated from their mothers, but are critical and lack empathy for the mothers who are separated from their children because they had to leave them behind to travel to a foreign country to work. Although it is easy for social scientists, practitioners and ordinary citizens to see the emotional and psychological pain the children suffer as a direct result of the mother's absence, as well as the toll transnational parenting takes on the mothers, very often the reasons for transnational parenting are viewed as an individual choice made by the mothers and family members only. The structural issues that drive the parents' decisions are not easily recognized as a significant part of the decision making process. This narrow view focuses blame on individuals such as the mothers, fathers, and employers, as opposed to the discreet structural interaction between developed and developing countries that goes back to colonialism.

Irrespective of the cause, transnational parenting is difficult for everyone involved, particularly the mothers and children. While many of the mothers who have personally experienced "mothering from a distance", experience it as painful, challenging and difficult, they harbor a common belief that parenting from a distance is a means to an end as well, given their limited options. In addition to the pain they experience, these mothers feel a sense of helplessness, regret and guilt (Cummings, 2009). Their feelings of concern for their children are often intensified by the fear that their absence from their children may increase their children's vulnerability to being abused and or maltreated. Since many of the mothers are undocumented and are given entry into the United States to work on a temporary basis without a path to citizenship or permanent residence, they are unable to send for their children or visit their country of origin for many years. Consequently, they are obligated to engage in transnational parenting/mothering from a distance.

This chapter gives voice to African Caribbean mothers who have personally experienced transnational parenting and documents their attempt to share their experiences (1). Additionally, it attempts to illuminate some structural issues through the intersection of gender, race, socio-economic status, national origin, and immigration status.

Caribbean Migration Patterns

African Caribbean people, specifically those from the English-speaking countries otherwise known as the West Indies, are very familiar with the migration experience, beginning with the involuntary movement of Africans from the African continent to the West, followed by voluntary migration within the Caribbean region and later, beyond. Since the 1960's, West Indian migration expanded greatly to the United States, Canada, and England. Although working class African Caribbean women have participated in the migratory movement historically, their role was more of a peripheral one as they followed their male counterparts either as wives or laborers in countries such as Cuba, the Dominican Republic, Trinidad, Aruba and other parts of Central and South America such as Panama and Guyana. Today, African Caribbean women workers are central to the migration story in the United States, Canada and parts of Europe-The United Kingdom. In many cases, they are the primary migrant in their family, which intersects with their many roles as mother, nurturer, wife, head of household, and recruiter.

Many of these women migrate from developing countries to North America as nannies and child care workers under restrictive immigration laws. The increase in women migrants from the Caribbean and the Philippines coincided with the 1965 U.S. Immigration and Naturalization Act or Hart-Celler Act that followed the passage of the civil rights legislations in the United States. The Hart-Celler Act of 1965 abolished the national quota system the United States had in place, which favored European immigrants and opened up opportunities for people of color globally to migrate to the United States.

The Data: African Caribbean People in the U.S.

Immigrants from the English-speaking Caribbean countries make up the majority of Black Caribbean immigrants in the United States, with Jamaica accounting for 36% between 2008 and 2009. Trinidad and Tobago, Barbados and Grenada together accounted for 16%. It is important to note that the number of black immigrants from the non-English speaking Caribbean countries have also increased tremendously with Haiti representing 31% of all Black Caribbean immigrants. The Black immigrant population from the Dominican Republic also grew by 686% between 2008 and 2009, specifically (Migration Policy Institute 2012; Agency for Children's Services, 2009).

Although the number of Black Caribbean immigrants is notably high for Black immigrants as a whole, when compared with the foreign born population in New York City, the numbers are remarkable. For example, the top 10 countries of birth for the foreign-born population in New York City are: the Dominican Republic (13%); China (11%); Mexico (6%); Jamaica (6%); Guyana (5%); Ecuador (4%); Trinidad and Tobago and Haiti (3% each); and India and Russia (2% each) (MPI analysis of 2008; ACS, 2009).

On a national scale however, the Black immigrant population, particularly the African Caribbean population, pales in comparison with other immigrant groups. Nationally, the top 10 foreign born countries are Mexico (29%); China, India and the Philippines (5% each); and Vietnam and Korea (3% each). The other countries represented in the 10 top foreign-born countries nationally are Latin American countries. They are Cuba (3%), El Salvador (3%), Guatemala and the Dominican Republic (2% each). The Dominican Republic is the only country represented nationally with a significant number of Blacks (MPI Analysis of 2008 and 2009 ACS).

Consequently, the African Caribbean population in the United States is small in comparison to other immigrant groups and for many social scientists, and politicians alike, West Indians are indistinguishable from other minority groups. Owing to their small numerical presence, they are often lumped together with other minority groups such as (1) African Americans, (2) minorities in general; (3) immigrants as a whole and specifically, (4) black immigrants, and at times they are referred to and identified as a part of the (5) inner city populous. While these categories/groupings sometimes serve a positive purpose, there is a need to distinguish West Indians at times because as a group, they have some unique issues that will require their input and contributions. Although West Indians are similar racially to African Americans, there are also some distinctive issues that differentiate them from African Americans. These issues include their culture, immigration status, national origin, accent, the acculturation process, religion, discipline and other child rearing practices, food, climate, music, and most of all for some West Indians, the separation from their children and loved ones indefinitely due to immigration legislations and other structural practices. While in many cases being part of a collective has many benefits politically, concurrently, the collective groupings contribute to the invisibility of West Indians. Therefore, many of them experience a sense of loss and a feeling of being misunderstood, misrepresented and overlooked.

Gender and Immigration

Since the early 1990's, there appears to have been a shift in the gender ratio of immigrants coming to New York City down to 92 males per 100 females from 98 male per 100 females in the 1980's (Salvo and Ortiz, 1992). This change in the male to female gender ratio was in part because of the special provisions that were permitted in recent immigration laws, like "sixth preference". Sixth preference is given to either skilled or unskilled workers in occupations where labor is in short supply. As a result, immigrants in nursing and other health-related professions, which attracted a high number of female workers (Donato, 1992; Houston, Kramer & Barrett, 1984), have increased. The "sixth preference" also allowed women who were unskilled to migrate to the United States to work as "live-in" domestic servants (Kasinitz and Verkerman, 2001).

Child Fostering

Support for mothers to engage in transnational parenting comes from a number of people. Many mothers use a family member to take care of their children when they migrate to another country to work indefinitely. This practice in which there is an informal transfer of parental rights from the mother or parent who has migrated to an extended family member or guardian, usually female, who is caring for the child in the country of origin during the mother's absence is referred to as child fostering (Soto, 1987). Child fostering is a common cultural practice in West Indian and many African communities. It is not uncommon for children of large sibling groups to be sent to live with other extended family members, such as an aging aunt or grandparent, to assist with the care of that family member.

Today, child fostering is an integral part of transnational parenting. For the women in the study who have family members such as mothers, sisters, uncles, fathers, cousins etc, leaving their children behind with these relatives is usually the optimal choice. However, for the women who do not have relatives to care for their children, fostering their children with friends and guardians are often their only available choice (Best-Cummings and Gildner, 2004).

Serial Migration

Given the restrictions in the immigration legislations, the migration pattern from developing countries such as those in the West Indies to developed countries such as the United States occurs in a serial (Chrisiansen, Thormley-Brown, and Robinson, 1982) or "step-wise" manner (Smith, Lalonde and Johnson, 2004)). What is different about serial migration from many of the women in the study and many West Indians is the fact that the first parent to migrate is usually the mother, which means she has to leave her children behind. This is especially true in single-parent families. In two-parent families, both parents migrate, leaving the children behind, or one parent migrates, usually the mother, later followed by her husband and then the children (Baptiste, Hardy, and Lewis, 1997b; Christiansen et al., 1982; Nicol, 1971). Prior to the Immigration Act of 1965, the migration pattern for African Caribbean immigrants were similar to the rest of the world with the male immigrant leading followed by the spouse and children.

The Role of African Caribbean Immigrants

The role of women as caretakers and nurturers of their family is universal and has historically supported the foundation of the family in many cultures. The phenomenon of transnational parenting, where the mother travels to a foreign country leaving her children behind, challenges this cultural intervention because it is counter intuitive and creates a gap in the family structure. Despite this, more and more mothers from developing countries are opting/required to parent from a distance and establish transnational households.

The African Caribbean women's migratory journey to the United States is unlike most other traditional immigrant women who migrate together with their spouse and/or children. For many African Caribbean women, their migratory journey consists of traveling by themselves, leaving both children and spouse behind in their country of origin, to work, find housing, and provide financial support to family members at home, including their extended family. In addition to traveling on their own and making a home in the foreign country, they are the breadwinners and financial supporter of the family. They are also expected to continue to be the caretaker and nurturer of their children while providing emotional sustenance to their family members as well.

METHODOLOGY

This study is based on a qualitative study conducted in 2008-09. The data collected were based on interviews of African Caribbean women living in New York City who migrated to the United States from the English-speaking Caribbean countries. When these women first migrated, they left their children behind in their country of origin with family and other adults with the goal of finding a "better life" for themselves and their children.

At the time of the study, all the mothers had been reunited with their children. Many of the women in the study were undocumented immigrants at the time of the study, while some had received permanent resident status or were in the process of acquiring it. In an effort to protect their identity, they did not use their real names, nor were they interviewed in their residences. They were recruited using a non-probability (snowball) sample. The sample size was small due to the growing negative immigration sentiments that emerged after the September 11, 2001 terrorist attacks. As a result of the attacks, many undocumented and documented immigrants, particularly those of color, developed a keen sense of fear of being stopped, questioned, frisked, and arrested/deported due to the increased vigilance and racial profiling conducted by Immigration Control Enforcement (ICE) officers and the New York City Police Department (NYPD).

The participants in the study migrated from five West Indian countries. They are Grenada (65%), Trinidad (10%), Jamaica (10%), Antigua (10%) and St. Lucia (5%). These women migrated to New York City in the last 20 years and engaged in transnational parenting for a number of years when their children lived in their country of origin.

Literature Review

Transnationalism describes the processes immigrants use to build and maintain multifaceted social relationships that connect their country with their host country. Immigrants of today have different experiences from earlier emigrants because the newer immigrants have access to the development, growth and improvement in technology. These new technologies help to sustain familial, economic, cultural, and political relationships across international borders and by so doing, they are combining their home and the host countries into one arena of social action (Basch, Glick Schiller, & Szanton Blanc, 1994 as cited in Foner, 2001). Even though these migrants live in the United States, they have their hands on the pulse and are heavily involved in issues in their country of origin, through frequent telephone calls and other forms of communication.

Transnationalism is not just specific to the migrant populations; it also includes global corporations, media and communication networks, social movements and criminal and terrorist groups (Vertovec, 2003). Additionally, transnationalism includes circular flows of persons, goods, information and symbols triggered by international labor migration. It also deals with how migrants create and re-establish their lives while simultaneously living in two different worlds.

Transnational Parenting: The Structural Context

Globalization has created an economy that has increased the gap between the haves and the haves not. Developed economies such as the United States and countries in Europe have created a high demand for female workers in the labor market as professionals. Hence, more women in the United States and Europe are seeking higher education and are entering the job market as professionals, in fields such as law, finance, accounting and consulting services which used to be areas of work primarily for their male counterparts. Consequently, this has created a gap that is filled by the labor of the women from developing countries such as the West Indies and the Philippines (Salazar-Parrenas, 2001). The growth in these professional employments by the middle class creates demand for low-wage, low-skilled, service jobs, which are more attractive and accessible to immigrants than native minorities, because of the immigrant's eagerness to work these low-wage jobs (Sassen, S. 1994). This dynamic of having access to the low-wage labor market only sets up the undocumented immigrant woman in opposition with the American-born minority who is in need of employment but is unwilling to work for the low-wage that the immigrant is willing to accept.

While having access to the low-wage labor market, the desperate immigrant woman accepts work that is fraught with immigration restrictions and constraints (Chin, C. 1998). Immigrants are recruited by citizens of developed countries to work in low-wage jobs without the benefit of a permanent visa. Many of these women are given temporary visas for themselves and not their family, which separates them from their family members (Chin, C. 1987 as cited in Salazar-Parrenas, 2001). Additionally, their visas do not allow them to travel back home to visit loved ones, so they go without seeing their family for many years. These structural restrictions are the main reasons why these women engage in transnational parenting. One mother in the study recalled her earlier years in the United States without her family/child and describes how she coped with the separation:

"It was difficult for my daughter because I could not bring her up and I could not go down to visit her, so I bought her stuff like a lot of clothes to make myself feel better but still you have this emptiness and guilt killing you, but on the other hand I was able to work and take care of myself and my daughter hoping I could send for her and take care of her."

Another mother reported the difficulty of reunifying with her children and due to the restrictions, she had to engage in serial migration over a period of 12 years before she was finally together with all of her children.

"My first daughter came up first 12 years ago; I was here five years before she came. Seven (7) years ago the fourth one came. Five (5) years ago, I brought up the last two".

Many of these women have to cross legal minefields in order to gain a permanent visa that allows them to work legally and to be reunited with family members. This journey is long, exhausting and filled with legal difficulties that have onerous financial and emotional costs to the migrant and her family. As a result, West Indian mothers out of necessity engage in transnational mothering. One of the mothers in the interview shared her experience.

"It was difficult to get them to come up. You have to get a permanent visa, invitation letter, and bank statement-not an easy thing to do. At the time, I lived with my sister. I didn't have an apartment of my own - couldn't afford one".

Developed countries such as the United States, Canada and Europe restrict the integration of migrant West Indian workers because they want to keep some aspect of their economies a secure low-wage job market. Furthermore, developed countries create a supply of low-wage workers for their economies, and when the economy becomes sluggish, they can easily send them back home (Salazar-Parrenas, R. 2001). The United States set a precedent for this practice during the depression when many Mexicans were sent back to Mexico. This practice sends a message to West Indians and other immigrants from developing countries that developed countries such as the United States only want their production labor and not their reproduction labor, further contributing to the increase of transnational families and the unequal treatment of immigrants.

While developed countries increase their need for immigrant women to ease the reproductive labor of privileged working women in developed countries, an international division of reproductive labor has been created. Under this system, migrant domestic workers do the reproductive labor of privileged women in developed countries and due to structural restrictions, have to leave their children behind. These migrant women in turn hire domestic workers in their country of origin to take care of their own children when family members are unable to do so or when their original childcare arrangements fail. As a result, there is a formation of three tiers of mothering between middle class women in developed countries like the United States, migrant domestic workers working in the United States who are engaged in transnational parenting, and domestic workers in developing countries who are too poor to finance the costs of emigration so they remain in the country of origin and work there caring for the children of the domestics in the United States (Salazar-Parrenas, 2001).

Remittances

Remittances have become the most visible evidence and measuring stick for the ties connecting migrants with their societies of origin Guarnizo (2003). Remittances are migrant workers' earnings sent back from the country of employment to the country of origin. According to the World Bank (April 2012), remittance flows to developing countries are estimated to have reached $372 billion in 2011, an increase of 12.1% over 2010.

Immigrant mothers play a major role in the economy both in the United States and in their country of origin. When they leave their children behind with relatives and other adults, it creates interplay between the caretaker and the mother as well as the economies between the host country and the country of origin. In exchange for caring for the children, the extended family members are paid in the form of remittances, either through cash or goods in addition to the money sent for the children's clothing and schooling and materials (Philpott, 1968 cited in Watkins-Owens, 2001). When the issue of remittance came up, one mother shared the following,

"I worked and bought a beautiful house back home. I also worked and helped my children and my nieces and nephews. When my brother died, I often sent money and clothes to his children. Later, as I got older, I sent for the oldest nephew so that he can help his brothers and sisters".

Studies of the impact of remittances have shown that they are utilized for investment purposes in the senders' countries of origin in small businesses such as manufacturing and crafts companies, market stalls, bakeries and transport agencies (Taylor, 1999; van Doorn, 2001 as cited in Vertovec, 2003). On the other hand, remittances have been shown to have some negative consequences such as the: displacement of local jobs and incomes; increased consumption spending (primarily on foreign imports); inflation of local prices of land, housing, and food; creation of disparity, and envy between recipients and non-recipients; and creation of a culture of economic dependency (Vertovec, 2003).

Social Networks

Almost all newly arrived immigrants to New York participate in an informal social network made up of family members and friends that help them adapt or acculturate to the new country and connect them with jobs (Kasinitz cited in Foner, 2001). Social networking is a significant part of the African-Caribbean immigrant woman's experience (Watkins-Owens cited in Foner, 2001). In their country of origin, these women participated in both a colonial and patriarchal society that dominated them on the basis of sex, class and color, while in New

York they experienced discriminations based on race, sex, color and location/origin. As survivors, these women have found ways to adapt to the challenges and developed strategies that have framed their historical experiences that are used in their transnational experience. These women are strategic, goal oriented, focused and practical. Migration to them is a means to an end, and together they are a great "human resource" in the Caribbean migrant communities (Watkins-Owens as cited in Foner, 2001). Best-Cummings and Gildner (2004) described social network as the fourth of six steps involved in the pre-migratory stage of emigration. It was found that networking is not just critical in the pre-migratory or decision-making stages, but it is also an important part of the migration stage and later the acculturation and reunification stage. The informal networks, both in the U.S. and at home, is perhaps central in helping the woman cope with feelings of guilt and regret.

"They told me that people left their children and travel all the time. All I had to do was send for my children when I got there" (Best-Cummings & Gildner, 2004, p.90).

After they have settled in the host country, the social network is also a refuge, a respite from the job and an asset to ongoing socialization of these women in the host country.

"I sometimes go to my friends on weekends. I buy food that reminds me of home and we cook together. It makes me feel good."

Another woman said, "When you work as a live-in, you have to work 24 hours a day. It was good to visit with my aunt and my friends on the weekends (Best-Cummings & Gildner, 2004, p.96)."

With access to telephones and computers, immigrants today speak frequently to their family and friends who are part of their network both in the host country and in their home of origin via cell phones and emails. These women get support from their network,

"When I call my friends at home, they would tell me, 'your kids are fine. You can take care of your children better if you stay in America than if you come back. Stay and take care of yourself, so you can help your children". (Best-Cummings & Gildner, 2004)."

The use of social networks for African-Caribbean immigrant women is a survival tool that is a valuable resource because it provides them with emotional and financial support if needed. It is also a clearinghouse for information on employment and housing as well as it provides knowledge of how to negotiate the challenges in the host country. In turn, when the woman becomes seasoned, after her children arrive, she then becomes part of the social network that offers assistance to other new immigrants such as her family and friends both at home and in New York.

Transnational Parenting

Many of the African Caribbean women engaged in transnational parenting are also ironically working in jobs that require their reproductive labor, caring for other people's children, while expected to care for their own children as well (Hondagneu-Sotelo, 1992). Due to the demands of their jobs, they often are sapped of the energy and resources needed to provide for their own families. However, the geographic distance between these women and their children is one of the primary challenges for them because the distance separates them from their children, which makes it even more difficult to provide emotional care to their children. In many cases however, regular and frequent contact is maintained between parents and children through telephone calls and letters, as well as through financial and material support sent to the country of origin (Foner, 2001).

In spite of the frequent contacts, however, immigrant mothers separated from their children experience a severe sense of loss. The pain of the loss for the mother who has left her children behind is unlike any other loss because it is unresolved (Boss, 1999). Unlike a death in the family where the surviving relatives mourn and bring some kind of closure to it, the loss of family as a result of migration, especially when the migrant is undocumented and cannot return to visit the family and home, causes the grieving process to go on for a very long time without resolution as is demonstrated by one mother's recollection.

"The separation was very hard. For a mother who really wants her kids and loves her kids, it's very hard to be separated from them. For me, it took about three years before I could stop thinking about her constantly and getting sad and crying for her and wondering what she is going through. I couldn't sleep well the first three years. I thought of her day and night".

In response to the question "What was it like being separated from your child?" One mother responded by saying:

"It was difficult living here without my daughter. I missed her a lot and would cry at times. Sometimes I would just call her on the phone and tell her I love her."

A second mother talked about her conversation on the phone with her daughter.

"When I left, my daughter was a week away from her third birthday and one day when I was talking to her on the telephone, she told me 'I know your voice, but I don't remember what you look like'. I was devastated, so I sent her a lot of pictures of me".

The Dynamics of Transnational Parenting: Staying Connected

The telephone is the primary and most commonly utilized means of communication, which over the years becomes a ritualized event that is used on specified days and at specific times throughout the transnational period. Often, these calls were made once a week usually on weekends, particularly on Sundays after attending church. One mother reported,

"I would call them every Sunday once a week sometimes during the week but mostly on Sundays after church I will call them".

Additionally, although the telephone was a good way of staying connected, it was also a way both the mother and child relived the pain of separation. Many of the mothers reported crying with their children on the telephone. The duality of the telephone communication for these mothers were heightened because it was the tool that kept them connected to their children but it also brought them pain because as Boss (1999) indicated, it also contributed to reliving the loss. One mother described this duality,

"You miss them a lot and that is very difficult but it was painful to stay long with them on the phone".

According to the mothers, the benefit of the telephone conversations is that they provide immediacy and intimacy. For many of these mothers, the telephone is preferred to letters or cards because hearing and speaking to their child on the phone provides an instant and deep connection through both the familiar words and expressions used, and in hearing the voice of one's loved one.

On the other hand, parenting from a distance via telephone for these mothers presented a multitude of challenges. As revealed in the study, many of the mothers felt guilty that they were not physically present for their children. However, their inability to physically express their love for their children in person was one such obstacle that the mothers communicated.

"It was difficult not to physically show the love I was feeling, the way I wanted to show it to my child. Although you say it verbally on the phone, it's not the same. But emotionally, your child cannot experience it and neither can you the mother."

The Essence of the Conversation

The mothers shared a variety of issues they discussed with their children in their weekly parenting sessions on the telephone. These parenting sessions have some common themes that emerged from the study for many of the mothers. The most common topic the mothers reported discussing with their children was related to the children's education. There seemed to be an ease among the mothers in discussing academic performance, attendance, recreational activities and friendships connected to school.

"We talked about everything. We talked about what was going on in school mostly. We also talked about family stuff. We also talked about what was going on with their friends".

For some, parenting by telephone included discussing such taboo issues that would normally cause a challenge for most parents to discuss in person, nonetheless some of the mothers seem to discuss them with ease. These discussions were about sexual development, including issues related to puberty, changes in the body, good touch-bad touch, and sex education.

"We talked about how they were doing in school. About them going to church because I would call them after they came from church on Sundays. We also talked sometimes about her menstrual and about boyfriends".

Another mother recalls the conversation with her teenage daughter,

"We had a lot of conversations. I spoke to her about menstruation and about having breast. I also sent her books to read up on those issues, and I think that helped".

For one mother, recalling her inept experience as a teenager provided her with the motivation to engage her son in conversations that focused on sex education.

"I remember when I was going through puberty I was ashamed to tell my mom. So I talked to my son about girls, sex and condoms ".

For others, it wasn't an easy thing to discuss and they left those topics up to the child's caretaker to deal with. As was stated by one of the parents,

"We talked about everything but sex. It was hard for me to do that on the phone. Besides, I'm sure someone at home where they lived did that, talked to them about sex, I mean".

The third theme that emerged was that of the children's behavior. Obedience and respectfulness were expected, encouraged and monitored by the mothers. The mothers were acutely concerned about their children being respectful and obedient to elders and to their caretakers. This was particularly concerning because it is part of the West Indian culture. However, their children's behaviors took on more significance because these mothers were very concerned that if their children were not behaving respectfully and if they weren't obedient to the adults caring for them in their country of origin, their misbehaving would fuel the child's caretaker to refuse to continue to care for the child. These mothers invested very heavily in their children's caretakers and depended on them so their children's life at home would be stable, safe, and have some sense of permanency until they were ready to be reunited with their children. The decision of reunification is also very much connected with the mothers becoming a permanent resident, which is a long, protracted, expensive experience. One of the mothers reported,

"Sometimes when I spoke to my son, I would speak to him about how to be a young man. How to grow up and be a good young man, and not to get into trouble. Be respectful of elders and women."

Another mother reported that although school work and educational achievement was important, obedience was also critical to her because it can make a difference between whether or not her child could stay with this family member or she would have to send her to live with someone else.

"I would call her and ask about school but I always wanted to know how she was behaving and I told her don't give them any problems because I don't want them to tell me you couldn't stay with them anymore and I have to come get you or they were sending you to someone else to live".

The fourth theme was the mothers' communication of their love for their children, while simultaneously connected to concerns about their children's well being. Many of these mothers would try to ascertain in the phone calls whether or not their children were treated well by relatives and caretakers.

"I would always talk to him and tell him I loved him, but I also wanted to know if they were giving him enough to eat". Another parent shared, *"I would tell her that I loved her and ask her how they were treating her, I didn't want them mistreating my child."*

Comforting Children

Overall, many of the mothers agreed that it was difficult to comfort their children on the telephone when they were upset. They found it very difficult to comfort a child who was upset because they found the telephone very obtrusive and somewhat limiting in addressing the issue the distance caused by the telephone. As a result, some of them relied on their children's caretakers to comfort them. Others, on the other hand, used the telephone to have long conversations with their children to get at the root of the problem.

"I would stay hours on the phone talking to her. I would ask her about everything and she would tell me what made her sad. But I always had to remember that I wasn't there to be with her and I did not like to make it worse for her when I hung up the phone. So I always had to bear that on my mind". Another mother revealed the challenge of the telephone when she reported, *"Whenever my daughter spoke to me she would get sad and cry and I would talk. But I also had to rely on my mother to follow up with her."*

On the other hand, one mother reported that her children did not share with her that they were upset because they did not want to upset her, - i.e. the mother. So she had to develop strategies of getting them to be truthful with her so they would let her know what was really happening to them.

"They didn't let me know if they were upset but if I called on a Wednesday or Friday out of the ordinary they would tell me more about the things that were upsetting them. Other than that, when I called on weekends, they only focused on the good things. I think they would tell their father or my parents about the things that upset them".

Yet another mother described her frustration and discomfort in this area of parenting.

"Whenever she was upset we would talk about it". Sometimes I was able to help, sometimes not. That was the most difficult part of it for me".

Challenges Inherent in Parenting from a Distance

While all the mothers engaged in transnational parenting reported it was difficult and challenging to parent from a distance, some reported finding transnational parenting relatively simple and uncomplicated. Some of the mothers, who did not feel overly burdened by transnational parenting, gave the following reasons for the ease of their particular situations: the separation from their children was brief; the children were too young to understand what was happening; and they had reliable childcare arrangements in relatives they trusted.

Another parent reported finding parenting from a distance 'effective' because she had her sister and her mother to discipline her daughter for her.

"I found it effective because I had my sister and mother to discipline her and to help me".

Another descriptive category that the mothers in the study reported on regarding parenting from a distance was that they found it 'uncomfortable'.

"It's very uncomfortable to parent your child from a distance because all you do is talk and they can't really see you".

This mother was frustrated because her son's caretaker called frequently to complain about him. *"It's not easy because they are always calling you to complain about him ".*

This mother put it succinctly when she said parenting from a distance is not easy because

"You are a voice on the telephone with no power".

On the other hand, one parent responded to the question that parenting from a distance is not parenting at all. She felt that parenting can only be done in person. Another parent thought parenting from a distance is "non-existent". The overall feeling is that parenting from a distance is possible, albeit difficult. The overall responses from the mothers indicate that they believed that it is possible to effectively co-parent from a distance, especially when the caretaker is someone who lives in the same household with the children and that person is trustworthy and supportive to the parent while being a caring, protective, nurturing, yet stern co-parent to the children.

"Parenting from a distance was not too difficult because my children lived with their father and my parents lived close by. We also had a family business, which helped to support them financially".

In all actuality, what the mothers described they did was co-parent their children with their caretakers.

SUMMARY

African Caribbean Mothers from English-speaking countries co-parented from a distance with a great deal of challenges. When asked if they would do it again, 45% of the women in the study reported they wouldn't do it again, while 40% reported they would and 15% were undecided. For the women who reported the rewards outweighed the consequences of migration, they referred to the educational achievements of their children as the rewards upon reunification in the United States. Those women who reported they would not do it again emphasized that being away from their children was one of the most difficult and traumatic things they had to do. One woman described the time she was separated from her children as one that is similar to "a death" of a loved one.

The study unearthed that many of the women saw themselves as co-parenting with the child's caretaker. Additionally, although in many cases the caretaker and the mother are often related to each other or to close family and friends, there are many parenting issues that are not explicitly discussed between the two parents prior to the mother's departure. As a result, they attempt to address these issues as they evolve in the best possible way.

It is also clear that the mothers are very connected to their children and use scheduled telephone communications to sustain emotional connection with their children and family members. Many of these mothers discuss a variety of issues with their children on the telephone ranging from school to friends to issues related to puberty. Remittance is a significant part of these women's method of taking care of their children. Remittances are sent in the form of barrels with dry goods and material resources such as clothes as well as in the form of financial support to pay for rent, food, school tuition and supplies, and medical needs.

Practice Implications

Practitioners working with immigrant families engaged in transnational parenting need to understand the nuances inherent in this painstaking experience that immigrant families must endure in order to fulfill the strict requirements needed to change their immigration status. This process is extremely stressful to the transnational mother because of its high stakes. It is important that practitioners working with transnational families become knowledgeable of and keep abreast of the changing immigration laws, so that they can inform their clients of the reforms as they occur or have a reliable, competent resource to refer people to. However, it is absolutely imperative that practitioners understand that they are never supposed to report or compromise the confidentiality of families they suspect to be undocumented. Sharing the confidentiality laws such as NYC's Executive Order 41 and the most recent immigration changes such as The Deferred Action for Young People Regulation of June 15th, 2012, with these families could help allay their fears and provide vital information to a population that is very much affected by the continuous changes that are occurring in U.S. immigration policies. Having knowledge of the most recent changes in immigration policy and rulings would certainly be an asset to staff working with transnational families. Sharing this information would certainly build confidence and expertise for the worker. More importantly, it could also promote goodwill and trust so that the family will experience the worker as contributing to the family's understanding of important immigration issues.

Having a comprehensive understanding of the issues that are relevant to the African Caribbean mother who is engaged in transnational parenting or who is recently reunited with her children is critical for practitioners. Practitioners should be aware of the mother's feelings of guilt, helplessness, depression, isolation due to being undocumented, possible aspects of exploitation by employers, domestic violence by partners as well as experiencing emotional difficulties as a result of the acculturation process, not to mention some cultural expectations of children when reunification occurs. For the children upon reunification, practitioners should be aware of issues related to separation and loss, such as feeling abandoned, lack of trust, anger and fear.

Additionally, practitioners working with African Caribbean families should utilize a strengths-based approach, which is based on the belief that when people focus on their strengths, they are more likely to solve problems and make changes in their lives. These families have demonstrated a great deal of strength and resilience while living under very stressful situations. Social workers working with African

Caribbean families should use Brief Solution-Focused Therapy given the fact that this population is not accepting of the therapeutic community and would most likely be resistant to long-term, traditional psychotherapy. It makes sense that a model that is time limited and promotes clients' abilities to find solutions to problematic issues would be better received than open-ended long-term therapy. This model would engage the family as a partner in the helping process and utilize the strengths found in this population.

Bibliography

Baptiste, D. A., Hardy, K. V. and Lewis, L. (1997a). "Clinical Practice with Caribbean Immigrant Families in the United States: The Intersection of Emigration, Immigration, Culture and Race". In J. L. Roopnarine & J. Brown (Eds.),*Caribbean Families: Diversity Among Ethnic Groups* (pp. 275-303). Norwood, New Jersey: Abex.

Basch, L. 2001. "Transnational Social Relations and the Politics of National Identity: An Eastern Caribbean Case Study". In Nancy Foner (ed.). *Island in the City: West Indian Migration to New York*. Berkeley: University of California Press.

Basch, L., Glick Schiller, N. & Szanton Blanc, C. (1994). *Nations Unbound Transnational Projects. Postcolonial Predicaments and Deterritorial Nations-States*. Amsterdam: Gordon and Breach Publishers.

Best-Cummings, C. (2009). "The Long Goodbye: Challenges of Transnational Parenting." *U.S.A. VDM Verlag* Dr. Muller Aktiengesellschaft & Co. KG.

Best-Cummings, C. & Gildner, M. (2004). "Caribbean Women's Migratory Journey: An Exploration of their Decision-making Process." *Journal of Immigrant and Refugee Services*. 2(3/4): 83-101.

Boss, P. (1999). *Ambiguous Loss: Learning to Live with Unresolved Grief*. Cambridge, Massachusetts. Harvard University Press.

Chin, C. (1998). In *Service and Servitude: Foreign Female Domestic Workers and the Malaysian Modernity Project*. New York: Columbia University Press.

Christiansen, J. M.; Thornley-Brown, A. and Robinson, J. A. (1982). "West Indians in Toronto: Implications for Helping Professionals." *Family Service Association of Metropolitan Toronto*. Ontario, Canada.

Donato, K. (1992). "Understanding U.S. Immigration: Why Some Countries Send Women and Others Send Men." In: Donna Gabaccia (ed.). *Seeking Common Ground: Multidisciplinary Studies of Immigrant Women in the United States*. Westport, CT: Praeger.

Foner, N. (2001). "Transnationalism Then and Now: New York Immigrants Today and at the Turn of the Twentieth Century." In Cordero-Guzman, Smith, and Grosfoguel (ed,). *Migration, Transnationalization, and Race in a Changing New York*. Philadelphia: Temple University Press.

Guarnizo, L. E. (2003). "The Economics of Transnational Living," *International Migration Review*. 37(3): pp. 666-699, Fall.

Hondagneu-Sotelo, P. and Avilla, E. (1997). "I am Here, but I'm There: The Meaning of Latina Transnational Motherhood." *Gender and Society* 11: 548-71.

Hondagneu-Sotelo, P. (1992). "Overcoming Patriarchal Constraints: The Reconstruction of Gender Relations Among Mexican Immigrant Women and Men." *Gender and Society* 6, 393-415.

Houston, M., Kramer, R. and Mackin-Barrett, J. (1984). "Female Predominance of Immigration to the United States since 1930: A First Look." *International Migration Review* 18: 908-63.

Kasinitz, P. and Vickerman, M. (2001). "Ethnic Niches and Racial Traps: Jamaicans in the New York Regional Economy". In Cordero-Guzman, Smith, and Grosfoguel (ed,). *Migration, Transnationalization, and Race in a Changing New York*. Philadelphia: Temple University Press.

MPI analysis of 2008 and 2009 ACS.

Nicol, A. R. (1971). "Psychiatric Disorder in the Children of Caribbean Immigrants". *Journal of Child Psychology and Psychiatry,* 12, 273-287.

Salvo, J. and Ortiz, R. (1992). *The Newest New Yorkers: An Analysis of Immigration into New York City during the 1980s.* New York City: New York City Department of City Planning.

Salazar-Parrenas, R. (2001). "Mothering from a Distance: Emotions, Gender, and Intergenerational Relations in Filipino Transnational Families." *Feminist Studies,* 27 (2) 361-390.

Sassen, S. (1994). *Cities in a World Economy.* Thousand Oaks, CA: Pine Forge Press.

Smith, A., Lalonde, R. and Johnson, S. (2004). "Serial Migration and its Implications for the Parent-Child Relationship: A Retrospective Analysis of the Experiences of the Children of Caribbean Immigrants". *Cultural Diversity and Mental* Health. Vol. 10 (2), pp. 107-122.

Soto, I. M. (1987). "West Indian Child Fostering: Its Role in Migrant Exchanges." In Constance R. Sutton and Elsa M. Chaney (eds.), *Caribbean Life in New York City: Sociocultural Dimensions.* New York: Center for Migration Studies.

Taylor, J. E. (1999). "The New Economics of Labour Migration and the Role of Remittances in the Migration Process." *International Migration,* 37 (1) 63-88.

Vertovec, S. (2003). "Migration and other Modes of Transnationalism: Towards Conceptual Cross-fertilization". *International Migration Review,* 37: 641-65.

Watkins-Owens, I. (2001). "Early-Twentieth-Century Caribbean Women: Migration and Social Networks in New York City." In Foner, Nancy (ed.). *Islands in the City: West Indian Migration to New York.* Los Angeles: University of California Press.

Chapter Five

Transnational Migration: The Elderly and Healthcare

Joyce Hamilton-Henry

and Beverley Russell

INTRODUCTION

According to the United States Census Bureau, the total United States population is 311,591,917 million of which 12.7% are foreign born. Of the Foreign born population, 12% are 65 years of age and older, most of whom resided in New York, New Jersey, Massachusetts, Florida, and California (Migration Policy Institute 2012).

Following a steady decline between 1960 and 1990, the number of older immigrants (those ages in the United States) almost doubled between 1990 and 2010, from 2.7 million to nearly 5 million. These seniors now account for 12% of the 40 million immigrants in the United States—-a share that is much lower than the historical high. In 1960, 33% of the nation's 9.7 million immigrants were 65 or older, mostly European who arrived during the early 20th century wave of immigration (Batalova, 2012).

According to the Migration Policy Institute, in 2009, 3.5 million of the foreign born population was from the Caribbean, representing 9% of the total foreign born population. In 2009, 90% of the Caribbean immigrants were from Cuba (28.6 %), The Dominican Republic (22.9 %), Jamaica (18.8 %), Haiti (15.5 %), and Trinidad and Tobago (6.4 %). Most resided in Florida and New York (McCabe, 2011).

In 2009, Florida had the largest number of resident Caribbean immigrants with 1,388,014, or 40% of the total Caribbean-born population in the United States, followed by New York (1,008,134, or 29.1%). Other states with relatively large Caribbean immigrant populations (greater than 65,000) included: New Jersey (253,010, or 7.3%), Massachusetts (136,578, or 3.9%), Georgia (83,735, or 2.4%), Connecticut (78,957, or 2.3%), Pennsylvania (77,527, or 2.2%), and California (72,251, or 2.1%).

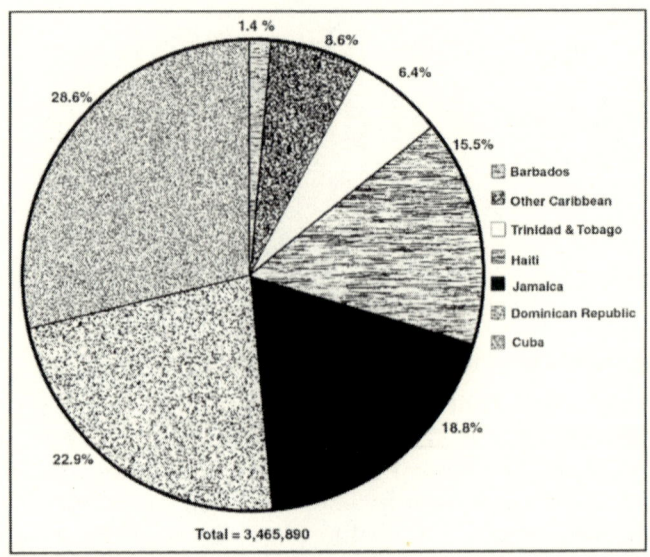

Figure 5.1: Share of Caribbean-born Population by Country of Origin, 2009

[Pie chart showing: 1.4%, 8.6%, 6.4%, 15.5%, 28.6%, 22.9%, 18.8%. Legend: Barbados, Other Caribbean, Trinidad & Tobago, Haiti, Jamaica, Dominican Republic, Cuba. Total = 3,465,890]

Note. Persons from "other Caribbean" countries include those reporting their birthplace as: Antigua-Barbuda, the Bahamas, Dominica, Grenada, St. Kitts-Nevis, St. Lucia, St. Vincent and the Grenadines, the West Indies, or Caribbean ns/nec (not specified or not elsewhere classified).
Source: US Census Bureau, 2009 American Community Survey.

Caribbean women are among the majority of immigrants who came in the early 1960s and 1970s in search of better employment and educational opportunities for themselves and their children. The Hart-Celler Act of 1965 made it easier for Americans to sponsor these women to work in their homes as domestics and as caretakers of their children or elderly family members. It has been over five decades since many of these women have resided in the United States. They have raised their children (first and second generation), have sponsored other family members to join them, and now have grandchildren who were born and raised in their adopted country.

As these early immigrants age, their exigent health needs make them increasingly dependent on formal institutions and their adult children for daily care. This phenomenon is associated with a crisis in Caribbean families as adult children of aging immigrants struggle to care for their aging family members (parents, aunts, uncles, and grandparents) while raising their own children. Many are faced with deciding whether to care for their aging family member in their country of origin, or in their adopted country. If the aging family member returns to their country of origin, the family must decide how best to navigate two societies. Transnational migration is the normal pattern for many of these immigrant families.

The information in this chapter is based on a review of the literature and informal interviews conducted with adult children and seniors in the United States. It is also based on informal focus groups held in Jamaica with aging Jamaicans, some of whom were returnees who lived in an adopted country for over 40 years.

The chapter examines and discusses the experiences of first generation aging Caribbean immigrants from English speaking Caribbean countries. It discusses how their families coped with social and healthcare issues within a transnational context. What is missing from the dimensions of transnational migration is the measure of prosperity or despair among the elderly, ostensibly determined by the availability of healthcare and other resources within the Diaspora. Incorporated in this discussion will be information on return migration and available resources when an aging family member who returns and resides in their country of origin becomes ill. It will also discuss healthcare services and possible policy strategies that will influence quality of care and ultimately, a better quality of life for seniors.

Transnational Migration

Transnationalism "refers to migrating populations whose networks, activities, and patterns of life encompasses both home and host countries" (Quirke, 2010; Reynolds, 2008; Plaza, 2008; Drachman & Ryan, 2001). Transnational immigrants are therefore individuals whose lives and networks span across national boundaries, and whose fields exist in two countries (Quirke, 2010; Levitt & Jaworsky, 2007; Drachman & Ryan, 2001; Schiller, 1995).

Drachman and Paulino (2004) defined return migrants as "persons who emigrate, live in a new country for years, and ultimately return to reside in their native land". Guzzetta (2004) states that unlike the perception of migration as one way, between 35-45% of immigrants return to their country of origin or migrate to a third country. The literature states that immigrants often emigrate intending to return to their country of origin (Small, 2007; Guzzetta, 2004; King, 2000; Weist, 2000; Suro, 1996; Rogers, 1984; Cerase, 1967). Guzzetta identifies two predominant reasons immigrants return to their country of origin, "because they fail or because they succeed".

Rogers (1984) identified eight reasons individuals return to their country of origin, four of which are: changes in the home country which made return feasible or profitable or both; awareness of being needed in the home country, either by family or for patriotic reasons;

changes in the adopted country which made staying there no longer feasible, or disappointment over inability to achieve the goals that had induced the original migration (Guzzetta, 2004).

Several factors determine who returns to reside in their country of origin. For instance, the type of services and support networks available to individuals will determine whether and how long individuals return to their country of origin (Drachman and Paulino 2004). A dimension of the returnees' experience is re-acculturation to their country of origin. Weist (2000) recognizes that little information is available about the experiences of returnees, "how they relate to people who stayed in the home country, or how the returnees are received by them" (Guzzetta, 2004). In some cases, the country of origin discourages return migration particularly among certain age groups (Reynolds, 2008). What are the characteristics of those who return and of their caretakers? What infrastructures exist in the Caribbean to care for the aging population?

Allegiance to one's country of origin does not end when one migrates. Most immigrants maintain an emotional connection to their country of origin, a bond which is reinforced by contact with family members at home, the extent to which they set down roots in their adopted country (United States, United Kingdom, Canada), and the political and socioeconomic conditions in their country of origin. There are other related factors, such as the year in which they migrated; their immigrant status at the time of migration; their marital status--single versus married and to whom (Suro, 1996); how often they returned to their country of origin; the family members who remain in the country of origin; the ability of family members in the country of origin to travel to the adopted country; home and property ownership in their country of origin; home and property ownership in the adopted country, and the sociopolitical climate in their adopted country. These factors determine the frequency of contact with family members, the number of visits to their country of origin and/or their desire to return to their country of origin.

There are three categories of transnational migrants. The first category are those who return to live in their country after living abroad for a period of time and who travel abroad to visit, shop or get medical services. The second category are those who retire to their country of origin after living abroad for decades; travel back and forth as needed, then due to illness, return to the adopted country. The third category includes those who decide not to return home but occasionally visit their country of origin. To understand the issues faced by Caribbean families and their aging family members when they return to their country of origin, we must examine aging within the Caribbean context.

Aging Populations and Health

It is well documented that the population of individuals 60 years of age and older has constantly risen worldwide. Influencing factors to the aging of baby boomers are attributed to declines in fertility, advancement in medical technology, overall better medical care, and awareness that maintaining health status is facilitated through changes in lifestyles (Russell, 2008; Lubitz, 2003). In general, the aging population is a great challenge for healthcare systems. As nations age, the prevalence of disability, frailty, and chronic diseases (Alzheimer's disease, cancer, cardiovascular and cerebrovascular diseases, etc.) is expected to increase dramatically.

According to information published by the World Health Organization, the leading causes of morbidity and premature death for people over age 60 worldwide are chronic cardio-vascular diseases such as ischemic heart disease, cerebrovascular disease, and chronic obstructive pulmonary disease. Other illnesses include Alzheimer's, other dementias, and diabetes mellitus (ECLAC, 2008; Crooks 2008). Some experts have raised concerns that mankind may become a "global nursing home" (Gavrilov & Heuveline, 2003; Eberstadt, 1997). This growth within the aging Caribbean population will put additional demands on an already stressed publicly funded healthcare system, and on long-term and income support programs in both developed and developing countries.

The Caribbean Context

Life expectancy of this population in Caribbean countries has increased tremendously. Many countries such as Jamaica have a life expectancy matching that of developed countries (Russell, 2008). In 2004, the Economic Commission for Latin America and the Caribbean (ECLAC) reported that although the region has the highest percentage of elderly people, it is difficult to determine the total elderly population in the Caribbean. The growth of this population is projected to increase worldwide from 6.9% in 2000 to 19.3% in 2050. Within Latin America and the Caribbean, the increase may be from 5.4% in 2000 to 16.9% in 2050 (Gavrilov, 2003). In fact, it was projected that during the 2005–2010 period, Jamaica's 60 and older age groups increased at a rate that is almost three times that of the total population. (Chukwudum, 2010; Palloni, 2002).

The elderly represents 10-13% of the overall English-speaking Caribbean. Of that total, 10% are in Jamaica, 11% in Trinidad and Tobago and 13% in Barbados (Rawlins, 2010). Aging comes with a number of challenges that impact every dimension of one's life including financial, family, health and, in general, every fabric of society such as living conditions, social and community supports/resources (Bourne, 2009). Caribbean seniors face a number of social challenges including high poverty rates, limited social security coverage and pensions, inadequate supportive infrastructure and diminishing family support due to the outmigration and changes in family structure and composition (Powell, 2011). They also face numerous health-related illnesses such as degenerative and non-communicable diseases such as arthritis, diabetes, hypertension, cataracts, glaucoma and heart disease that are becoming more prevalent among seniors, impacting their quality of life and increasing their demands for specialized healthcare services and social services (Edwards-Wescott, 2011; Powell, 2011; Chukwudum 2010; Palloni & McEntiry, 2007; Mullings, 2007; Hambleton 2005).

For the most part, many countries in the Caribbean provide assistance to seniors through safety-net programs such as social insurance schemes; contributory or non-contributory old-age pensions; social or public assistance; in-kind assistance, food stamps; social funds (communities, elderly, low income families); and residential homes. While many Caribbean governments offer free primary healthcare to all its citizens, the quality and quantity of services vary. Despite the free access to care, barriers such as high cost of drugs and inadequate transportation systems influence elder use. Apart from Barbados, almost no specialized healthcare programs exist in the English-speaking Caribbean for seniors who become affected by the aforementioned diseases and most countries make such provisions within the general public health services system (Rawlins 2010; Cloos, 2009, ECLAC, 2004).

We want to highlight three (3) Caribbean countries (Trinidad & Tobago, Barbados and Jamaica) that have implemented systems to respond to the needs of their aging population. Jamaica will be used as the backdrop as we have both professional and personal experiences within the transnational context.

In 2007, the first country, the Republic of Trinidad and Tobago (T&T), with their elderly population estimated to reach 20% of their total population by 2025, initiated a National Aging Policy in collaboration with the private sector, non-governmental organizations (NGOs), community-based organizations (CBOs), faith-based organizations (FBOs), schools, the media, academicians and international organizations. T&T has projected to implement programs to support seniors such as training and provision of homecare service in geriatric care; provision of affordable houses and a range of health and social services to seniors; collaboration with aging interest groups, NGOs, public and private sectors providing social and cultural programs, events that foster intergenerational interactions and honors seniors in the community; a radio series that provides both educational and general information on aging and age-related topics; and an annual Public Open Forum for Older Persons to allow older persons to share their issues and ideas directly with government officials (Rouse, 2008).

For the second country, the President of the Barbados Elderly Care Association reports that by 2020, the island's elderly population would account for more than 25% of the total population. Their National Policy on Aging includes legislation to protect older persons from discrimination and abuse, and provides access to adequate housing, offering both residential and recreational programs and universal pension coverage. Persons 60 and older are provided universal access to healthcare and medication services through polyclinics and outpatient service stations (ECLAC, 2004).

The government's Alternative Care of the Elderly Program, a contractual agreement between government and the private sector, provide alternate and/or additional means of care for the elderly. Other services for seniors such as community day care centers are provided by NGOs supported with government funding. Institutional care is available through government run geriatric hospitals and privately run nursing homes. Overall, the Barbados government is focusing on issues facing their population of seniors and is committed to creating programs and environments to continue improving their quality of life.

In 1976, the third country, Jamaica, was the first Caribbean country to establish a National Council on Aging to advise on and develop programs to improve the quality of life for seniors. Since then, at least 16 other Caribbean nations have undertaken initiatives to address their aging populations. Most countries establish such initiatives within the general public health services system (Cloos, 2009; ECLAC, 2004).

To further address the health issues of its aging population, Jamaica implemented the Drugs for the Elderly Program (JADEP) in 1996. This is a public-private sector collaboration to reduce the high cost of prescription drugs for seniors aged 60 and older. JADEP allows seniors with certain chronic diseases to obtain their medication at a low out-of-pocket cost (Russell, 2008). In 2001, the Jamaican Parliament approved the establishment of the National Health Fund that covers services for a wider range of illnesses and medications for a larger sector of the Jamaican population.

Jamaica has approximately 49 nursing homes that are recognized by the Ministry of Health (MOH). The MOH has oversight of these facilities to ensure consistency in the quality of care. The average monthly cost of care in a nursing home ranged from $30,000 to

$80,000 Jamaican dollars, based on the type of care needed (Reid 2007).

In 1997, the National Council for Senior Citizens (NCSC), under the auspices of the Ministry of Labour and Social Security, was established to assist individuals and families faced with crises such as an untenable financial burden. The Ministry of Labour and Social Security is the oversight agency for the NCSC. Both agencies work in collaboration with international and local organizations on behalf of senior citizens. This agency's role is to find and screen trained professionals to work with families that provide peace of mind for families in Jamaica. Seniors 60 years and older are eligible to receive services from these trained professionals.

Based on the projected doubling of the elderly population from 10 to 20 percent by 2050, the Minister of State in the Ministry of Labour and Social Security responsible for senior citizens announced the need for a revision, a year after the tabling in by the Parliament of the National Policy for Senior Citizens. This National Policy is based on the approach that acknowledges individuality and the diversity among older persons and aims at assisting the elderly in maintaining a maximum degree of independent living. The Policy focused on the need for the elderly to actively participate in decisions affecting their lives and ensures that no discrimination in availability of services exists. A first of its kind in the Caribbean sub-region, the policy attracted wide international attention, with a number of countries seeking Jamaica's assistance in shaping their own senior citizens policy (JIS, 2011).

According to Reid (2007), Jamaica is experiencing a trend that has mixed reviews. On the one hand, it is a necessity for busy families and on the other hand, it goes against the tradition. In Jamaica, the elderly are categorized as: a)'Well Older People' whose basic financial needs (food, clothing and shelter) are the same as everyone else's; b)'Frail Older People' (usually over 80 years old) who need help with activities of daily living, demanding the "additional cost of a caregiver, not necessarily a nurse; and c) 'Sick Older People' (people who have had a stroke or have Alzheimer's) who need constant care. (Eldermire-Shearer, 2007).

These distinctions highlight the need to create a variety of services tailored for the elderly to maintain their dignity and independence. The elderly are faced with growing health concerns. Cancer, degenerative and non-communicable diseases such as arthritis, diabetes, hypertension, and heart disease, have become more prevalent among this group and families struggle to negotiate these challenges (Edwards-Wescott, 2011).

Returnees to the Caribbean

Local social and public health services are greatly impacted when the aging family member decides to return to their country of origin. Though few adult children of older immigrants return to their homeland, the conditions and circumstances that lead to the aging family member's return and the systems in place to support them are among the issues considered.

Many returnees who lived abroad were afforded access to specialized medicine, home care services, Meals on Wheels, and Senior Centers that address a wide range of health, social and cultural needs. Upon their return to the Caribbean, many anticipate having access to similar programs and services. Returnees usually experience a cultural shock having to adjust to under-resourced communities where these programs and services may not be available. Instead, they must now cope with fewer shopping facilities, higher prices, frequent electrical cuts, water shortages, and domestic tasks that are harder to complete (Conway, 2006).

The aging family member who retires to their country of origin brings certain resources with them because they have saved for their return and have the financial resources to pay for the services they need. For instance, they can afford to hire a Helper to do household chores and to provide assistance for those who are less mobile. However, while they are pleased to be "home", neighborhoods have changed; several younger generations now live in the community where they grew up and many of their peers are now deceased. For others, their family members may be living busy lives and are less available to care for their aging family members, particularly when their needs are medical, labor intensive and/or are outside their areas of expertise.

If the returnee did not maintain close contact with family and friends in the country of origin, they may have fewer peers with whom they can socialize; they no longer have the support network they once had and are unaware of organized social activities specifically tailored for older individuals. Those who migrated during the 1950s-1970s are likely to be characterized by stubbornness and reactionary attitudes towards the changes that have occurred since they left their country of origin.

Safety is among the challenges returnees face. Living in a home protected by burglar bars is practical, but it is also a constant reminder that safety is an issue. Having lived abroad, they are perceived to have acquired many material possessions, the aging family member may feel vulnerable to theft, which is compounded by age, health status and/or mobility. Individuals residing in urban or rural areas rely heavily on public transportation or taxis to get around and transportation in rural areas can be particularly challenging.

Access to Resources

Caribbean seniors face a paucity of primary care physicians, unreliable transportation, long waiting periods and inadequate health facilities (Powell, 2011). They are concerned about medical emergencies and how quickly they can get to a hospital or receive medical attention. If they do not have a private physician, they must rely on public clinics and may experience very long waiting periods to receive medical care.

The lack of adequate pension schemes and targeted health programs in their countries of origin often make the aging family member vulnerable and dependent. With recent economic challenges world-wide, many Caribbean countries have faced declining public health systems due to foreign and domestic debt servicing obligations (Mullings, 2007). This responsibility is more or less entirely taken on by the family network, often supported through an informal community-based support system (ECLAC, 2008). Consequently, such disparities in the quality of healthcare between the home country and host society often dictate decisions about the health and welfare of the aging family member.

The aging family member residing in the Caribbean fears experiencing a medical crisis and being unable to access medical care in a timely manner. Another related factor is the cost of medical care, especially for those who have retired and live on a fixed income. They are usually reliant on the social security benefits from abroad and remittances from children and other family members living abroad. The high cost of medical care remains a global problem.

Having health needs that require constant care and supervision, having few people who can relate to the lifestyle or experiences they had abroad, and being vulnerable due to their age and perceived resource needs are additional challenges this aging population face. Involuntary living arrangements, such as co-residence of two or even more generations out of dire economic needs, along with rising demands on caretakers may also result in increasing tensions over scarce resources (Powell, 2011; ECLAC, 2008). Consequently, the aging family member may become at risk for abuse, neglect, or maltreatment by unscrupulous individuals.

Anxiety about the quality and availability of health and social services, issues of safety, and how to handle a health crisis are all issues that may arise for both the aging family member who returns to the Caribbean, and the adult child caretaker living abroad. The adult child is usually dependent on others, including strangers, to provide the best care possible for their aging family member and to maintain a certain level of health and quality of life. If the aging family member is in a convalescent or nursing home in the Caribbean, the adult child is also faced with financial and emotional challenges. Visiting them often will ensure consistency in the quality of care affecting their overall well-being, and aids in reducing the sense of isolation often felt by the aging family member. These fears can be a major adjustment for both the aging family members who were used to taking care of themselves, and for the adult child who oversees their family members' primary healthcare needs while living abroad.

Caribbean Immigrants in the US

Caribbean immigrants in the United States are racially, ethnically and linguistically diverse individuals from the English, Spanish, French and Dutch speaking Caribbean countries. It is estimated that they represent about 10% of the total US foreign-born population in 2000. In general, they migrated in search of employment and educational opportunities. In their adopted country, they worked to build a support network by connecting with others from their country of origin, with a church, or by sponsoring family members to join them. During the period of separation, they sent money, barrels of food, and durable items for family members in their country of origin even while they attended school, or even if they are relatively poor in the adopted country (Crawford, 2004; Healy, 2004). Most individuals migrated with the intention of returning to their country of origin. The observed trend is that those who migrated in the 1960s and 1970s are now retired, and made the decision to remain in their adopted country. Some returned to their country of origin, leaving their adult children abroad.

In the United States, an industry exists that caters to the medical and social needs of the elderly. Healthcare providers can specialize in Gerontology or Geriatrics. This industry offers services ranging from home care (including visiting nurses, home health aides, social workers, physical therapists, etc); meals on wheels for those who are not able to prepare their own meals, and convalescent or rehabilitation centers for short-term and intermediate care. There are assisted living facilities for individuals who can live on their own, but require occasional assistance for illnesses such as Alzheimer's or dementia, adult-day care services for daily respite, and hospices for individuals with terminal illnesses.

Caribbean immigrants face a wide range of obstacles in the use and access to healthcare services in their adopted country. Those employed in sectors where they worked long hours often received inadequate or no health benefits, have questionable immigration status, or faced the stigma associated with mental illness. In many of those instances, the use of traditional health beliefs and practices increased (Wheeler et al, 2008; Williams, et al 2007; Livingston, et al, 2007).

The challenges families face pertains to the ability to afford the services or the long waiting lists for care. In cases where individuals cannot afford the services, family members usually assume responsibility for the care of their aging family member. In situations where there is a short-term health crisis or when long-term care is needed, the family must decide on a plan of action that could entail remaining in the United States, or having the aging family member return to their country of origin. They must deal with realities such as: Does the aging family member want to return to their country of origin? Should the aging family member return? What are the resource needs of the aging family member? Are they able to take care of that aging family member? Is the adult child prepared (psychologically, financially, and emotionally) for the responsibility? What financial and other obligations are attached to caretaking? What is the nature of their relationship with the aging family member? What impact will it have on their life and lifestyle? If there are unresolved issues between the aging family member and adult child stemming from early migration, these issues must be resolved. The decisions that aging family members and their adult children face in the adopted country include lack of family support, isolation, access to affordable healthcare and issues of independence versus dependence.

Lack of Family Support—"Everyone is busy": Upon arrival in the U.S., some family members maintain a tight bond and have regular contact with each other. They remained very close to their parents, siblings or cousins and relied on each other when needed. Others lose contact over time and although they live in the same town or state, they are not in regular contact. Consequently, fewer family members are available to provide short-term or long-term care for sick and aging family members.

The sick or aging family member who does not want to be a burden to their family now becomes highly reliant on them, which may cause some psychological stress. While other family members may offer to assist in their care, the adult child who lives closest to that sick aging family member or to the healthcare providers and has the space to accommodate that aging family member, or has a medical background may become the lead primary caretaker.

Caribbean adult children who reside abroad may lead very busy and demanding lives. Because they do not have the same social networks common in their country of origin, they usually rely on paid and/or professional care for their children, sick family members, or during family emergencies. Living in the adopted country, work schedules, daily demands of raising children and other family obligations make it a cultural challenge to take on the care of an aging family member.

Isolation: If the aging family member becomes homebound because of the nature of their illness, she or he may be confined to the home or have to remain close to home, often feeling isolated from their peers, their family and/or their neighbors. If no one has any time to visit or to help out, church members are often the ones who call regularly, visit with shut-ins, provide an occasional meal, or run an errand.

If they reside in the northern sections of the U.S., the cold winters or merely living in an apartment/apartment building adds another layer to their sense of isolation. Unlike the Caribbean, the aging family member is not able to sit on the verandah (a common practice among the elderly); instead, they are confined to the home and if they are living alone, may feel safer staying indoors.

Access and the Cost of Medical Care: The cost of and access to medical care are among the reasons a decision is made for the aging family member to remain in the U.S. versus returning to their country of origin. With the growing number of elderly persons living longer with two (2) or more chronic diseases, the cost of care for the elderly at home will increase. Many elderly immigrants, having worked in the US, can rely on health insurance to cover the expenses of health-related care. Aging Caribbean family members living in the adopted country have relatively easy access to medical services. Transportation is accessible through utilizing a family member or a neighbor with a car, by local community resources, taxicab or ambulance.

There are broad arrays of healthcare and homecare services accessible to the aging family member. For instance, if they were formally employed in the US, Medicare or Medicaid covers the cost of these services. Nursing homes, convalescent homes, assisted living residences, and elder day care centers are also available to support the aging family member. In the event of an emergency, they are able to call an ambulance or the police whose response is generally timely and efficient. As extra precautions, lifeline alarms are available to the aging family member during emergencies if they are unable to dial for help. Family members can also keep in touch throughout the day by telephone.

Independence versus Dependence: Once a Man, Twice a Child: Due to age, medical and physical status, and lack of support networks, the aging family member reported having difficulty with the few choices available to them. Aging family members who were once vibrant and self-sufficient may become dependent and tend to feel vulnerable and confined. Similarly, adult children must cope with the reality of their aging family member's health status, age, mortality, and increasing dependence. Often, neither the aging family member nor the adult child is fully prepared for the role reversal or the permanency of the situation. As a result, the relationship may be strained due to the aging family member's struggle to maintain control and the adult child's resistance to take control.

From a Caribbean cultural perspective, adult children are programmed to care for an aging family member in the same way they provided opportunities and support for other family members to migrate to the adopted country. They are aware of the many sacrifices that their aging family members made to create new opportunities for them and their family. Usually, the adult children's personal and professional success is directly due to the risks and sacrifices their aging family members have made. First generation adult children of aging Caribbean immigrants remember growing up in a culture where several generations of family members resided together.

Adult children are aware of the sacrifices their aging family members have made on their behalf and how hard they worked to achieve the "American Dream". As direct beneficiaries of the aging family member's struggle, the adult child may feel culturally bound and obligated to give back to their aging family member. Adult children fulfill this obligation whether or not their aging family member receives governmental benefits in the United States or in the Caribbean; the adult children know that they are their aging family members' social security, taking care of them "in their old age"(Clarke, 2009).

Migration has placed extra demands on both individuals and families. They must function within the context of two countries while coping with challenges without an adequate support network. A cultural shift often occurs when the practice of taking care of the aging family member in the home changes, or when the family is faced with crises, as in a medical emergency, requiring intensive medical and physical care. These events can quickly deplete the emotional and financial resources of the family. Depending on the nature of the illness and the type of care needed, related costs and the availability of family network, decisions are increasingly being made to utilize outside resources such as a nursing homes, convalescent homes, and assisted living facilities.

Adult children are often conflicted about their responsibility to the aging family member and their own children and their spouse. They are often "busy with their own lives". Consequently, the aging family member may become confined to their home, regardless of the nature of their illness. If ill, they may rely on more than one professional caregiver either in or outside of the home while receiving intermittent care from family members.

There is cultural dissonance whenever an individual must make a decision to place a family member outside the home, even when the situation necessitates that the best quality of care can only be provided by professionals in a skilled long-term facility. Adult children often struggle with feelings of guilt that they have failed to fulfill their familial obligation and duty. Some place their aging family member in a nursing home or an assisted living residence. Others provide support to their aging family members who reside in the Caribbean. Regardless of the decision to stay in the adopted country or to return to their country of origin, Caribbean as well as other immigrant families engaged in transnational migration patterns must examine existing resources, policies and practices affecting seniors and influence changes that will promote the best quality of life.

Implications for Transnational Practice and Policy

With the projected growth of seniors in the Caribbean, policies and services to effectively respond to their growing needs and health challenges must be implemented. Critical to this process is the need for comprehensive, multidisciplinary and preventative care and resources for seniors (Powell, et al., 2011). There are many lessons to be learned from policies and practices in countries such as the United States and from best practices that already exist in the Caribbean.

Sharing Best Practices

With the growing number of transnational families, a focus on international social work is necessary, especially when the welfare of these families is impacted by laws, resources and practices that incorporate the policies of two or more countries (Healy, 2004). Institutions in the United States, Canada, the United Kingdom and the Caribbean should explore partnerships that allow for the sharing of best practices, training for service providers and resources that will support the aging population. For example, Caribbean social workers or providers could receive training in the use of the latest technology and in the field of gerontology/geriatrics to understand and respond to the psychosocial needs of seniors. In turn, practitioners and providers in the United States could learn from Caribbean social workers and medical practitioners about providing culturally relevant care to Caribbean nationals residing in the United States. As Caribbean immigrants interface with medical institutions in their adopted countries, they encounter practitioners who are not familiar with their culture, traditions or language.

Healy (2004) states that "increased cross-national collaboration between sending and receiving countries (must occur) to improve migration practice in the context of an uncertain future". This process will ensure that social workers are fully prepared to work with Caribbean families within a transnational context to improve inter-country casework, ensure application of appropriate interventions (Healy, 2004), and also impact social and health policy design.

Policies and Practices in the Caribbean

In 2004, The Caribbean Regional Charter on Aging and Health adopted in 1999 by the Caribbean Community (CARICOM), called for all governments in the sub-region to acknowledge aging as a priority in health and social planning. Since then, most of the governments in the Caribbean have begun to develop national policies and programs to address this growing elderly sector. Programs and policies vary from providing free medications, medical services and health insurance to designated senior housing.

It is evident that many of the Caribbean countries have developed comprehensive policies on aging that consider the social determinants of health (poverty, housing, environment, safety) affecting the elderly, as well as the availability and quality of health and social services. What is challenging for these countries is the ability to implement aging policies within the current world economic climate.

Several gaps in elderly programs and services exist in the Caribbean. They include the need for more advanced technology in hospitals and clinics, more housing and home care resources for seniors unable to care for or live on their own, more clinics in rural areas, up-to-date equipment and supplies in clinics and hospitals, and more providers skilled in caring for clients with Alzheimer's, dementia and other cardiovascular diseases.

Because of the growing senior population with short-term and long-term care needs in and outside the home, Caribbean countries must ensure that there are infrastructures to support the growing demand for resources such as facilities that can provide quality and accessible care. There is a need for professional and formalized care in convalescent homes, nursing homes and assisted living facilities. All these facilities must be licensed and inspected regularly for accountability in compliance with meeting standards, policies and quality care. Where possible, the facilities should be linked with a university and/or a medical facility to provide training for professionals in the field, ensuring the delivery of high quality of care for seniors for additional oversight. There should be a 24-hour hotline to identify deficiencies in senior programs and facilities and to report incidents of senior abuse or neglect.

For many Caribbean countries, the present staffing for public sector programs is insufficient to execute the many programs outlined in the National Policy agenda. Non-governmental organizations are often lacking resources for capacity building and infrastructure to carry out their programs. More exchanges between Caribbean countries and adopted countries regarding best practices and models of care with adequately trained staff are needed. A more efficient system must be devised to handle requests for medical information such as an established process or communication between healthcare providers in the Caribbean and those in the adopted country.

As a whole, the general public needs to be informed about the full range of diseases affecting aging populations such as cardiovascular diseases, the cause and how to prevent and/or care for these conditions. Whether living in the country of origin or in an adopted country, Caribbean immigrants need to be more engaged in preventative health to improve the quality of healthcare and ways to address dietary and other needs of those who are afflicted by the range of cardiovascular illnesses. Short-term and long-term plans need to be developed for the care of Caribbean residents and their aging family members. The plans should include adequate provisions for medical crisis, including out-of-home options.

Eldermire-Shearer (2007) states that "Jamaicans need to start making long-term plans to avoid many of the problems and pitfalls that currently plague the society, including the stress of properly caring for old people." She further suggests that Jamaicans should not be dependent upon the National Insurance Scheme (NIS) as a supplement. She encourages families to develop a plan about whom and how they will care for their elders.

"Recommendations for healthcare providers, caretakers and policy makers are outlined below."

Health Care Providers

Ensure that healthcare providers are trained in gerontology to work with diverse populations and are culturally competent.

Identify one or two family members to communicate with and work with the family to ensure the best possible care. This may not necessarily be the primary caretaker.

Make time to understand the needs of the elderly and their experiences in self-care related to their illness.

Find out about the individual's support network and access to services

Help families to fully understand short-term and long-term health needs, the types of resources available to address those needs and how to advocate on behalf of their family member.

Caretakers

Learn about medical resources in the area in which the person resides and maintain close contact with medical providers. Keep a record of service providers, appointments, medications and medical history.

Connect with relatives, neighbors or friends who can stop in regularly and possibly at short notice to check on the status of the home and quality of care being provided.

Create a support network for the aging family member. Find trustworthy people who can provide direct care. Create a support network to provide relief to you and others in the caretaking role

Accompany the aging family member to their medical appointments. They may not always understand or recall what they are told by the providers and are not always able to negotiate the myriad of agencies/providers.

Secure access to transportation in case of an emergency and finances for medicine and pay attention to the dietary needs of the aging family member.

Visit the aging family member often to monitor the quality of home and health care.

Policy Makers in the Caribbean

Develop standards of care for the aging population. Monitor and evaluate services for elders, caregivers and care providers.

Develop standards and quality improvement mechanisms for nursing/convalescent homes, assisted living and in-home care for elders that maintain their independence, integrity and dignity.

Develop training for caregivers to provide the necessary medical, psychological and technical skills to deal with the aging population.

Develop and strengthen community infrastructures such as adult day services for elders.

Create community support systems for the growing elderly population.

Develop preventative care programs that will assist seniors in maintaining the highest level of health.

Conduct further research regarding the living conditions and the needs of the elderly in rural and urban areas.

CONCLUSION

Caribbean families both in the country of origin and the adopted country are faced with the growing challenge of caring for their elders. Remittances from family members who migrated decades ago have contributed to the quality of life in terms of material or financial support for those who remain in their country of origin. This same migration pattern, however, impacts the nuclear and extended families. Fewer family members become available or are able to care for the elderly.

Families migrate and reside where there are educational and job opportunities. In the case of a sick child or relative, there are often not enough family members living in close proximity to each other to care for the sick or the elderly. Second and third generation Caribbean individuals are often younger, busy with school, caring for their family, or in the workforce. Consequently, when an elderly family member becomes ill, it results in a crisis for families. Some families may have difficulty getting time off from work, or are unable to afford healthcare on a short-term or long-term basis. They often do not have the finances to support the aging family member. Instead, a patchwork of resources is created that are short-term measures and those become inadequate over time.

Depending on the health status of the aging family member, stress is placed on family members and caretakers who must comply with providing a prescribed diet, strict medication regime and/or frequent doctor's appointments. Families would prefer to care for their sick or aging family member at home, however: the complexity of the health issues and the need for consistent professional care dictates otherwise. Consequently, a growing number of Caribbean families turn to formal institutions and agencies such as home care, convalescent homes, nursing homes and assisted living facilities for supplemental and long-term care for their aging family member.

Clearly, to better understand the needs of our aging populations, more studies need to be conducted to assess the existing living conditions of the elderly, with a focus on those residing in rural areas. An in-depth look will allow us to determine existing housing situations, caretaking, transportation needs, availability and accessibility of basic social and healthcare services. The changes instituted by the Affordable Health Care Act are expected to enhance the capacity of both healthcare service providers and family members to assist the elderly in the United States. Perhaps certain aspects of it can serve as a prototype for healthcare systems in the Caribbean.

There is a growing need for affordable interim and long-term facilities in the Caribbean. There are lessons to be learned from medical and social work practitioners at home and abroad. This chapter outlines how service providers, caretakers and policy makers can create a network service to supplement and support families in crisis.

Bibliography

Batalova, J. (2012). "Senior Immigrants in the United States". *Migration Policy Institute*. May.

Bourne, P. A. (2009). "Growing Old in Jamaica: Population Ageing and Senior Citizens' Wellbeing". *Health Research Scientist*. University of the West Indies, Mona Campus. Department of Community Health and Jamaica.

Cerase, Francesco. "A Study of Italian Migrants Returning from the U.S.A.," *International Migration Review* (1967): 67-74.

Clarke, Egerton (2009). "Population Trends and Challenges in Jamaica". *Journal of Aging in Emerging Economies*, Vol. 1 – No. 1, January, pp. 24-32.

Chukwudum, U., C. O'Connor, Y. Beersingh & C.Walters. (2010). "Quality of Life of Jamaica's Elderly Population". *Journal of Aging in Emerging Economies*, Vol. 2 – No. 1 January, pp. 40-58.

Cloos, Patrick; Allen, Caroline F.; Alvarados, Beatriz E.; Zunzungui, Victoria; Simeon, Donald T. and Eldemire-Shearer, Denise. (2009). "Active Aging: A Qualitative Study in Six Caribbean Countries". *Aging & Society* 39, 2010, 79-101. Cambridge University Press.

Conway, D. and R.B. Potter (2006). "Caribbean Transnational Return Migrants as Agents of Change". *Geography Compass*: 10.1111/j. 1749-8198.

Crawford, C. (2004). "African-Caribbean Women, Diaspora and Transnationality". *Canadian Woman Studies* Journal, Volume 23, Number 2, pp97-103.

Crooks, Donneth (2008). "Aging in Jamaica: An Analysis of Patterns and Trends" Paper presented at the annual meeting of the *American Sociological Association Annual Meeting*. Sheraton Boston and the Boston Marriot Copley Place, Boston, MA, July 31.

Drachman, D. and A. Ryan (2001). "Immigrants and Refugees". In Ed. Alex Gitterman, Handbook of Social Work Practice with Vulnerable *and Resilient Populations*. New York: Columbia University Press, p. 652-686.

——, and A. Paulino (2004). "Thinking Beyond United States Borders", In Eds. Drachman, D. & Paulino, Ana, *Immigrants and Social Work: Thinking Beyond the Borders of the United States*. New York: The Haworth Social Work Press, p. 1-9.

Eberstadt, N. (1997). "World Population Implosion?" *Public Interest*, 129: 3-22.

ECLAC (2004). Economic Commission for Latin America and the Caribbean, "Population Ageing in the Caribbean: An Inventory of Policies, Programs and Future Challenges". May 11.

ECLAC (2008) Economic Commission for Latin America and the Caribbean, "Population Ageing in the Caribbean: An Inventory of Policies, Programs and Future Challenges. December 8.

Edwards-Wescott, P., K.A. Gittens-Baynes, and C. Metivier (2011). "An Examination of the Interaction between Poverty and Health Status in the Elderly Population of Jamaica". *International Journal of Humanities and Social Science*. Vol. 1 No. 11 (Special Issue – August).

James, K., Eldemire-Schearer, D., Gouldbourne, J., Morris, C. (2007) "Falls

and Fall Prevention in the Elderly: The Jamaican Perspective". *West Indian Med J.* Dec.; 56(6):534-9.
Gavrilov, L.A. and P. Heuveline (2003). "Aging of Population." In: Paul Demeny and Geoffrey McNicoll (Eds.)*The Encyclopedia of Population*. New York, Macmillan Reference USA: Available at:http://www.galegroup.com/servlet/ItemDetailServlet?region=9&imprint=000&titleCode=M333&type=4&id=174029
Guzzetta, C. (2004). "Return Migration: An Overview". In Eds. Drachman. D. & Paulino, Ana, *Immigrants and Social Work: Thinking Beyond the Borders of the United States*. New York: The Haworth Social Work Press, p.109-117.
Hambleton, I. R., K. Clarke, H.L. Broome, H.S. Fraser, F. Brathwaite and A.J. Hennis (2005). "Historical and Current Predictors of Self-reported Health Status among Elderly Persons in Barbados". *Rev Panam Salud Publica* Vol.17 No.5-6 Washington May/June, pp. 342-352. Available from:
<http://www.scielosp.org/scielo.php?script=sci_arttext&pid=S1020-49892005000500006&lng=en&nrm=iso>.   ISSN   1020-4989. http://dx.doi.org/10.1590/S1020-49892005000500006.
Healy, L. (2004). "Strengthening the Link: Social Work with Immigrants and Refugees and International Social Work". In Eds. Drachman. D. & Paulino, Ana, *Immigrants and Social Work: Thinking Beyond the Borders of the United States*. New York: The Haworth Social Work Press, p. 49-67.
Heuveline (2011). National Council for Senior Citizens. "Senior Citizens Policy Protects Ageing Population." *Jamaica Information Systems.* 29 September.
King, Russell; Warnes, Tony; Williams, Allan. (2000). *Sunset Lives: British Retirement Migration to the Mediterranean.* Berg. Oxford International Publishers, Ltd.
Levitt, P. and B. N. Jaworsky (2007). "Transnational Migration Studies: Past Developments and Future Trends". *Annual Review of Social*, 33:129-156.
Livingston, I. L., M. Neita, L. Riviere and S.L. Livingston (2007). "Gender, Acculterative Stress ad Caribbean Immigrants' Health in the United States of America". *West Indian Medical Journal*, 56 (3): 213-222.
Lubitz, J., L. Ca; E. Kramarow and H. Lentzner (2003). "Health, Life Expectancy, and Health Care Spending among the Elderly". *New England Journal of Medicine* 2003; 349:1048 -1055. September 11.
McCabe, K. (2011). "Caribbean Immigrants in the United States". *Migration Policy Institute*, April.
Migration Policy Institute (2012)
Mullings, J. and P. J. Tomlin (2007). "Health Sector Challenges and Responses beyond the Alma-Ata Declaration: A Caribbean Perspective". *Rev Panam Salud Publica/Pan Am J Public Health* 21(2/3).
NCSC. (1997) National Council for Senior Citizens, Jamaica.
O'Neil, K. (2003). "Remittances from the United States in Context". *Migration Policy Institute*, June.
Palloni A. and M. McEntiry (2007). "Aging and Health Status of Elderly in Latin America and the Caribbean: Preliminary Findings". *J. Cross Cult. Gerontololy*, Sep:22 (3):263-85.
Plaza, Dwaine (2008). "Transnational Return Migration to the English-Speaking Caribbean". *Revue Europeenne des Migrations Internationals*

(Online), Vol. 24 – n 1. Online since 01 April 2011, Connection on 12 June 2012. url:http://Iremi.revues.

Powell, D. L., Price, Addie J., Burns, Faith A., McConnell, Eleanor S., Hendrix, Cristina C., McWhinney-Dehaney, Leila, and Lombardi, Marilyn M. (2011). "Pillars for the Care of Older Persons in the Caribbean", *Public Health Nursing* (2011), Vol. 29 No. 1, pp 80-90.

Quirke, E.; R.B. Potter and D. Conway. (2010). "Transnationalism and the Caribbean Community in the UK: Theoretical Perspectives". *The Open Geography Journal*: 3, 1-14.

Rawlings, Joan. (2010). "Ageing in the Caribbean: Exploring Some Major Concerns for Family and Society". Paper prepared for the SALISES Conference, Turmoil and Turbulence in Small Developing States: Going Beyond Survival." Hyatt Hotel and Conference Centre, Port of Spain, Trinidad, March 24-26.

Reid, T. (2007). "More Seniors Off to Retirement Homes". *The Jamaica Observer*: April 29.

Reynolds, T. (2008). "Ties That Bind: Families, Social Capital and Caribbean Second-Generation Return Migration". Working Paper No 46, 2-29. February,University of Sussex, Sussex Centre for Migration Research.

Rogers, Andrei and Castro, Luis J. (1984). *Migration, Urbanization, and Spatial Polulation Dynamics*. Westview Press.

Rouse, J. (2008). Ministry of Social Development. The Government of the Republic of Trinidad and Tobago Delegate to the International Federation 9th Global Conference on Ageing, September 4-7. Montreal, Canada.

Russell, B. (2008). *The Impact of the Jamaican Drugs for the Elderly Program on Access to Care and Spending on Prescription Medications*: VDM Verlag Publishing.

Schiller, Nina Glick (1995). "From Immigrant to Transmigrant: Theorizing Transnational Migration". *Anthropological Quarterly*, 68:1, Jan, 48-63.

Small, John (2005). "The Dynamics of Return Migration". *The Caribbean Journal of Social Work,* Vol. 4/August. Special Volume, pp 122-136.

Suro, Roberto (1996). *Watching America's Door: The Immigration Backlash and the New Policy Debate.* Twentieth Century Fund Press, April 1.

Wheeler, D. P. and A.M. Mahoney (2008). "Caribbean Immigrants in the Unites States – Health and Health Care: The Need for a Social Agenda". *Health and Social Work*, August.

Williams, David R., Haile, Rahwa; Gonzalez, Hector M.; Neighbors, Harold; Baser, Raymond and Jackson, James S. (2007). "The Mental Health of Black Caribbean Immigrants: Results for the National Survey of American Life". *American Journal of Public Health,* January, Vol. 97, No. 1. 52-59.

Chapter Six

Caribbean Immigrant Families: Transnational Identity

Annette Mahoney

and Lear Matthews

INTRODUCTION

In this chapter, the authors examine the unique challenges faced by English Caribbean immigrant families that demand a merging of the dominant and often unfamiliar host culture with their own native practices. The chapter further examines the role and functions of family/kinship networks within transnational communities, the level of transactions conducted across national boundaries, and explores the manner in which English Caribbean families create shared identities.

Baptiste, et al (1997) argue that the term "Caribbean family" is a misnomer because such families are not monoliths about which we can generalize, but are heterogeneous groups representing many cultures, ethnicities and races. They further posit that there are many racial, cultural and inter-territorial variations in the way Caribbean families are structured and the manner in which they function. Although this chapter focuses on the Afro-Caribbean Family, there are some implications for Indo-Caribbean families whose kinship network has unique cultural characteristics that will not be addressed here.

The English Speaking Caribbean Family in the US

Each year, thousands of English Caribbean nationals continue to migrate to the United States for a variety of reasons. Many seek to reunite with family members, but a majority, like millions before them seek to improve economic, employment and educational opportunities for themselves, and more importantly, for their children than was possible in their respective native countries.

Maintaining and participating in transnational links with the community of origin, family/kinship relations and some forms of rituals serve both symbolic and practical functions for immigrant families. Culturally-consonant communities can make a critical difference, especially in the lives of newly arrived immigrant families in the United States who often feel excluded and marginalized. Invariably, survival of bi-national families requires the learning of new skills in order to facilitate living in "two places at once". Drawing from the work of Goulbourne (2002), Reynolds (2005) notes, "for Caribbean people, the maintenance of family relationships is not constrained by national boundaries and instead operates within a transnational context"(p. 10).

Caribbean immigrants come to the United States as family units or individually. Many migrate in a staggered pattern in which one family member - a parent, spouse or sibling - immigrate alone initially and over time is joined by other sanguine family members and often extended family members.

One axiom of immigrant life is the fractured bonds of family networks resulting from the transition. Specifically, when families immigrate they leave behind a network of extended kin who provide mutual aid and support and upon whom they depend in good times and bad times. These networks include sanguine (e.g., parents and siblings), non-sanguine (e.g., in-laws) and even fictive kin (e.g., godparents, informal adoptees). Additionally, although not officially a part of the support networks, children left behind, secondary to serial immigration, and awaiting reunification with their parents, engender much of the same feelings of loss and emotional cut-off as members of the "official" support networks. Often the bond developed between a child and the home-based relative is so strong that it can be traumatic when broken.

This is poignantly depicted in Mason Richardson's Film, "The Seawall", in which a child left in the care of his grandmother when his mother emigrated to the US finds it emotionally distressing to separate from his surrogate caregiver as he was about to join his mother (Nelson, 2012). Potential loss of these networks and the desire to maintain contact with family members left behind have contributed to a number of English Caribbean immigrants living a trans-context lifestyle and as transnational citizens after migration (Turner, 1991; Basch et al. 1994).

In this regard, Baptiste (1997) notes that trans-context immigrants function in two life spaces called 'home', their pre-immigration culture and the US culture, and strive to function in both concurrently and effectively. For example, parents whose children are left behind as a result of serial immigration engage in non-residential parenting although they reside physically in North America. Other challenges arise in the family resettlement stage. Drawing from the analysis of Pessar and Mahler (2001), Levitt and Glick Schiller (2004) noted, "Transnational family life entails renegotiating communication between spouses, the distribution of work tasks, and who will migrate and who will stay behind via long distance"(p. 18).

The role and functions of transnational communities and family/kinship networks in identity formation, and the role of immigrant Caribbean families in creating shared identities are central to the transnational process. In support of this observation, Levitt and Glick Schiller note, "Even children who never return to their parent's ancestral homes are brought up in households where people, values, goods and claims from somewhere else are present on a daily basis"(p.19).

Change in gender roles following migration is a characteristic that has impacted Caribbean families. It was found that the primary reason many Caribbean women migrate was to uplift the welfare of their family (Vernez, 1999). Mary Spooner (this volume) notes that a significant number of Caribbean women were head of households in the home country. As a result, the experience of being household decision-makers may prepare them for the independence expected of them as transnationals.

Enhancing the Caribbean family's resources and capacity to adjust to their adapted home is their Labor Force Participation Rate. For example, males from Jamaica have a Labor Force Participation Rate of 81.3% and females 85.7%, Guyanese males have a rate of 84.2% and females 71.3%, while the Trinidad and Tobagonians have an 82.3% male and 82.3% female rate (US Census Bureau, 2009).

Most of these families own homes. In addition, 30% of the men were in professional jobs (cited in Roopnarine and Shin, 2003). While the socio-demographic profile of Afro-Caribbean immigrant groups in the United States has been found to be less impressive on certain measures than that of Indo-Caribbean immigrant groups (see Roopnarine), in general, Afro-Caribbean peoples are making remarkable strides in areas such as education, income, labor force participation and other indicators of social mobility (Kasinitz, 1993; Foner, 2001; Waters, 1999; Mahoney, 2004).

Entrepreneurship among Caribbean families is also a likely contributing factor to the impressive profile of some Indo- and African Caribbean families, along the lines of education income and home ownership (Roopnaraine, 1999). In addition to their valuable entrepreneurial histories, the high level of success by segments of the immigrant Caribbean community has also been associated with such factors as high levels of English competency, strong work ethic and high aspirations. These attributes have served English Caribbean immigrants in the United States very well. Caribbean immigrant families have proven to be quite adept at building vibrant transnational alliances that subvert elements of the imposed social, economic and cultural order of their host country. Other notable strengths of the English Caribbean family include the presence of supportive fellow immigrants from the Caribbean region and an extended kinship network in the home country that lends support in such crucial areas as childrearing and caring for elderly kin.

Their extensive transnational fields, that often extends beyond family and kin in their home countries to include those in the broader Caribbean Diaspora (United Kingdom, Canada, etc), often serve various functional roles, especially for new immigrants. In part, the migrant's heightened interactions with home societies after 1980 can be related to the ready availability of cheap, frequent and fast communications and transportation, and by the 1990's, to advances in cyberspace (Basch, 2001). Emerging from these advancements, are various innovations in parenting.

Caring for and interacting with children constitutes a major part of transnational activity among Caribbean parents. In discussing this phenomenon, it was noted that "While adults make family decisions, children are the central axis of family migration and often a critical reason why families move back and forth and sustain transnational ties"(Levitt and Glick Schiller, 2004, p. 19). Among the practices bridging such ties is "parenting from a distance", a concept that aptly describes the practice of new immigrant parents who often precede their children in the migration process and their efforts to maintain vital elements of their parenting functions (Best-Cummings, 2004). Some parents also make frequent visits to their home countries in order to support the children's development. Even as these parents participate in the very vital US economy, thereby increasing their ability to provide for themselves and their children, they also make an enormous contribution to the development of their respective home countries and of the Caribbean region as a whole. Regular transfers of money to families in the Caribbean countries have emerged as one of the most reliable sources of foreign exchange in the region. For example, private remittances to Jamaica during the latter half of the 1990's totaled US$3.2 billion dollars.

On an annual basis, these inflows have equaled between 9% and 10% of GDP (http://www.iadb.org/mif/v2/files/grassless.doc). Recent trends suggest that a higher percentage of Jamaica's GDP is being supported by remittances from the U.S, Canada and the United Kingdom. A more moderate, but significant trend could be found in Guyana, Trinidad and Tobago, and Grenada (Edwin, 2011). Increasingly, immigrants from these countries are attempting to leverage their home countries for productive policies and projects.

Governments in the Caribbean have also come to see communities of their emigrants abroad as valuable resources on which to draw, and as a valued part of their nationhood. Consequently, they are seeking to extend voting rights and other acts of citizenship to them across geographic boundaries (GUYD Project, 2012; Karran, 2012).

Identity and Marginalized Neighborhoods

The concept of transnationalism provides an insightful conceptual understanding of the complex factors that are associated with the integration of English Caribbean families in the United States. For those immigrants who are never exclusively residentially based, the very notion of their citizenship takes on new dimensions. The frequent questioning of their loyalty to their adopted country often precludes the understanding of transnational social fields as important sites of opportunity for immigrant families, as well as their host society. For example, the interim strategy of leaving children behind to be cared for by close kin is one with economic benefits to the U.S. On the one hand, the State is spared its usual expenditure for education and other social costs, and on the other, the work force benefits from the very active involvement of immigrant parents in the labor market, as a result of the removal of some of the direct parenting responsibilities.

The relationship between immigrant youth and their parents provide some insight into the dynamics of transnational connections. The experiences of second generation English Caribbean immigrants have been widely discussed (Waters, 1999; Kasinitz, Waters, Mollenkopf and Anil, 2002). The desire of some Caribbean immigrant parents to continue their heritage through their children and grandchildren may not be easily realized. Although, as Reynolds (2004) found, some young Caribbean immigrants use the family as an interpersonal and social resource to reaffirm "their connections to their family's country of origin"(p. 12), Levitt and Glick Schiller (2004) argue, "Clearly, transnational activities will not be central to the lives of most of the second generation and those who engage in them will not do so with the same frequency and intensity as their parents"(p.20).

Various writers, including Waters (2001) have observed the complex nature of the relationship between immigration, identity formation and assimilation among English Caribbean families. What is of significance in understanding how Caribbean immigrants identify in relationship to their host society is largely located in the pre-eminence of race over other social-economic factors. Consequently, even the most accomplished of Caribbean immigrants can only expect an acknowledgement of social worth that is tinged with simultaneous experiences of marginality and privilege.

To avoid such characterizations, some families have abandoned the notion of ever achieving full integration into the US society and have instead sought to achieve a level of social citizenship by maintaining a strong cultural identity and a sense of community through the solidarity with their ethnic community ties in the US and in their home countries. Others have sought and have achieved some level of social integration. The stark reality of being an "immigrant of color" holds important implications for the success or failure of the immigrant family.

Race and Racism: Implications for Family Well-Being

Recognizing the hegemony of race and racism that are embedded in the structures of the United States and the unique dilemma that these forces create for the mostly non-white Caribbean immigrants, Kasinitz (1993) and others have observed that these immigrants enter a society that is far more prosperous than the ones they left behind, but they also join the ranks of America's most frequently oppressed group. Having come from societies where peoples of African and East Indian ancestry are in the majority, their new racialized identity and the racial and ethnic divisions that they encounter do not escape their attention.

Portes and Zhou (1999) argue that Caribbean families, particularly in US cities, have the difficult task of navigating complex cultural clashes, sometimes facing job loss, discrimination, harsher treatment and scrutiny in a post-9/11 world, few opportunities for meaningful employment, high rents, impoverished communities, few social services, religious differences, and low-income high-crime neighborhoods. This segment of the immigrant Caribbean population faces added challenges as a result of living in communities that are populated chiefly by native minorities. The stark reality of living in communities of color includes further realization that their host communities are notorious for characteristics that make them poor indicators of success for themselves and their families (see Matthews and Mahoney, 2005).

In describing the segregation indices for black Americans in many US cities, Massey and Denton (2006) in their book "American Apartheid", note that many of these cities, including those with substantive numbers of Caribbean immigrants, consist of hyper segregation - indeed a form of the racial separation of apartheid (cited by Water, 2001). Additionally, many of these neighborhoods face daunting problems of poverty, drug-use, and other indicators of poor health

(Mahoney, 2004). Caribbean immigrants and their families often suffer enormous consequences for living in such socially disorganized neighborhoods. Fear that they will lose their children to the street or suffer the consequences of deportation is a real concern for segments of the English Caribbean population in the United States.

Immigration Laws: Impact on Caribbean Families

Increased deportations have clearly affected the Caribbean family and its capacity to adapt to the new society. Leyland (2012) argues that among the consequences of implementing the U.S. Department of Homeland Security's Safe Communities Program is the separation of thousands of immigrant families. The burgeoning deportation rates of family members and friends have become more prevalent with the 1996 Immigration Law by provisions of the USA PATRIOT Act (Uniting and Strengthening America by Providing Appropriate Tools Required to Intercept and Obstruct Terrorism). The policy has resulted in increased deportation rates, particularly since 2008 (Hong, 2012). Immigrant parents of U.S.-born children "were among 396,906 immigrants removed from the United States in the 2011 fiscal year and the extreme hardship they could face by losing their parent. . . . that means parents have to either take their children to their native country, where they are not citizens or leave them here"(Foley 2012, p. 2). The impact of detention and deportation is troubling to some Caribbean immigrants. Not only is it potentially traumatic for immigrant families, but the resulting social costs on both sides of the Atlantic in continuing this trend could be unprecedented.

The separation of parents and children occur as they struggle to survive in the new society. Children are left behind, while some adolescents rebelliously seek to return to the home country. Moreover, detention and deportation figures for Caribbean countries are disproportionate to the size of these countries, thereby giving rise to the belief among many that there is a bias against Caribbean nationals. Under the provisions of the Illegal Immigration Reform and Immigrant Responsibility Act of 1996, the US Immigration and Naturalization Service, the Department of Homeland Security (DHS) received sweeping powers to determine admission, deportation and detention of immigrants who had committed crimes (Clarke, 2004, p.155). Unfortunately, some who did not fit the criminal immigrant profile have been swept up in this process.

This massive deportation scheme has had a devastating impact on countries in the region and on remaining English Caribbean families in the United States. The financial consequences are not only felt by remaining family members in the U.S., but by kinship networks and the Diasporic economies of the home country and by the individual countries and region as a whole. Simultaneously, the social and emotional impact of immigrant detention and deportation remain a major concern for Caribbean families in the United States. Implementing such policies affect parents' capacity to provide adequate child rearing. For example, when the sole breadwinner of a Caribbean immigrant family faced deportation under the DHS Safe Communities Program, his American-born children were at risk of being referred to the Child Welfare Department. This situation potentially separates families, diminishing parents' ability to provide, and forges transnational parenting, a tenuous alternative. A growing number of immigrant parents are reportedly in Dentention Centers across the US and if deported, many children face the possibility of ending up in foster care. However, in June of 2012 in an effort to make immigration laws fair and efficient, the Department of Homeland Security announced it will focus "enforcement resources on the removal of individuals who pose a National Security or public safety risk—by removing the threat of deportation for young people who came to the US as children and are low enforcement priority." (NILP, 2013)

Various countries in the Caribbean, including Jamaica, Guyana, and Trinidad and Tobago, have reported dramatic increases in their crime rates. Although not accurately documented, much of these increases have been blamed on "deportees." The United States Department of Immigration and Customs Enforcement (ICE) reported that during fiscal year 2004-2005, 6,000 Caribbean immigrants were deported, and of these only 4 were considered "criminal aliens"(Hardbeat News, 2005). Many of these deportees spent most of their lives in the US. Faced with less vibrant economies than that of the US, many must rely on relatives and friends, who are often stretched across vast transnational fields, for their survival in the home countries.

Gendered Constraints

Caribbean women often dominate in the outflow of immigrants from the English Caribbean region. For many of them, emigration promises a higher standard of living for themselves and their families, perhaps removal from violent domestic relationships, and an opportunity to escape oppressive political ideological forces that often limit their power and choices. The literature on Caribbean women shows a strong pattern of caring for themselves and their children regardless of male support. Historically, many of these women worked as domestics either as "live-ins"or "day workers", providing for their families in both the home country and adopted home, invested in their children's education, and belonged to mutual aid societies (Vergel, 2009). Once in America, many immigrant women will be caught up in various dimensions of gender politics, and according to Ho (1999), their responsibility "goes beyond that of mother to include that of worker and constructor of social relationships that crosses boundaries (p. 1).

Many will experience the intersecting forces of immigration, gender, race and class and understand the role that they play in shaping the contours of their experience in the United States. Some researchers (Ho, 1999; Levitt and Glick Schiller, 2004) found that transnational relations are not only racialized, but gendered within the rubric of globalization. In particular, family networks across nation-states "are marked by gendered differences in power and status and can be used exploitatively . . . Kin networks maintained between people who send remittances and those who live on them can be fraught with tension"(Levitt and Glick Schiller, p. 5).

Such tensions have been exacerbated by changes in the international domestic labor market, in which immigrant women can be separated from their families intermittently or for extended periods of time. Pierrette Hondagneu-Sotelo (2012) in her article, Transnational Motherhood, argues that post-industrial economies bring with them a labor demand for immigrant workers that are differently gendered than that typical of industrial or industrializing societies. She further notes that an increase in demand for jobs dedicated to social reproduction was observed in all post-industrial nations. These include jobs in convalescent homes, private household cleaning, and childcare. These jobs are traditionally coded as "women's jobs,"but today these jobs have entered the global marketplace. Not only are many of these women working long hours for meager wages, many are constrained by care-giving expectations within the home, and in providing transnational support for family left behind.

The Role and Function of Transnational Communities

Transnational activities serve vitally important functions that are mutually beneficial to the immigrant and to the family network in the home country. Goulborne's (2002) study identified the following functions of Caribbean Trans nationality across the Atlantic: Providing Care and Affection Across National Boundaries and Trans nationality of Self and National Identities. He found that kinship networks were primary institutions for equipping individual members for fulfilled lives in a competitive and generally hostile world. He argues that family members tended to utilize the kinship network as a primary source of transnational activity across the Atlantic. Similarly, Carten, et al. (2005) note that Caribbean families, like other ethnic groups, develop support systems as they settle in certain neighborhoods forming "natural helping networks"which facilitate resettlement.

Family members in the Caribbean play mutually beneficial roles in the lives of the immigrant families in the United States who have to contend with a range of socio-economic challenges. In this light, the Caribbean family can be viewed as a catalyst in the transaction between the home country and the adopted home. This process is not only constantly reshaped by the changing needs of global capitalism as noted by Ho (1999), but is also affected by draconian immigration policies.

Creating Shared Identities

In the experience of some observers, resettlement is likely to result in loss of one's culture and identity (Prasad, 2012). However, at the core of family and community networks among Caribbean immigrants is a shared identity that underscores the very fabric of their transnational character. In this regard, Thomas-Hope (1992) notes, "Trans-Atlantic family and kinship relationships are highly valued and represent a key aspect of a Caribbean identity"(cited by Reynolds, 2004, p. 10).

Notwithstanding the influence of a dominant American culture that tends to modify immigrants' identity via assimilation, Caribbean immigrants continue to identify with their own cultural group, preserving the values and norms reminiscent of the home country. For example, it is not uncommon to find the practice of many artistic, social and political activities that are informed by beliefs and customs prevalent in the Caribbean. In addition, immigrants' receiving indigenous goods from relatives, communicating through the Internet, telephone, and exchanging photographs, "reinforce continuity and bonding across distance and come close to influencing day-to-day activities"(Goulbourne, 2002, p. 169). The Calling Card and Internet Café have become staples in this cross border family communication process. Furthermore, the family functions as a source and conduit for the transmission of traditional customs, beliefs and practices. The immigrant family/household, then, has become the central milieu for cultural heritage and continuity(p.3).

Symbols of Caribbean culture such as pictures of tropical themes and a potpourri of Caribbean flavored artifacts are seen in the homes. Speech patterns, mannerisms and food are also typically Caribbean. In her assessment of immigrant Caribbean mothers, Reynolds

(2004), asserts, "Caribbean mothering identity include the maintenance of cultural and kinship connections to the Caribbean, childrearing strategies to respond to racism, employment and labor market, community mother, and the role and participation of Caribbean men in the family."She further notes that "the thematic issues of protection, advice, security and education form the central elements of these mothers' childcare"(p. 23).

Modification in post-migratory childrearing methods and the relationship between home and school can have a tremendous impact on the family, creating notable challenges. Due to differences in child rearing practices and the degree of enforcement of Child Protection Laws in the English Caribbean and the United States, some immigrant parents have been conflicted about the potential erosion of their parental authority. Physical corporal punishment has long been an acceptable form of child discipline in the Caribbean. However, in his research, Goulbourne (2002) found "such punishments were administered not out of hate, malice or cruelty, but out of deep concern for the long-term well-being of children"(p. 164). He reported that respondents justified harsh disciplinary measures as necessary to teach 'good manners', not bringing 'shame' to the family, and appropriate presentation of self in the larger society.

In the authors' research on the topic, the case of a Guyanese woman who migrated to New York City with her two adolescent daughters, graphically exemplifies this dilemma. Her parenting style was undoubtedly informed by engrained cultural beliefs and customs. One of the girls violated the home curfew set by Mom, who engaged corporal punishment in a manner that is customary in her home county. She soon found herself being questioned by case workers from the Agency of Children's Services and the possibility of having the child placed in foster care. Traumatized by the experience, though supported emotionally by relatives, who empathized with her situation, she was referred to a mental health facility for counseling "to improve her parenting skills". Although complying with the mandated "treatment", she vehemently protested: "I am not crazy, I disciplined my child the way I always did. This was clearly a cross-cultural dilemma [1]."

David Baptiste (2005) reported in his study that rearing children in the US revealed some challenging post-immigration challenges for English Caribbean families. Not only are there different rules for parenting, but many parents felt that their authority over their children was weakened. He concluded, "Some parents perceive their children to be too American in behaviors, values, and outlook, complaining that children are too ready to disparage any parental values that are reflective of the 'old country. Raising children, especially adolescents, in the US, is analogous to living with foreigners" (p. 354). Nevertheless, the assumption that the use of physical punishment among Caribbean immigrant parents is congruent with culturally defined behaviors, needs to be re-examined. In a study of child abuse among Barbadian families, Carten, et. al. (2003) conclude that the use of physical punishment in disciplining children was not sanctioned by culturally determined child-rearing norms and practice, but rather influenced by the intricate "interaction of interpersonal, economic, social and environmental factors"(p.1).

Demographic shifts and structural acculturation patterns also play a significant role in identity formation and adaptation to the new social environment, particularly among immigrant children. Matthews and Mahoney (2005) note that the school is one of the frontline institutions that children encounter early in their adopted home. Many families expect the school to play an instrumental role in the socialization, achievement and overall success of their children. The expectation by parents for their children's achievement of the American Dream is attached to the schooling process and outcome. However, various migration and acculturation-related stressors threaten to impede the learning process and overall psychosocial functioning of these children. These include structural barriers due to ethnic and cultural attributes, placement in a grade level lower than their academic capability, and referral to Special Education or ESL (English as a Second Language) classes.

Caribbean parents have been sending their children to private schools managed by Caribbean educators who attempt to adhere to practices such as the wearing of uniforms, and strict discipline, traditions preferred by many parents. For these parents, such an educational milieu represents the hallmark of character building and identity formation by a continuation of the values inculcated in the home country. However, because of the economic crisis that has resulted in financial hardship for many families, the nascent trend has shifted to the Public School System being a feasible alternative.

Certain ideological principles among Caribbean immigrants, such as pooling of resources through group savings (e.g. "Susu"and "box hand") continue to promote a common heritage of cooperation and mutual support in the areas of entrepreneurship and political involvement. Such practices also enhance the economic support capability of the family. The formation of Caribbean Cultural Organizations, including those that encourage family activities, serve to promote a shared identity through shared activities and interdependence. It is important to note that such intra-group reciprocity and identification enhance rather than retard adaptation to the new society. The initial phase of acculturation often requires a supportive and familiar cultural context, including a strong family network.

Among Indo-Caribbean immigrants, religious practices, in particular Hinduism, serve to reinforce a common social identity and facilitate interaction within and among families. Many Afro-Caribbean immigrants have continued the practice of the Christian religion in the United States and do conduct both religious and philanthropic missions in the home country. In describing ethnic identity formation, Goulbourne (2002) observes "ethnic identification continues to be expressed through individuals' transnational kinship networks. Consequently, young people's familial and cultural connections to their Caribbean country of origin often supersede their place of birth or residence, understanding and defining their ethnic identity"(Cited by Reynolds, 2004, p. 10).

Health Disparities: Implications for the Family

The lack of access to quality healthcare and educational resources is among the major concerns faced by English Caribbean immigrant families. These factors spiral together in a vicious circle to undermine the functioning of the entire family system and communities. The 1996 Welfare Reform Act imposed wide restrictions on the eligibility of support services, including Medicaid for non-citizens. Although certain waivers could be obtained, lack of knowledge about eligibility, fear of deportation and unavailability of culturally competent services undermined the receipt of such services.

Also influencing the new immigrant's access to healthcare is the fact that an increasing number of employers fail to provide health benefits for their employees. In addition, many immigrants work in sectors of the American economy that do not provide health benefits. In support of this observation, Shedlin, et al. (2006) found that "immigrants are more than twice as likely as citizens to have no health insurance - of the 33 million immigrants in the US, one third (11.2 million) have no health insurance"(p. 7). Bayne Smith et al. (2004), in their study of Infant Mortality Rates among Caribbean immigrant families in New York City, found vast disparities between Caribbean families and other groups.

Another area of concern has been the prevalence of HIV/AIDS in the immigrant population. Sheldon, et. al. (2006) warns, "Because the HIV pandemic undergoes continual change in its locations and affected populations, it is crucial to study HIV risk behaviors among mobile and immigrant groups within and across borders"(p. 1). The incidence of HIV/AIDS infection among Caribbean immigrants has had a devastating impact on families, particularly in cities such as New York, where the HIV/AIDS rate of 46% among persons of

Caribbean descent was reported (Office of AIDS Surveillance, New York City Department of Health (March 2000). Spooner, et.al. (2004) found that HIV positive individuals "often become fearful that the news of their diagnosis will reach relatives in their home country, bringing dishonor upon the family. It therefore becomes natural for individuals diagnosed with HIV/AIDS to keep their diagnoses private, thereby unwittingly pushing the epidemic underground"(p. 63). The psychological stress of migration and the impact on Caribbean families has also been an area of interest for a number of migration scholars (Sher and Vilens, 2010; Matthews, 1994). However, more research on the mental health needs of immigrants considering the impact of the world economic crisis on families in general would shed some light on adjustment issues and coping.

Considering the New Transnational Generation

It has been variously documented that females usually predominate in the Caribbean migration process, often leaving their children behind with childcare and protection provided within a transnational context (Ho, 1999; Best-Cummings, 2004). Discrete social arrangements dictate that the immigrant parent(s) provide financial and other forms of support to the caregiver and others in the family and community, while the caregiver reciprocates by building a network of caring and trust to guide the child's development.

The expectation of many of the children left behind, although usually temporary pending Visa arrangements, can have a negative effect on their commitment to social and educational progress after the parent's(s) departure. Bacon (2008) sees the young as having the tendency to view migration as a more attractive alternative to education. He notes further that the consequences of the migration process exacerbate "social and economic divisions, as some families have access to remittances and others don't. But it has also become an economic necessity and the families of those who take the road north often do benefit, although they risk danger and debt to receive its rewards" (p. 252).

The time between the migration of the adults and reunification with the children can be many years. Although lengthy separation from parents can result in parent/child adjustment problems, negatively impacting children's emotional well-being, children are likely to derive considerable social capital from participation in transatlantic family/kinship relationships and rituals. Addressing this issue, Gardner and Ralph (2002) argue that transnational rituals (based on ingrained cultural practices) make statements about membership, or at least ongoing claims to membership in the community of origin, and as such these statements have both symbolic and practical significance. According to Reynolds (2004), family rituals and celebrations provide a key opportunity for transnational links to develop between family members residing in various parts of the world. Indeed, when the child arrives in North America and is faced with challenges of ethnic identity, her/his participation in family rituals and cultural community celebrations enables her/him to consolidate such an identity.

CONCLUSION

This chapter has outlined critical issues regarding the structure and function of the Caribbean immigrant family and its role in identity formation within a transnational context. The paradox of the transnational lifestyle that has emerged is that it liberates as well as constrains immigrants in their efforts to keep the fibers of this changing social institution intact. Yet, situated at the crucible of a cross-continental relationship, these immigrants depend on the family and kinship network to cope with the vicissitudes of their transnational experience.

Drawing from research findings and observations by scholars, the chapter brings important concerns to the forefront of the discussion on the topic. As such, it offers a perspective on exploring key dimensions of the way in which the life space of English Caribbean immigrant families is shaped by both traditions of the home country and culture of their adopted home, sustaining a transnational lifestyle. For most of these immigrants, having left their places of origin in search of a 'better life', one of the principal objectives is to enhance the economic and educational opportunities for themselves and family members, invariably against multiple structural odds.

The issues presented in this chapter are critical to understanding the experiences of English Caribbean immigrants of African descent, although they only scratch the surface of the subject matter, focusing on one of the predominant ethnic groups in the region. More research on the experiences of other Ethnic-Caribbean immigrant groups in the region (e.g. Indo-Caribbeans) would be useful for comparative purposes. Hopefully, the issues examined and conclusions drawn in this chapter will contribute to the on-going discussion about this important dimension of the immigrant experience in the 21st century.

NOTES

1. In recent years, Child Care and Protective Agencies throughout the English-Speaking Caribbean have been more responsive to reports of child abuse and neglect, buttressed by an ongoing debate about the harmful effects of some traditional customs, thus seriously addressing a perennial domestic problem.

CHAPTER SIX
Bibliography

Acosta, Y.D. and G.P. de la Cruz (2011). "The Foreign Born from Latin America and the Caribbean: 2010 American Survey Briefs": *U.S. Census Bureau.*

Bacon, D. (2008). *Illegal People: How Globalization Creates Migration and Criminalizes Immigrants.* Boston: Beacon Press. P. 252.

Basch, L.G. (2012). "The Politics of Caribbeanization: Vincentians and Grenadians in New York". *Center for Migration Studies Special Issues.* Volume 7, Issue 1, p. 147-166. Retrieved 10/16/12.

———, (2001). "Transnational Social Relations and Politics of National Identity: An Eastern Caribbean Case Study". In N. Foner (Ed.) *Island in the City: West Indian Immigration to New York.* CA: University of California Press. P. 117-141.

———, N.G. Schiller and V. Blanc-Szanton (1994). *Nations Unbound: Transnational Projects, Post Colonial Predicaments and De-Territorialized Nation States.* Longhorn, PA: Gordon & Breach.

Baptiste, et al. (1994) "Clinical Practice with Caribbean Immigrant Families in the United States: The Intersection of Emigration, Immigration, Culture and Race". In L.L. Roopnaraine and J. Brown (Eds.), *Caribbean Families: Diversity among Ethnic Groups* (pp. 275-303). Norwood, New Jersey: Abex.

Bayne-Smith, M., Y. Graham, M. Mason, and M. Drossman (2004). "Disparities in Infant Mortality Rates Among Immigrant Caribbean Groups in New York City". In A. Mahoney (Ed.) *The Health and Well-Being of Caribbean Immigrants in the United States.* New York: Haworth Social Work Practice Press.

Best-Cummings, C. (2004). "Caribbean Women's Migratory Journey: An Exploration of Their Decision-Making Process". In A. Mahoney (Ed.) *The Health and Well-Being of Caribbean Immigrants in the United States.* New York: Haworth Social Work Practice Press.

Bonnett, A.W. (2009). The West Indian Diaspora in the USA: Remittances and Development of the Homeland. In *Wadabagel: Journal of the Caribbean and its Diaspora.* 12.001, 6-32.

Carten, A., P. Crawford-Brown and A. Goodman (2005). "An Educational Model for Child Welfare Practice with English-Speaking Caribbean Families". *Child Welfare.* Sept-Oct, 84(5): 77-89.

Carten, A., L. Rock and C. Best-Cummings (2003). "Dimensions of Child Abuse and Neglect Among Native and Immigrant Caribbean Families." In *Journal of Immigrant and Refugee Services.* Volume 1, Issue 2, pp. 41-57.

Edwin, J. (2011). "The Grenada Diaspora Organization. Diaspora Matters". http://diasporamatters.com/the-grenada-diaspora-organization/2011. Retrieved 8/21/11.

Fletcher, B. (2010). "Race, Racism, Xenophobia and Migration. Speech to World Social Forum on Migration". *The Black Commentator.* www.BlackCommentator.com.

Foley, Elise (2012). "Immigration Enforcement Separated Thousands of U.S.-Born Children from Parents". *Caribbean Daylight.* Friday, April 6th. P 2.

Foner, N. (2001). "Introduction: West Indian Migration in New York". In, *Islands in the City: West Indian Migration in New York.* University of

California Press. P. 1-21.
———, (2001). "Transnationalism Then and Now: New York Immigrants Today and at the Turn of the Twenty-First Century". In Cordero-Guzman, Smith and Grosfoguel (eds) *Transnationalization and Race in a Changing New York:* Philadelphia: Temple University Press.
Gardner, K. and R. Grillo (2002). "Transnational Households and Ritual: An Overview". *Global Networks.* Volume 2, Issue 3. P. 179-190.
Goulbourne, H. (2002). *Caribbean Transnational Experience.* London: Pluto Press. Pp 3, 164, 169.
GUYD Project (2012). "Guyana Diaspora Project: Let's Build Guyana Together". *IOM Development Fund:* Developing Capacities in Migration Management.
Hamilton, J. (1997). "Race, Ethnicity, and Identity: West Indian Immigrants in the United States". Third Triennial Conference of Caribbean and International Social Work Educators. Trinidad and Tobago. July 6-10.
Hardbeatnews, "Deportees to Caribbean Close to 6,000", *USICE.* www.HardbeatNews.net, Retrieved 10/29/05.
Ho, C. (1999). "Caribbean Transnationalism as a Gendered Process". *Latin American Perspectives* 26, no. 5: Pp 1, 34-54.
Hondagneu-Sotelo, P. (2012). "Transnational Motherhood". *NNIRR's Network News.* Retrieved 10/30/12.
Karran, B. (2012). "The Guyanese Diaspora in the United States as a Factor in National Development". . Retrieved 1/26/12.
Kasinitz, P. (1993). *Caribbean New York: Black Immigrants and the Politics of Race. New York:* Cornell University Press.
Kasinitz, P., M.C. Waters, J.H. Mollenkopf and M. Anil (2002). "Transnationalism and the Children in Contemporary New York". In *The Changing Face of Home: Transnational Lives of the Second Generation.* (Ed.) P. Levitt and M. Waters. New York: Russell Sage Foundation. Pp. 96-122.
Leland, J. (2012). "Divided By Immigration Policy". *The New York Times.* September 8th.
Massey, D. and N. Denton, (2006). *American Apartheid: Segregation and the Making of the Underclass. In Waters, M. Black Identities: West Indian Immigrants and American Realities.* Massachusetts: Harvard University Press.
Matthews, L. (1994). "Social Workers' Knowledge of Client Culture and Its Use in Mental Healthcare of English-Speaking Caribbean Immigrants". *Doctoral Dissertation,* UMI.
Matthews, L. and A. Mahoney (2005). "Facilitating a Smooth Transitional Process for Immigrant Caribbean Children: The Role of Teachers, Social Workers and Related Professional Staff". *Journal of Ethnic and Cultural Diversity in Social Work.* Vol. 14, Nos. 2/3.
Mahoney, A. (2004). "Introduction". *The Health and Well-Being of Caribbean Immigrants in the United States.* New York: The Haworth Social Work Practice Press.
Morgenthau, R. (2012). "Deportations: Still a Nightmare". *New York Daily News.* Sunday June 17.
Nelson, Havelock (2012). "Film Maker Mason Richards Brings Guyana's Stories to Global Audience." *Of Note Magazine.* Retrieved 9/20/12.
NILP (2013) "Fixing the Immigration System for America's 21st Century Economy." www.latinopolicy.org.Retrieved 2/13/13
Portes, A., Haller, W., and Guarnizo (2001). *Transnational Entrepreneurs:*

The Emergence and Determinants of an Alternative Form of Immigrant Economic Adaptation. Los Angeles: University of California Press.

Reynolds, Tracey (2005). *Caribbean Mothers: Identity and experience in the UK*, United Kingdom, The Tufnell Press. P 10.

———, (2004). *Caribbean Families, Social Capital and Young People's Diasporic Identities*. London: Families and Social Capital. ESRC Research Group.

Schiller, N.G., Basch, L.G., and Blanc-Szanton (1994). "From Immigrant to Transmigrant: Theorizing Transnational Migration". *Anthropological Quarterly*, Volume 68, Number 1 pp 48-63.

Sewpaul, V. (2008) "Social Work Education in the Era of Globalization". *Caribbean Journal of Social Work*, Col. 6 & 7, December, pp. 16-35.

Shedlin, G. et al. (2006). "Migration and HIV/AIDS in the New York Metropolitan Area". *Journal of Urban Health*: January: 83(1) 43-58.

Sher, L. and A. Vilens (2010). "Immigration and Mental Health: Stress, Psychiatric Disorders and Suicidal Behavior among Immigrants and Refugees. New York": *Nova Science Publishers*.

Thomas-Hope, E. (2002). *Caribbean Migration. Barbados*: University of the West Indies Press

———, (1992). *Explanation in Caribbean Migration*, London: Macmillan.

Turner, J. (1991). "Immigrants and their Therapists: A Trans-context Approach". *Family Process*, 30(4) 407-419.

US Census Bureau (2009). Selected Socioeconomic Characteristics of New York City's Top 10 Foreign-born Groups. American Community Survey-Public Use Microdata Sample. Population Division-New York City Department of City Planning.

Waters. M. (1999). *Black Identities: West Indian Immigrant Dreams and American Realities*. New York and Cambridge, MA: Russell Sage Foundation.

Chapter Seven

Hometown Associations: Needs and Challenges

Lear Matthews

INTRODUCTION

Diaspora connections among English speaking Caribbean immigrants, involving Hometown Associations (HTAs) and their contribution to development, is a growing phenomenon that has not been given much attention. In this chapter, the author examines the activities of HTAs among this population and argues for a prominent role of the 'helping professions' to enhance transnational practices. An HTA is an organization formed by immigrants from the same village, town, region or shared institution seeking to support their place of origin, maintain connections, through cash or in kind, while retaining "a sense of community as they adjust to life in their new home countries" (Orozco and Garcia-Zanello, 2009, p. 1). Specifically, the goals of this chapter are to explore the needs and challenges of HTAs among English-speaking Caribbean immigrants in the U.S., examine the role of social work in facilitating Diaspora development activity, and, drawing from a transnational model of practice, suggest a framework for intervention.

Informal transnational ties have been maintained by relatives and friends through the continuous flow of remittances such as cash or material goods sent from overseas. In addition, immigrant groups, some amorphous in nature, religious and savings institutions, including Rotating Credit Associations and Trust Networks, have flourished among Caribbean immigrants (Tilley, 2007; Bonnett, 1981; Hevener, 2006). However, global economic changes have caused fluctuations in migration patterns from the region, partially accounting for the robust growth of HTAs. Significantly, the World Bank reported that $338 billion was sent by immigrants to their homeland in 2008 (Levitt, 2010).

Remittances to the Caribbean account for the transfer of billions of dollars (U.S) in cash, material and non-material resources annually

(Newland, 2010). Levitt and Glick Schiller (2004) bring to our attention studies that examine "the relationship between immigration and development, categorizing transnational migration as a product of late capitalism which renders small, non-industrialized countries incapable of economic autonomy and makes them dependent on migrant generated remittances" (p. 4)

Against this backdrop, the author explores the attributes and challenges of these emerging immigrant associations and explores the ways in which the helping professions, particularly social work, can effectuate the changes and development they pursue in a transformative practice environment.

The Anglophone Caribbean Experience: HTAs and the Role of Social Work

Global challenges have caused the profession of social work to expand its focus on cross-cultural issues. Specifically, Negi and Furman (2010) argue that in recent years, there is an increase in interest "about how the interconnectedness of global institutions (transnationalism) and movement of people, resources, and ideas back and forth across nation-state boundaries (transmigration) have influenced the profession of social work" (p.4). In light of this development, transnational social work is at a vantage point to facilitate the activities and effectiveness of HTAs. Activities include Volunteerism and Diaspora philanthropy such as healthcare missions and disaster aid, educational services, community development projects, and workshops for immigrants to mutually support, intermingle and converse about life experiences in the host society and home communities.

HTAs vary in structure, organization and size and for decades there has been a disproportionate number of them in North America among Latin American and African migrants compared to those from other regions. Not unlike other migrant associations, HTAs among English speaking Caribbean immigrants "have gained potential as development players, given the link between philanthropic activities and the economic development of migrants' homelands" (Orozco and Garcia-Zanello, 2009, p. 3).

With increasing globalization, the social work practice landscape is changing. The life space of service recipients is shaped, directly or indirectly, by their social, economic, political and personal experiences in both place of origin and place of settlement. This paradigm shift, which sets new parameters for assessment and intervention, must be recognized. As Mills (2005) observes, "Community social organizations abroad and access to the internet as an organizing tool allow transnational connections to flourish and provide much needed aid to the home community. The transnational network fosters an organized and effective way of providing development aid on a larger, community-wide scale" (p.1). Furthermore, studies by Orozco (2008) and Somerville (2007) conclude that (a) these organizations foster integration in the country of destination and (b) belonging to them is an important way of remaining attached to the home country.

In making a convincing case for social work's contribution to enhancing the activities and practices of HTAs, this author reiterates that social workers are agents of social change who empower people and institutions to improve their lives and become self-sufficient, helping to alleviate poverty. These core principles and goals are reflected in what HTAs seek to accomplish and social work can provide the impetus, guidance, skills and basic tools needed. Having similar objectives, these organizations can also benefit from engagement strategies familiar to social work partitioners and necessary for the success of their efforts.

HTAs function within a multiple context, including "providing a sense of community and political influence in the new and home communities, pursuit of small-scale development goals in the home communities and helping new immigrants adapt to their new life, assistance in finding housing, employment, and resources to integrate themselves in the community." (Negi and Furman, 2010; p. 44-45). These operational areas coincide with the objectives of social work, intended to meet the needs of a range of recipients.

There has been an unprecedented proliferation and visibility of these organizations among English speaking Caribbean immigrants over the past ten years but no serious attempt has been made to examine this phenomenon. Their activities have resulted in the solidifying of systematic relationships among immigrants and between the recipient and sending society. In her discussion of transnational migration, Levitt (2001) notes that "in many cases, the magnitude, duration, and impact of migration is so strong that migrant social networks mature ... spanning the sending and receiving country" (p. 197). The increase in the number of HTAs appear to reflect the changes in the number and diversity of migrants from the region, stricter immigration laws, economic hardship, and a desire to strengthen relationships with the home country (Negi and Furman, 2010).

HTAs tend to attract a broad network of expatriates, regardless of occupation or ethnicity, who are eager to support hometown causes, by participating directly or supporting social and cultural events. They engage in fundraising activities, generating resources to provide material and non-material support for selected communities or institutions in the home country.

The English-speaking Caribbean immigrant community is replete with models of such practices. For example, Guyanese, Jamaican and Grenadian HTAs across the United States account for the largest number of remittance senders to the Caribbean region. More than 200 Guyanese HTAs were identified in the U.S. Karran (2012) notes that overseas Guyanese are "increasingly being viewed as a significant element within the country's national development thrust" (p. 1). There are over 40 Grenadian HTAs in New York City alone; and a massive increase in the mailing lists of Jamaican HTAs (Orozco, 2009; Edwin, 2011; Murphy, 2006). Table 7.1 shows that 29% of Guyanese immigrants sending remittances belong to HTA's and 16% of Jamaicans are either HTA members or supporters.

This would indicate that large numbers of immigrants contribute either monetarily or in kind to HTA's of their choice. Orozco (2006) notes that membership "may reflect specific patterns associated with political culture, family links, material circumstances, cultural identity, and integration which differentiate them from those who do not form part of these associations" (p. 7). In assessing the significance of HTA's to Caribbean nation-building, expatriate St. Lucian entrepreneur, Eroline Lamontagne asserted, "Diasporic relations must be central to our development strategy . . . remittances, travel, investment and philanthropy are four areas in which members of the region's expatriate community contribute the greatest" (2012, p. 2). As these organizations grow in numbers and impact on international development, the need for strategic engagement, program coordination and culturally competent intervention, will increase. Professional social work can respond effectively to such needs.

Table 7.1 Remittance Senders Who Belong to an HTA by Country

Country	%
Guyana	29
Jamaica	16
Ecuador	10
Haiti	10
Honduras	7
Columbia	6
Nicaragua	4
El Salvador	4
Mexico	4
Dominican Republic	3
Guatemala	3

Bolivia	1
Average	9

(Source: Orozco, 2006)

The relationships that follow from this cross-continental linkage tend to forge a pattern of institutionalized transactions among immigrants and between immigrants and non-migrants. Levitt (2001) refers to these as examples of a "transnational social field" in which participants "are exposed to a set of social expectations, cultural values, and patterns of human interaction that are shaped by more than one social, economic, and political system" (p. 197).

Despite the surge in popularity of these associations among English speaking Caribbean immigrants, there has been a dearth of comparable data on the topic. Moreover, social work research on Diaspora philanthropy and related development activities with regards to this population has been virtually nonexistent. Exploring how these organizations sustain development in hometown communities is essential to understanding transnational experiences in the 21st century. There appears to be more than an ephemeral interface between HTAs and the home country. How entrenched they are in the fabric of transnational connections, the impact on sustaining communities and institutions, and how social work can best contribute to these processes, are central to this study.

In his study of HTAs among Mexican immigrants, Orozco (2006) found that membership is voluntary, with the principal officers drawn from the more established, settled, legal immigrants. With such attributes, Ellerman (2003) notes their willingness "to interact with government officials, sources of funding and other similar groups. Owing to members legal status, professional grounding their incomes tend to be higher. Leaders of formal HTAs have usually lived longer in the United States than other members have, their standard of living is relatively higher, and they are likely among the most successful of the members" (p. 44-45). This appears to make them more confident in their ability to organize and commit to organizational goals. The intent is to form associations that would harness resources to help develop their home community and retain cultural traditions in their adopted home.

Psychologically, the desire to 'give back' is described in Erik Erikson's seventh stage of human development, generatively versus stagnation. According to this view, mature, middle-age adults tend to develop a wish to establish a foundation for the next generation. "People who do not find an outlet for generativity become self-absorbed, self-indulgent, or stagnant . . . volunteering for community service or a political cause is an expression of generativity" (Papalia, et al. 2009, p. 519). Understanding the social and individual experiences, purpose and motivation for participation in HTA activities are instrumental for effective intervention in this transnational process.

HTA Activities: Emerging Issues and Unintended Consequences

Somerville (2008) posits that HTAs have an integrating function in the host society, forging cultural cohesion and solidarity and providing needed social services to newly arrived immigrants. However, as the number of these organizations increase, it is important to assess the extent to which they serve as integrative entities or risk competition among immigrants, help institutions in the home countries or cause divisions among communities therein due to uneven resource distribution.

One of the inadvertent outcomes of the unilateral flow of remittances from HTAs is the potential dependency this could create. Although on a smaller scale, dependency theory in which underdevelopment in the region is viewed as stemming from the dependent incorporation of developing nations into the world's capitalist system is applicable here.

In their discussion of the collateral impact of family remittances, Negi and Furman (2010) observe that some community members "do not seek work or engage in productive activity, creating dependence on the periodic supply of money from abroad" (p.40). This could negatively affect interpersonal and social relationships. Similarly, as hometown infrastructural development from HTA resources and activities occur, there is likely to be unequal growth between communities that are assisted and those communities that are not assisted because the latter are not connected to an HTA.

With the abundance of remittances from hometown associations, as Roberts (2011) notes, they serve to ameliorate personal and institutional economic hardship in the Caribbean. Nevertheless, other unintended consequences must be noted. Efforts to achieve institutional self-sufficiency in the home country may be compromised by the provision of the virtually unrestricted resources from overseas. Furthermore, where local governments encourage support from HTAs, the intent may not only be to complement social development, but could absolve them from full responsibility of providing critical aid for their constituents.

Indeed, the sending of resources sustains communities and helps people cope, but it can also raise expectations to unachievable levels. Furthermore, this transnational phenomenon shapes opinions locally and abroad about the role of Diaspora contributors. Should they be a voting constituency? To what extent should they have a voice in institutional and nation-building? These questions and issues are critical to policy makers and development foot soldiers of change and development. A leading Caribbean government official espoused the importance of "tapping into the Diaspora", including skills and best practices acquired from abroad as a resource for nation-building (Ramotar, 2012).

HTAs Sustaining Identity, Social and Personal Attributes

Transnational ties through organizational networks also sustain a hometown identity, facilitated by exchange of an array of material and non-material cultural forms. The transnational community field spanning the United States and the Caribbean region has enveloped what Mills (2005) describes as the emergence of "a vibrant network that fosters development aid, providing critical support for the home community" (p. 174). HTAs serve as an extended safety net for the welfare of hometown communities.

HTAs, described as the "pioneers of collective remittances" Negi and Furman (2010, p. 49) have also formalized networking among immigrants. Members often view what they do not merely as charity or benevolently reaching across nation states, but as seeking to stimulate institutional and personal change of recipients, while transforming their own lives. The networking fabric formed by the activities of these organizations presents opportunities for significant individual and social change (Orozco, 2003). For some, executive membership may have a deeper socio-cultural meaning. Notably, Misir (1997) concludes that the decision to affiliate with these organizations appear to be typically associated with an attempt to cope with alienation, reduce stress, improve self-image or regain social status—albeit a nostalgic recreation of the past. At the same time, poor management, lack of transparency and accountability has caused intra-organizational tensions and mistrust by supporters.

The continuous connection to HTAs imbues a sense of identification with the home country, and perpetuates the culture while simultaneously helping with adjustment to the host country. It also presents an opportunity to give back through altruistic endeavors, and perhaps as an investment for returning 'home'. Orozco (2006; 2003) found that altruism is a principal motivation for remitting, and further notes, "Members mix their commitments to both homes, signifying a transnational membership. This pattern of belonging as an affirmation of a transnational identity is relatively important"(p.8). Such transformational, feet-in-both-worlds, life-changing experiences can create opportunities and risks. Bonnett (2010) argues that Diaspora nationals "use the instrument of their remittances to spur development in the Hometown Associations, and utilize dual citizenship status arrangements to ensure that their advice is taken seriously" (p. 600).

Many of these organizations offer community assistance such as language classes, employment counseling, housing and entrepreneurial advice and other adjustment services to new immigrants in the country of destination (Somerville, et. al., 2008). At the risk of politicizing their activities, some HTAs have sponsored fundraisers for hometown political candidates who increasingly value immigrants as an important constituent. Recognizing the significant contribution of expatriates, a leading candidate for one Caribbean country's general elections pledged to establish a Department of Diaspora (D. Granger, Personal Communication, 2011). In this regard, Turner (1991, p. 409), found that participating migrants often "developed networks that support the trans-context lifestyle both politically and socially", a process imbedded in HTA functions.

Conceptual Framework

The impetus for interposing social work as a key player in this process is drawn from a transnational social work perspective espoused by Negi and Furman (2010), who posit that social workers need to restructure their thinking to accommodate an expanded, transformative, cross-cultural practice environment. They affirm that "more and more people are living transnational lives providing us with the ethical and moral imperative to develop models and methods to respond to their needs" (p.4). This view is supported by Claiborne (2004) and Drachman (2004) who urge increased participation of human service professionals in international service-based and leadership positions, and ways in which they can intensify their involvement in organizations such as HTAs which "are pursuing progressive transnational connections" (Drachman, 2004, p 177).

Somerville (2008) and Orozco (2009) help us to understand the contributions of HTAs in capacity building, where critical needs such as training of HTA members in areas of accessing services, relying on the work of volunteers with minimum community organizing skills, the professionalizing of service delivery, perfecting decision making skills, and increasing community participation, are identified. These perspectives provide the lens for examining the role of social work in comprehending the dynamics, functions and efficacy of HTAs as a vital source of transnational development and in facilitating intervention tasks. One essential way for these organizations to sustain their effectiveness in economic and psychosocial development is to solicit the unique knowledge and skills of social workers.

Methodology and Sample

To achieve the goals of this research, an exploratory, qualitative study using a snowball approach in which HTA members were asked to identify similar organizations, was adopted. Goulbourne (2002) insists that these aspects of the modern world must be empirically validated in order to verify important dimensions of the transnational experience. Leaders from HTAs in New York, New Jersey and Florida, states with a high concentration of Caribbean immigrants, were asked to complete a survey. Information regarding the characteristics, needs and challenges of their respective organizations was solicited. Selection of countries-of-origin, Jamaica, Guyana, Grenada, St. Lucia and St. Vincent was based on their high usage of HTAs. A 10- item self-administered questionnaire was e-mailed to the participants, who were instructed to complete it to the best of their ability and return it to the researcher.

Follow-up telephone interviews were conducted by two trained associates familiar with English speaking Caribbean culture, to obtain additional information and/or clarify stated responses. Fifty (50) questionnaires were sent out and 39 were returned completed, reflecting a 78% response rate. Questions were asked about organizational goals, primary activities, collaboration with other organizations, and challenges encountered in the host and home countries. Space was provided for respondents to express personal comments and observations about their experience as HTA members.

An 8-item questionnaire also was sent electronically to one recipient organization in each of the five selected countries. Questions included their experience in working with HTAs, benefits of support received, and views about the role of social work in accomplishing goals. The questionnaire and interview data were reviewed and grouped into categories and themes. Comparisons, trends and frequency distributions were used to analyze the data.

Findings and Analysis: Characteristics of English Speaking Caribbean HTAs

The HTAs in this study represent a range of immigrant organizations. Some key patterns conform to the findings of Somerville (2008) and Karran (2012) in related research, i.e. their formation is on the basis of shared interests and experience, professional or ethnic affiliation from the same hometown. Most have a stable structure, with an active executive body and standing committees of about eight members. Donations are collected from various social and cultural events. A counterpart group is expected to identify needed projects and coordinate disbursement of remittances in the home community. Examples of the stated goals are:

To promote and preserve the economic, cultural and social health of West Indians and West Indians in North America. We target the youth in particular, in the US and at home to encourage good citizenship.

To support Caribbean nationals and to give financial, medical and educational assistance to the homeland.

To enhance the cultural and educational development of Caribbean-Americans as responsible and productive residents of the United States and maintain the mutual interests of members of the association.

To promote, through medical, humanitarian and social programs, the welfare of fellow Caribbean people, especially those who are needy.

A relatively small number (7.7%) is focused on fundraising for hometown political candidates. Bonnett (2010) notes that with dual citizenship status, Caribbean immigrants may cast their votes in the home country and insist that "the home governments establish cabinet level agencies to deal reciprocally with their concerns" (p. 600). One executive of a Guyanese HTA reported that the objective was,

To create awareness of the nationals' (hometown political party) status and work in North America. To garner support for the party in New York and to facilitate participation of our nationals in the affairs of political development at home.

Implicit in these goals is support for the hometown and organizing of immigrant communities. In this regard, Orozco (2009) found that apart from projects in the Caribbean, these organizations promote social, cultural and political awareness and identity in the U.S. Not only do hometown political parties support Diaspora groups, but as Karran (2012) observes, "....in addition to providing funding for political campaigns and carrying out political activities abroad, these organizations make material contributions to their constituencies . . . " (p. 4).

This bi-national commitment, truly transnational in nature, buttresses their effectiveness as they seek approval and sanction from both sending and host societies. Somerville (2008) suggests that policy makers should view the roles of domestic immigrant integration and transnational development "as complementary and concentrate on enhancing associations' capacity to deliver for communities at home and abroad" (p. 1).

"JAMPACT", a Jamaican immigrant group states its goal in this way:

Our common bond is the belief that an informed and active overseas community can contribute significantly to the improvement of so-

cial and economic conditions at home.

Despite having similar objectives, collaboration among these HTAs appears to be in its embryonic stage. Negi and Furman (2010) argue that a consortium among organizations would increase the impact in political and economic spheres in the country of origin and host society. Otherwise, a non-cooperative approach may lead to competition for recognition and resources. Although fundraising events are supported primarily by persons from the same hometown, some organizations provide aid to other communities, but less than 6% have served communities in countries other than their own.

While a minority of respondents acknowledged the role of the helping professions, social workers served either in an advisory capacity or as visiting team members in only three HTAs. The goals of one of these include:

Serving and empowering those in need through educational workshops, technical assistance, individual and group counseling, provision of food, clothing and other supplies. Target population includes individuals, groups and communities: e.g. women, children and families are our primary focus.

Another whose team visits annually, stated the objective as, *The provision of medical supplies, assessment, treatment and other healthcare services to various communities in the Caribbean.*

This coincides with the findings of Orozco and Welle (2005) who conclude that these organizations seek to promote social change and intervention that benefit vulnerable populations and communities, certainly areas to which social work is amenable.

Table 7.2 shows the frequency distribution of HTAs and the primary transnational connections vis-à-vis material or other assistance. Of the 39 organizations studied, 16 identified as educational, 7 as community development organizations, 6 as medical missions, 3 as political groups and 3 as cultural organizations. In addition to their manifest and on-going infrastructure developmental mission, some responded specifically to disaster mitigation in the region, while others reported engagement in multiple activities.

For example, the majority of the High School Alumni Associations provided educational resources, in addition to disaster aid, while financial assistance and community medical services were offered by other organizations. Many (46.2%) supported educational institutions, including providing scholarships. Comparatively, Orozco (2006) found that a significant number of HTAs in the Caribbean "invest resources in education or relief assistance for natural disasters" (p. 5). Primary support activities include financial assistance (23%); healthcare (15.4); special community projects (10.3%); and counseling services (5.1%).

Collectively, the organizations have been in existence for an average of eight (8) years. However, there was minimum reporting of consulting with, or intervention of helping professionals in HTA activities, although trained social workers are among supporters.

Table 7.2 HTA Characteristic & Primary Support

Type of HTA	No. of HTAs	%
Educational	16	41.0
Cultural	3	7.7
Political	3	7.7
Medical Mission	6	15.4
Community Development	7	17.9
Other (Not Specified)	4	10.3
Total	**39**	**100**

Primary Support	No. of HTAs	%
Educational Aid (including Scholarships)	18	46.2
Financial Assistance	9	23.1
Healthcare	6	15.4
Special Community Project	4	10.3
Counseling Services	2	5.0
Total	**39**	**100**

As indicated in table 7.3, the majority (25 or 64%) of HTAs in this study have been in existence for more than ten years. Financial membership varied from 50 to 100 individuals with a significantly larger number of non-member supporters. Of the target countries studied, the longest established HTAs were among Jamaicans and Guyanese (more than 10 years). Although the large representation of immigrants from these nations may account for this trend, other causal factors are beyond the scope of this study.

Table 7.3 Demographics of HTAs

Time in Existence	No.	%	Approx. Financial Membership
More than 10 years	25	64.1	50
5 to 9 years	8	20.5	100
Less than 5 years	6	15.4	50

Needs and Challenges

Transnational activities are driven by complex individual and social dynamics. An overwhelming majority of respondents expressed the desire to 'give back' to their hometown by supporting infrastructural development of local institutions such as a former high school, community center or health facility. While some executives express concern about the lack of resources and lack of motivation of some recipients, a number of supporters worry about the appropriate use and accountability of funds. Nevertheless, most HTAs were found to be certified by the respective states of operation (e.g 501c3, in New York) and maintain management transparency through websites and General Membership reports.

According to Orozco (2003), decisions about structure and activities, HTAs "depend on factors like availability of resources, relationship with their hometown, and preferences of members" (p.4). However, the quality of relationship between HTAs and the home country government is central to their success. Tensions between them appear to emanate from two sources. While some contributors question the motives of the organizations' principal officers, others blame a lack of confidence in the home country government. One HTA leader recalled a supporter's passionate lament,

There is suspicion of 'hidden motives' among foreign leaders and inconsistencies with some stakeholders. The level of commitment is questionable.

An executive, who described the mission as educational and cultural, sees the main challenges as the inability to obtain sustainable funding and indifference of nationals to participate in educational and political events. Another stated that some people who attend fundraisers express a lack of confidence in the Government's capacity to coordinate and distribute sent items affectively,

The government at home will do what they want with what is sent for the school. I support the cause, but that is why I am so skeptical. I do not trust the government. This is an investment in the children and the future of our country.

This is supported by the findings of Karran (2012) asserting that "Diaspora communities generally have a pervasive mistrust of government institutions and are often politically fragmented . . . factors which affect the nature and level of contributions" (p. 9).

Executive respondents reported that they regularly deliberate about project feasibility, relying on their organization's counterparts or government officials in the home country to determine needs. Although some reported successful collaboration with local governments, skepticism was expressed by supporters:

Why should the government decide what to do with the money we send home? I honestly can't say that I trust them. I want the things we send to go toward building the community center.

I do understand the need to make the local authorities aware of what we plan to do, but it should be up to us and the communities we are trying to help, to say what they need and what changes we can help them with. To interface with government is tough.

Such questions are often raised by supporters of organizations, whose targeted recipient institutions are under the direct auspices of the government. These issues also point to concerns regarding the planning and distribution of HTA resources. Ideas about the level and extent of related decision-making are at the core of the relationship between these organizations and the hometown government. The contributions of HTAs may be valued by the local authority, but their influence on decisions relating to development plans remains peripheral. Nevertheless, in an attempt to address this relationship, Lamontagne (2012) urged, "a more deliberate approach . . . formalizes our ties for their impact to be even better felt and their contributions to be better appreciated" (p. 2).

The data also show that those HTAs with dependable, committed liaisons in the home country are successful in fulfilling their mission, while those with unreliable counterpart groups or no such group reported difficulty in realizing goals. As two New York based executives observe,

It is difficult to get dedicated groups or individuals at home to maintain a program to facilitate their receiving our aid and to be accountable once the aid gets there. It is hard to find intermediaries to make contact and execute action with targeted agencies. This has af-

fected our mission.

There is a different work ethic in the Caribbean. They are laid back and not as proficient in getting things done. This is frustrating and delays our program plans. We cannot attract reliable persons to coordinate programs to effectively disseminate information nationwide.

To offset this problem, some members travel to the home country to ensure the intended distribution of donations, realizing that, in light of the highly valued resources channeled through these organizations, accountability to stakeholders is vital. There appears to be some disconnect between HTAs and the government, although one third of the respondents reported that they depend solely on the government to identify community needs.

The organizations do maintain visibility in the host community by advertising openly. More than half of them have strategically sponsored at least one charity project in the community where they are located, not only as a way of 'giving back' to the community of residence, but also to guarantee recognition, legitimacy and corporate sponsorship therein. Among other immigrants, Jamaican and Guyanese HTAs have participated in local and national social causes including "Walk for the Cure" which coincides with Breast Cancer awareness Month (Clarke, 2012).

One of the most consistent findings was the difficulty in recruiting new members. Fifty-five percent (55%) of the organizations reported this problem. As one HTA representative noted:

Many of our supporters attend fundraising activities, but seem unwilling to join the organization, or if they become financial members, fail to keep up with the payment of dues.

Another reported:

Many would attend the events sponsored by our organization, but are not there to vote at the annual general meeting. We try to build a strong membership in order for us to fulfill our goals. Getting members to meetings is hard.

Although not fully borne out in the data, it appears as though leaders are unwilling to be replaced or unaware of strategies to recruit new members. As a result, the principal officers tend to rotate leadership positions, representing only a certain age-group, resulting in the extended tenure of a core body which may restrict innovation and risk 'burn out'. The following comment addresses this issue, but does not provide a solution:

We are trying to get members to understand that this is a voluntary group and nepotism must not be one of the ways to do business. Not changing the old guards is bad for the organization.

One executive suggested that more extensive use of the Internet, including Facebook, may be appealing to potential members.

Concerned about the capability of novice recruits to manage effectively and the ambivalence of relinquishing leadership, one executive worries,

We have to be careful about who we select to continue this association. They may not be as dedicated and committed as we are. It would be a shame if the organization dies after all the hard work we put in over the years. I feel strong about this.

The Role of Social Work

Most respondents (69%) acknowledged the need to improve ways of providing services to recipient communities. Of particular relevance to making the case for trained social workers to expedite transnational activities are the needs expressed by respondents for (1) follow-up services in the home country communities (2) the general lack of problem-solving skills and (3) connecting effectively with locals. To illustrate, the following are observations reported. The first is an HTA executive, a Social Worker who states,

These organizations are labor intensive, members mean well, but lack problem-solving skills and scientific approach to management. Social workers know what best practice is, and can help with organizing and intervention. The evaluative piece and dealing appropriately with interpersonal issues is wanting.

A home country counterpart, focusing on coordinating needs, offers this:

There is a need to guide and encourage communities' involvement in sustainable development activities, such as capacity building and organizational strengthening to develop the capacity to better manage its affairs. Social workers would then 'step back' and allow the community or local organization to conduct its own affairs. Social Workers would oversee implementation and play a consultative role.

Such attributes are supported in Orozco's (2009) delineation of criteria for evaluating HTAs' developmental potential. He suggests that community members should participate in decision making, project implementation and must have control after completion. To be successful, projects should also meet basic needs that are prioritized and implemented in coordination with other institutions. Social Workers' community organizing skills are essential for the realization of these potentials.

One HTA member, a Social Worker and part of a humanitarian team stated,

It is not easy to connect to locals. They are sometimes unprepared and inefficient. There is very little or no follow-up services when we

leave and limited resources to provide support. Often we can only engage in crisis intervention. No local facilities to make referrals. There is a dire need for Counselors and Social Workers.

Another respondent emphasized the need for clinical social work skills, particularly in medical missions and working with disaster survivors. She puts it this way:

After we leave the island, many clients do not return for treatment, including renewal of prescriptions because of a lack of trained personnel and medical facilities in the areas we serve. Our experience in working with survivors of natural disasters is similar. We need social workers and psychologists.

A poignant demonstration of such a need is seen in the following comment:

It is a case that people refuse to travel to the medical facilities either because they feel the distance is too great or they do not receive the kind of attention they need or simply because they feel uncomfortable outside their district. The result is that medical missions attract large crowds.

Based in these findings, the case for social work as a major "development player" in both humanitarian needs and infrastructural development can be made from a number of fronts. Specifically, respondents identified organizational problems in the areas of group and community organizing, and program evaluation, which social work can address. Karran (2012) argues that although HTAs have been generally viewed as charitable organizations with a structure and well-intended goals, they lack the organizational and intervention skills of social work that would enhance "the formulation and execution of projects" (p. 3). Furthermore, there were three (3) promising indicators regarding the potential role of social work: (1) one of the few HTAs with youthful participants, has collaborated with the Ministry of Human Services to enhance the effectiveness of various programs (2) two retired Social Workers were part of an HTA treatment team and (3) one medical mission official sought to recruit social workers for his group. He stated: "I have been desperately looking for social workers to join our team".

The need for counseling, service coordination and follow-up services, particularly in response to medical and humanitarian missions, was emphasized by almost half (16) of the respondents (See table 7.4). This confirms that input from both clinical/mental health and concrete service areas is recognized as important. It must be noted, however, that mental health intervention is to be undertaken with caution and awareness regarding desired outcomes[1].

Table 7.4 HTA Needs/Challenges
(Areas for Social Work Intervention)

Needs & Challenges	No.
Recruitment of New Members	15
Follow up Services	8
Lack of resources	5
Counseling Skills (Humanitarian)	4
Service Coordination	4
Working with Hometown Govt.	3

One finding related to the work HTA members do on location is noted with keen interest. Mandatory government registration of visiting Diaspora caregivers, including social workers, nurses, and medical doctors, has been instituted in Jamaica and Guyana. The significance of this process is reflected in the need to monitor the work of overseas practitioners, barring which they would intervene only on the merits of membership to an HTA. This practice should be emulated throughout the Caribbean. Establishing local standards ensures quality care and social justice for developing communities, core values of social work. A permanent credentialing system for practicing social workers in the Caribbean is of paramount importance. This can be accomplished by Regional Professional Social Work Associations setting standards for practice, informed by relevant cultural and international principles.

Fostering Development and Integration or Creating Dependency?

Orozco (2005) points to the important policy implications for exploring the relationship between transnationalism and development. Specifically, he noted the role of HTAs in this process, observing that "some of the infrastructural and economic development work performed by these associations provides momentum for development agents to partner in local development" (p. 1). Respondents did not support the notion that HTA philanthropic acts create dependency among communities in the home country, but there was some concern that while many HTA-aided communities flourished, others remain underdeveloped. One of the Alumni Associations rebuilt a huge section of its alma mater, following major damage caused by a fire.

Although an emergency response, neighboring, non-HTA supported schools that were in disrepair for an extended period did not have the same benefit. Similarly, Bacon (2008) argues that this situation "exacerbates social and economic divisions, as some families have access to remittances and others don't" (p. 252).

Nevertheless, in some instances, such disparity has motivated the local government to establish competing structures in communities that are not connected to HTAs. As one executive reported,

The Minister of Education was so impressed, that the government plans to use this (HTA-supported) high school as a model to institute a nationwide computerized system.

Similarly, Orozco (2009) emphasizes the importance of project replicability, which "allows for the establishment of regional strategies focusing on achieving a development goal beyond the effects on a single community" (p. 9). If instituted, this would decrease the potential for developmental dissonance between communities.

The manifest purpose of HTAs is community and institutional development, but a secondary objective is bringing together hometown nationals through a variety of events, including family fun days, awards ceremonies, and seminars. Respondents cherish the opportunity to meet, greet and reminisce with fellow countrymen, as the comments indicate:

I love socializing with my buddies from home, so I attend the parties as often as I can. The nostalgia and emotions I share mean a lot to me. It's like home away from home. I go to these events because I want to help the children at home (in the Caribbean). But being with people I can identify with also is very important to me too. It makes me feel at home.

The integrating effect is further noted:

We are building an organization that reaches across ethnic boundaries, including our Caribbean brothers and sisters to provide our help in the home country and the Diaspora.

It is clear that HTAs serve as a conduit for social networking and cultural identity and in some cases, collaborate in development projects. Mutual support of members and their families is also a valued expectation. Nevertheless, some respondents expressed concern about the fragmented, self-serving approach of HTAs. As one executive stated:

These groups are all for themselves. Although they may be from the same hometown, they seldom work together. There is no identification with the country of birth.

Bridging Diaspora Transnational Activities and Social Work: A Framework for Action

In order for professional social work to be in sync with the realities of a changing global world, it is imperative that practitioners adapt to the challenges of a transnational practice environment. Similar to other fields such as adult education, social work "is uniquely positioned to make an empowering intervention on behalf of the underprivileged, and at the same time, influence macro policy" (Ramadas,1997, p. 36). Other studies have examined the impact of Caribbean transnationalism on social policy, concluding that in analyzing social welfare issues and the development of social policy across nation states, global factors must be seriously considered (Acevedo, 2005; Melendez, 1991).

This study extends the discussion, calling for a re-conceptualization of social work practitioners' approach in response to the rapidly growing conduits of transnational development. This process can be effectively served by transnational social work intervention, which is designed to help transnational populations, operates across nation-state boundaries, and is informed by and addresses complex transnational problems (Negi and Furman, 2010). The practice foundations of social work center around precisely the welfare concerns HTAs attempt to address. These include housing discrepancies, quality education, physical and mental health issues, community development and the problems caused by spiraling emigration rates. Social workers have the skills set to help prioritize the needs of recipient communities and institutions "based on an understanding of the status of health-care delivery, education, public and financial infrastructure and other related activities" (Orozco, 2005; p. 5). While HTAs in this study symbolize a bridge between Pan Caribbean communities, social work is equipped to address the socio-cultural challenges that emerge from the crossings. The bridge metaphor emphasizes the role of a Diaspora community and how social work practice and research can engage structural and human interactional forces that strengthen transnational activities.

Nurse (2004) argues that diasporization is not likely to modify the "fundamental structure of peripheral economies" (p124). However, Diaspora development activities are a significant indicator of economic, political and cultural links between sending and receiving countries. Representing a major arm of contemporary transnational linkage, HTAs bridge an unprecedented development gap in the Caribbean region. Within this context, social work skills are essential to the emergence of a cadre of development actors, whose bases of operations are these organizations. Their work provides an arena for demonstrating what Healy and Link (2012) describe as "competence as a helping profession, embracing a more global agenda and role". Social workers have the potential to galvanize the unique strengths of these groups, not only in the area of psychosocial needs, but in shaping public policy in both donor and developing country. By helping participants understand the dynamics of Diaspora philanthropy, they can make informed decisions regarding their on-going transnational efforts.

Owing to the international scope of contemporary social problems, cultural competence and professional identity in the Caribbean must be realigned. This realignment is poised to occur within a framework that is conducive to best practices in a transnational context. Based on the findings, four steps are recommended to affirm social work's role in building essential delivery and engagement skills to promote development: (1) Assess the capacity of HTAs relative to the needs and resources of communities or institutions in the home country. This would minimize cross-continental operational discrepancies cited. (2) Identify areas in which social work knowledge, values and skills would be most effective. (3) Develop intervention strategies for executing HTA functions in a culturally competent manner. The findings indicate that there is a need for more consideration of cultural characteristics of recipient communities. This was reflected in the voice of one respondent who stated that "social workers could work with local communities to identify and prioritize needs". (4) Establish evaluation criteria for HTAs, informed by transnational experiences. Social work can also mediate between HTA expectations and government policy to ensure sustainable development. Drawing from the expertise of social workers who are HTA members or supporters would be instrumental in implementing these steps. Levitt (2010) found that such implementation could also be done by partnering with other organizations (immigrant or non-immigrant) to further their specific project goals.

Transnational social work must be included in college curricula. It should also be part of the training agenda of social service agencies, where practitioners are working with a growing number of trasnationals.

CONCLUSION

This study brings into perspective the urgent call for today's social work professionals to respond to issues that enhance the international exchange of resources and ideas (Healy and Link, 2011). Its importance and timeliness is threefold. (1) The Caribbean region is among the largest recipients of remittances, proportionate to the population, (2) systematic transnational activities among English speaking Caribbean immigrants have increased significantly over the past decade and (3) social workers are needed to provide the underpinnings of transnational practice in light of global challenges.

The findings reveal that the activities of Hometown Associations have become an integral part of transnationalism in the Caribbean region. Viewed as institutionalizing the process of collective remittances, these organizations no longer respond only to emergencies or small-scale charity work. They play a crucial role in the development of hometown communities, cross-continental cultural and political connections, and simultaneously fortifying the strands of immigrant networking. The impact of HTAs, though not conclusively measured, have significant implications for social and economic change, often stymied by unanticipated delivery barriers. Consequently, an earnest commitment from social work, with its unique skills set to help sustain development and influence policy, is strongly recommended. Social work can complement the effectiveness of HTAs efforts to improve the welfare of their hometown communities. Karran (2012) argues that a potent mechanism for Diaspora involvement in the development process is to strengthen and consolidate the activities of HTAs. This study lends credence to that recommendation. Working with regional organizations such as CARICOM, NGO's and agencies such as the International Organization for Migration can also enhance the work of HTAs.

This study has limitations. Owing to the relatively small size of the sample, generalizations about immigrant groups across the U.S. and the development impact in other Caribbean nations cannot be made. Nevertheless, the findings set the stage for unraveling the dynamics of an intriguing 21st century phenomenon. The central role of the social work profession in influencing development transformations as nations struggle to cope with the global economic crisis is highlighted. It is hoped that students, practitioners, educators across disciplines, and policy-makers draw from the findings as they conceptualize and implement change. Further research is needed to acquire a more in-depth understanding of the sustainability of HTA-supported development projects, ethnic differences in response to development needs in the Caribbean and the broader impact on modernity and immigrant networking.

NOTES

1. The Inter-Agency Guidelines for Psychological Intervention in Emergencies issued by UNICEF and NGOs caution against extensive use of external mental health counselors in emergency situations, including the risk of causing more harm than good.

Bibliography

Acevedo, G. (2005). "Caribbean Transnationalism and Social Policy Formation". *Caribbean Journal of Social Work.* Volume 4, August.

Bhaba, H.K. (1993). "Cultures In-Between". *Artforum International.* Volume 32, September.

Bonnett, A.W. (2012). "The West Indian Diaspora to the USA: Remittances and Development at Home". . Retrieved 6/6/12.

———, (2011). "Wendell Bell, The Democratic Revolution in the West Indies: Some reflections on the past, present, and future". *Futures.*

———, (1981). *Institutional Adaptation of West Indian Immigrants to America: An Analysis of Rotating Credit Associations.* Washington, D.C.: University Press of America Inc.

Claiborne, N. (2004) "Presence of Social Workers in Non-governmental Organizations". *Social Work,* 49 (2), 207-218.

Clarke, T. (2012). "OSHAG Celebrates 10th Anniversary". *Caribbean Life.* September 28th – October 4th.

Edwin, J. (2011). "The Grenada Diaspora Organization. Diaspora Matters". . Retrieved 9/7/11.

Ellerman, D. (2003). "Policy Research on Migration and Development". Working Paper 3117. Retrieved 8/13/11.

Fletcher, B. (2010). "Race, Racism, Xenophobia and Migration". *The Black Commentator.*

Glick-Schiller, N., L. Basch and C. Blanc-Szanton (eds.)(1992). *Towards a Transnational Perspective on Migration: Race, Class, Ethnicity and Nationalism Reconsidered.* New York: New York Academy of Sciences.

Goulbourne, H. (202) *Caribbean Transnational Experiences.* Kingston, Jamaica: Arawak Publications.

Healy, L. and R. J. Link (2012). *Handbook of International Social Work: Human Rights, Development, and the Global Profession.* New York: Oxford University Press.

Hevener, C. C. (2006). *Alternative Financial Vehicles: Rotating Savings and Credit Associations (ROSCAs).* Philadelphia, Federal Reserve Bank of Philadelphia.

Karran, B. (2012), "The Guyanese Diaspora in the United States as a Factor in National Development". Pp 1-4, 9. Retrieved 7/25/12.

Lamontagne, E. (2012). "Caribbean Call to Build Diaspora Bridge. P. 2. . Retrieved 7/23/12.

Levitt, P. (2010). "It's Not Just About the Economy, Stupid" – Social Remittances Revisited. *Migration Policy Institute.* Migration Information Source. http://www.migrationinformation.org/USfocus/display.cfm?ID=783

———, (2001). "Transnational Migration: Taking Stock and Future Directions". *Global Networks*: July, Volume 1. Issue 3, p 195-216.

Melendez, E. , C. Rodriguez and J. Figueroa (1991). "Hispanics in the Labor Force: An Introduction to Issues and Approaches". In *Hispanics in the Labor Force: Issues and Policies.* Ed. E. Melendez, C. Rodriguez, & J. Figueroa. New York, NY: Plenum Press.

Mills, B.H. (2005). "The Transnational Community as an Agent for Caribbean Development". *Southeastern Geographer.* Vol. 45, Issue 2. P. 174-191. (November)

Misir, P. (1997). "Toward an Understanding of Division in Community

Organization". *Caribbean Journal*, 17.
Murphy, M. (2006). "Trans-national Community of Jamaicans Need Hometown Associations". *Jamaica Primetime*.
Negi, N. J. and R. Furman (2010). *Transnational Social Work Practice*. New York: Columbia University Press.
Newland, K., A. Terrazas, & R. Munster (2010). "Diaspora Philanthropy: Private Giving and Public Policy". Diasporas & Development Policy Projects. *Migration Policy Institute*.
Orozco, M. & E. Garcia-Zanello (2009). "Hometown Associations: Transnationalism, Philanthropy, and Development". *Brown Journal of World Affairs*. Volume XV, Issue II: Spring/Summer, pp. 1,9.
———, (2006). "Diasporas, Philanthropy, and Hometown Associations: The Central American Experience", *Draft*. (March, 22nd).
———, (2005). "Hometown Associations and Development: Ownership, Correspondence Sustainability, and replicability". In (ed.) B.J. Mertz, *New Patterns for Mexico: Observations for Remittance Giving, and Equitable Development* (Cambridge, MA: Harvard University Press).
Orozco, M. (2003). "Remittance Back Home and Supporting the Homeland: The Guyanese Community in the U.S. U.S." *Agency for International Development*, January 15th.
Papalia, D., Olds, S.W. and Feldman, R.D. (2009), 519. *Human Development*, (11th edition), Boston: McGraw Hill.
Portes, A. and R. G. Rumbaut (2006). *Immigrant America: A Portrait*. Berkeley, Los Angeles: University of California Press.
Ramadas, L. (1997). "Adult Education, Lifelong Learning, Global Knowledge: The Challenge and Potential". *Convergence*, 30 (4), 34-37.
Ramotar, D. (2012). "Utilize Skills of Diaspora – Ramotar Urges Guyanese Diplomats". *Guyana Times International*. July 15.
Roberts, D. (2011). The Development Impact of Remittances on Caribbean Economies: The Case of Guyana. Central Bank of Guyana. Retrieved July 27.
Somerville, W., J. Durana and A.M. Terrazas (2008). "Hometown Associations: An Untapped Resource for Immigrant Integration". *Mpi Insight*. Migration Policy Institute. July.
Thomas, R. (2011). "Remittances and Development in the Caribbean". Paper Presented at the Tenth Biennial Conference of the Association of Caribbean Social Work Educators. July 11-15. Martinique.
Tilley, C. (2007). "Trust Networks in Transnational Migration". *Sociological Forum*. Volume 22, Number 1. March.
Trotz, D. A. (2006). "Rethinking Caribbean Transnational Connections: Conceptual Itineraries". *Global Networks*. January, vol. 6 Issue 1, p. 41-59.
Turner (1991). "Migrants and Their Therapists: A Trans-Context Approach". *Family Process*. Vol. 30 (December)

Chapter Eight

English Speaking Caribbean Immigrant Students: Providing Culturally Competent Educational Services

Lear Matthews and

Rosalind October-Edun

INTRODUCTION

School-age children from the Caribbean represent one of the most rapidly growing single-immigrant groups in North America. These youthful immigrants and their guardians inevitably transpose their own values and expectations as they attempt to adapt to the new environment, including changes relating to learning, teaching and mental health. This chapter is based on data from a qualitative study which examines the factors that impact the efforts of teachers and other school personnel in providing culturally competent services to English-speaking Caribbean or West Indian immigrant students in the United States.[1]

Since the mid-1960's, immigrants from the Caribbean have been among the largest numbers of foreign-born residents in North America where a demographic transformation in major social institutions has occurred. Concomitantly, school-age children of immigrants, particularly in cities such as New York, Miami, Atlanta and Toronto, have been swelling the public school student population.

More than half of the students in the NY City public school system are immigrants and make up 20% to 30% of the student population in the suburbs (Lee, 2004). Data obtained from the Office of Support Services, NYC Board of Education, reveal that 17,251 newly arrived children from the West Indies entered NYC schools during the period 1997-2000. Of this number, 9,439 or 54% entered at grade 7 through 12, with about 45% entering at the elementary level. In addition, the births to foreign-born mothers by country of birth in New

York City shows that 6% of the birth parents were Anglophone Caribbean (Dept. of Health and Mental Hygiene, 2009), while MaCabe (2009) found approximately 1.2 million children in the US had at least one Caribbean-born parent in that same year. These demographic changes are likely to fundamentally impact major institutions of society—families, communities and especially schools.

The school system is one of the first institutions that immigrant children encounter in their adopted home. For many immigrant families, the expectations for their children's achievement of the American dream are closely tied to schooling processes and outcomes. Yet, various migration and acculturation-related stressors threaten to impede the learning process and the overall psychosocial functioning of these children. Suarez-Orozco and Suarez-Orozco (2003) describe recent studies examining the performance of immigrants in US schools as presenting a complex picture. They argue that many of these children are successfully navigating the American educational system, while a significant number struggle academically, leaving schools without acquiring the tools that will enable them to compete in a complex society. They argue further that some of these students are likely to gravitate toward the world of gangs and will face the danger of incarceration in the new country—a country that today has the largest prison population in the post industrial world.

Newly-arrived immigrant students and parents often do not receive the guidance anticipated and may initially find it difficult to understand an unfamiliar education institution. This could be particularly exasperating for those who do not have host relatives to assist in the transition. Coming from societies in which the education system has fluctuated in standards, resources and preparedness, the students are often confronted with the demands of a foreign curriculum and educational milieu to which they are expected to adapt. Invariably, however, they are exposed to acculturative stress (i.e. the stress likely to result from the process of adjusting to a new social institution) these demands may produce.

In this transitional process, teachers and related service providers such as social workers and counselors, many of them unfamiliar with the culture (customs, practices, and beliefs) of their students/clients, have been in the challenging position of instructing, evaluating, assessing and ultimately influencing their adaptation to a new social structure. London (1980) posits that the purpose of education in the multiethnic United States will be adequately fulfilled only if the unique characteristics of Caribbean and other immigrant students are considered. Consequently, the extent to which professionals work effectively in cross-cultural situations is paramount to the success of the helping process, in education and other milieus of social intervention.

This qualitative study examines the factors that impact the efforts to provide academic instruction and clinical services to English-speaking Caribbean immigrant students in New York City. Specifically, the objective is to explore the experiences and responses within the public education system, with the aim of developing cultural competence, an essential ingredient in engaging newly arrived and second generation immigrant students.

Although studies have addressed the relationship between the host society's educational institutions and Caribbean immigrants, primarily those of African descent (Herman, 2004; London, 1981; Bushell, 1992; Gopaul-McNicol, 1993), there has been no serious attempt to examine the experiences of teachers and clinicians (Social Workers, Psychologists, Counselors), who work with the increasing numbers of Caribbean students of African and East Indian heritage, within the New York City public school system.

The Problem

Newcomers to the United States, especially children and adolescents who were born or raised in the Caribbean, rely on both the family network and the school as primary sources of guidance, inspiration and support in their attempt to achieve academic success and become well adjusted adults in their adopted home. While newly arrived families and host relatives struggle to stymie the risks of resettlement and promote opportunities for successful adaptation, immigrant children have been faced with the often underrated task of familiarization with the school system and ambivalent responses by teachers and other practitioners.

Among the concerns identified in previous studies are: stress caused by unfamiliarity with the new school setting; speech patterns, spelling and writing styles; cultural adjustment; the struggle to master the curriculum; discipline related conflicts; teachers' difficulty understanding students and vice versa; placement in a grade level lower than their academic capability; referral to special education or ESL (English as a Second Language) classes; self-esteem problems related to stereotyping by teachers and ridicule by non-Caribbean peers (London, 1980; Rubin, 1989; Richmond and Mendoza, 1990; Gopaul-McNicol, 1993; Smith, 2000; Singleton, 2003). An understanding and appreciation of the difference between the education system in the Caribbean and the United States is also essential. Singleton (2003) reminds us that education in the English-speaking Caribbean "is based on the British system and children who come to the United

States must become familiar with a different educational structure. At home, the Caribbean parents would not involve themselves in school decisions as parents are expected to do in the United States. As a result, some children excel while others require remedial help to meet educational expectations" (p.8).

In her research on the experiences of Caribbean immigrant adolescents in New York, Smith (2000) reported a number of rather revealing difficulties. The first was a general disappointment among newly arrived students about the lack of any sort of orientation procedure to help them adjust to the new school. Secondly, owing to the differences in school structure, policies, procedures (including the absence of uniforms) and the presence of multiethnic personnel to whom students have never been exposed, they face "the task of reorganizing their mental processes" to cope in the new environment that did not appear "immigrant friendly". Sometimes the fear of ridicule because of their speech patterns "prevented them from participating and contributing in class discussions or making friends with fellow students" (p. 354). Some students were reportedly beaten up because of their foreign, Caribbean accent (English, 2001). Although such experiences have been associated with immigrants who speak a foreign language, accented English-speaking students and their parents have also had to contend with this problem.

The perceptions and attitude of educational service providers, peers and parents undoubtedly influence the young immigrants' Cultural awareness. Participants of an educational forum on teacher cultural awareness held in New York City (Yearwood, 2003) agreed that teachers in New York City Public schools are not sensitive enough toward Caribbean students. Further, while "American teachers are educating children trying to adapt to a new society with a different behavior and style, as any immigrant. . . . they are ignorant of patterns of cultural differences in the classroom and may be unable to effectively transmit instructions to learners whose cultural orientation is different from their own" (Yearwood, 2003, p. 8).

Certainly, a number of American or American trained teachers and other educational personnel demonstrate a sense of caring and interest in the educational development of their students/clients, but Rubin (1989) notes the tendency by educators to view newcomers as a population presenting new problems instead of a source of rich cultural diversity for the school system and society at large. In this regard, Brendtro (2007) posits that immigrant youth may succumb to chaos within the school environment in the form of apathy, alienation, rebellion and delinquency. Further, as Matute-Bianchi (1991) found, schools play an instrumental role in shaping the self-definition of immigrant students by providing an arena for association and detachment. Even though it was further observed that as school children interact "with groups differentiated by their own self-perceptions and perceptions of external observers... especially when they equate success with power attained through conflict and physical force (as in the case of youth gangs), those groups can exert a strong downward pull on immigrant children" (Matute-Bianchi, 1991, p. 49).

Although Caribbean immigrant parents value education as key to upward mobility (Foner, 2013), they tend to view school personnel as having little control over the students, some of whom may not adjust to the teaching style that is more informal than in the home country. These students were taught to value non-verbal behavior and attentive listening. As a result, they generally display respect, deference and silence toward teachers and other service personnel, which in American schools may be viewed as resistance, sloth or a non-cooperative attitude. Consequently, the students' progress in the public school is often compromised by a combination of resentment, insecurity, identification and cultural dissonance. It is important to note that there has been an increase in the number of Caribbean owned and managed private Elementary and Middle schools in New York City, giving parents an option to the formal education of their youngsters (personal observation).

In her study of second generation Caribbean immigrants, Mary Waters (1996) reported that newly arrived immigrant students of middle-class parents did extremely well academically, primarily because of their superior educational foundation in the Caribbean. Although new arrivals, regardless of social background do excel in academic skills, a growing number of students are challenged by the realities of a new and different academic and social environment. In addition, the combination of arrival at an early age, the effects of teacher "brain drain" among schools in the Caribbean, identification with American peer culture in the inner city, inadequate school facilities and incidence of violence, has resulted in serious adjustment problems. Concerned about the labeling of Caribbean immigrant youths with discipline problems, Una Clarke, a Caribbean-born New York City Councilwoman sternly remarks, "I'm sick of hearing that it's the Caribbean children that have become the behavioral problem, ending up in juvenile detention and joining youth gangs" (English, 2001, p. A7).

Some of these students reported overt racial/ethnic discrimination and stereotyping for the first time in their lives within and outside of school. In this regard, Rumbaut (1996) suggests that for many immigrant students, the experience of social injustice may decrease the acculturation process, give rise to depressive symptoms and increase parent-child conflict. This situation is exacerbated by a "crisis of loss" and a "crisis of load" (Rumbaut, 1985). That is, not only have the youngsters lost home, friends and a familiar school environment, but they have to cope with the demands of a New York City Public education system that is consistently and severely criticized for mismanagement and miseducation, often with the sole support of peers from the same country (Smith, 2000).

Addressing the clinical concerns pertaining to children of Caribbean immigrants, Baptiste et al. (1997) observed that psychosocial problems could be attributed to difficulties adjusting to school and disappointment in other support systems in helping to ensure successful adaptation in the new society. Student performance and adjustment to school are also indirectly affected by the children's burdensome role as family mediator or hampered by the immigration status of their parents. Teachers and other personnel in several New York City Public schools reported that students often act as interpreters and facilitators for parents and grandparents to help them access services and "to get them to conform to American society" (Hedges, 2000). Furthermore, not only do the parents rarely attend PTA meetings, but fearing deportation, some parents choose not to sign school permission forms for the students' participation in important school activities.

These conditions create stress among students and their parents, with potential negative repercussions to their learning experience and to the bewilderment of teachers and clinical service providers. Acculturative stress among students is manifested in psychological and behavioral changes, which are influenced by factors such as alienation, racism and the nature of social support systems, as well as prior experiences with other cultures (Nwadiora, 1995; Gopaul McNicol, 1993).

Conceptual Framework

Within the framework of the above-mentioned adjustment problems, it is the contention here that possible solutions must be viewed within a culturally competent educational system. Cultural competence is "a set of congruent behaviors, attitudes and policies that come together in a system, agency, or among professionals and enable that system, agency or those professionals to work effectively in cross-cultural situations" (Cross, 1989, p.13). This study is conceptualized in relation to theoretical formulations on empowerment strategies in human service settings. It is therefore guided by concern for human dignity, equality, equity, self-determination, and the acknowledgement of cross-cultural elements in transnationalism. Further, it emphasizes strength rather than pathology and recognizes the impact of oppressive forces on individual functioning. This emphasis on understanding and meaning is especially useful for working with immigrant children. Grounded within a system of values and beliefs that is consistent with post-modernist formulations such as the strength perspective, these principles are also embedded in the National Association of Social Workers (NASW) Cultural Competence Standards. These standards address several key areas of social work practice, including ethics and values, self-awareness, cross-cultural knowledge, cross-cultural skills, service delivery, empowerment and advocacy, workforce diversity, professional education, language diversity, and cross-cultural leadership. Educators, social workers and other professionals whose work is influenced or guided by these principles must therefore be concerned about ways in which marginalized persons may be given voice and empowerment.

Sample and Method

A survey was used to gain insight into the experiences of teachers, social workers, guidance counselors and school administrators who work with newly arrived and American born second-generation English-speaking Caribbean students. While teachers are invaluable in their role of providing academic instruction, school social workers, guidance counselors and school psychologists are pivotal in assessing interpersonal and social needs, and cognitive skills. The study utilized open-ended and structured interviews, observation and focus groups. Using an interview guide approach, a list of questions was generated from the review of related literature and from the researcher's own interests and experiences. Access to the population was made by the researcher's visit to two New York City Public Schools, in districts where significant numbers of children of Caribbean descent are enrolled, specifically in such areas as the Flatbush/Canarsie section of Brooklyn and Greater Richmond Hill, Queens. Their ages ranged from 6 to 15 years. A total of 32 service professionals participated in the study, 20 of whom were female and 12 male. Three trained interviewers conducted focus interviews with one group of 14 respondents (8 teachers, 2 guidance counselors, 1 social worker, 1 school psychologist, 1 assistant dean and 1 principal) and distributed a 12-item self-administered questionnaire to a second group.

The purpose of the focus group was to acquire more detailed information from respondents. Approximately 75% of the students for whom they provided services were either born or raised in the English-speaking Caribbean, many of them Indo-Caribbean. Twenty-five (25) questionnaires were sent out to the second group (who worked with predominantly Afro-Caribbean students) and 18 were returned completed. This accounted for a response rate of 72 percent.

They included 9 teachers, 3 social workers, 5 guidance counselors and 1 After-school coordinator. Of the two groups, 14 were Caucasian, 8 Caribbean, 9 African-American and 1 Latino. Table 8.1 describes key characteristics of the study sample.

The selection of respondents was based on their willingness to participate in the study and their access to English-speaking Caribbean immigrant students. Following the suggestion of Yegidis and Weinback (1991), the researchers used the respondents' judgment and prior knowledge to choose a group of people who are familiar with the study population. They vary in gender, age, years of employment and ethnic background and their primary responsibilities were education, counseling or school-related social services. The data was first organized in accordance with the methodology, i.e., questionnaires and focus group, followed by the description of patterns, themes and experiences of the respondents. Of importance was the development of systemic categories, which were determined by "recurring regularities" in the data (Patton, 1989).

Analysis of demographic information obtained through the structured interview process generated quantitative data, while qualitative data emerged from content analysis of in-depth interviews. Five focus groups were conducted. They were tape recorded (with permission of participants), transcribed and categorized into themes. Each session lasted for about 45 minutes, with an average attendance of 6 informants from a cross-section of school service providers. This format allowed for in-depth discussion on issues pertaining to this population and for eliciting suggestions and possible solutions. Observation was used as a check on what was reported in the interview. In addition, interactions between school personnel and immigrant students (in such areas as hallways, cafeterias, and school libraries) were also observed, where possible, and provided a realistic profile of an immigrant student within the school setting.

Table 8.1–Sample Characteristics

		N=32	%
Gender	Male	12	30
	Female	20	70
Ethnicity	Caribbean	8	25
	Caucasian	14	44
	African American	9	28
	Latino	1	3
Position/Title	Teachers	19	50

	Social Workers	4	17
	Counselors	8	30
	Psychologists	1	3
Place of Residence	Within school Community	8	25
	Outside school Community	24	75
Cultural Competency Training	Yes	16	50
	No	16	50
Total		32	100%

FINDINGS

Data from those responding to the questionnaire will be reported first. Most of the respondents of this group worked at their respective schools with a significant number of Caribbean immigrant students for more than 5 years. Seven (7) of them reported having no difficulties with these students, but did express concern for their adjustment, while 6 indicated problems relating to language/dialect, 5 reported lack of class participation and 11 mentioned behavioral problems. Most respondents (13) would talk to the student and their parents about the problems and 5 said that they have referred students to another service provider within the school.

A crucial starting point for a culturally competent system of care is the institutional capacity to develop cultural sensitivity among practitioners and administrators (Matthews, 1994). Fifty percent (50%) of the respondents had no cultural sensitivity training, but those who did receive such training thought that it was either very helpful or somewhat helpful. The majority of them resided outside of the community where the school was located. Some respondents were aware of community based organizations within the school environ, but have had very little connection with the immigrant community beyond the boundaries of the school. Five (5) of the respondents did not know of any English-speaking Caribbean community organizations, although there are several such organizations (Ramadar, 2001). The concerns of the professionals who completed the questionnaire were grouped into three categories, namely, adjustment to the school environment; challenges to teaching and learning; and impact of cultural difference on behavior.

Adapting to the School Environment

The problems of adapting to the new school environment centered on the lack of proper introduction to the novel school setting and assessment of students' adjustment needs. The following were reported:

These students are put into a school that may be different from what they have encountered in their home country. Newly arrived Caribbean students should not be thrown into a foreign classroom. It would be beneficial to spend a week or so in an orientation class to help them learn the new system and way of life. They are in need of some type of social adjustment upon entering this country.

Many of the students need to have a feeling and experience of welcome ... be assigned a buddy system. Students should receive an orientation when they enter the school and after the term has begun.... this is vital. These immigrant students should be given more time when they enter the system, they seem so lost.

Other comments on the adjustment to school environment focused on the need for a basic knowledge of American history, particularly if the student had elementary schooling outside of the U.S.

In comparing American students and immigrant students, one teacher observed,

The school system here in New York is different from the school system in their island.... most of these children are further ahead than their American counterparts, which I think cause some of the children to be bored, which leads to behavioral problems.

Challenges of Teaching and Learning

Generally, service providers' experiences with immigrant students from the Caribbean have been somewhat positive. Some informants used the following terms to describe their interactions with the students:

Usually respectful, quiet, disciplined, seems to have good work habits

Despite these positive descriptions, informants identified various challenges that they have encountered in their work with Caribbean immigrants students. Among these are:

Inadequate preparation for students and service providers; a broad range of communication difficulties; behavioral/disciplinary problems; and difficulties in home-school relationships.

Regarding problems related to interaction between students and teachers/clinicians, responses included:

They have difficulty adjusting to the teaching style of teachers. One Social Worker reported, through dialogue with the students, I learned that the teachers spoke too fast so they had problems understanding what was being said.

One of the Guidance Counselors stated:

Teaching methods are different, which cause confusion on both the teacher and student side, for example, spelling words (British to American) . . . math problems are worked out differently from their island, but it's correct, which confuses the teacher here in New York.

Another Social Worker reported that enough cultural sensitivity training is not accessible to service providers.

It would greatly benefit the English-speaking Caribbean student if all staff had cultural sensitivity training workshops.

There was very little planned interaction between school and community, and parents reportedly did not regularly attend Parent Teachers' Association meetings. The dissonant nature of the relationship between school personnel and immigrant parents was demonstrated when the Principal reported that he was troubled by the practice of some parents, who habitually removed their children from school during the term and take them to the home country for two to three weeks without proper notification. He indicated that, not only does this action jeopardize the child's educational progress, but it violates school attendance policy. "I told them time and again that it is unacceptable, but to no avail".

Table 2 outlines some critical areas of challenges that emerge in the interaction between immigrant students and educational providers. Nineteen (19–59%) of the informants reported that they were inadequately prepared for work with diverse populations; while seven (7–21%) deemed themselves as prepared. Respondents viewed the lack of knowledge of the students' pre-migratory educational background, customs and experiences as immigrants, as major barriers to providing adequate educational and related services.

Other barriers identified were absence of an introductory protocol to address the transition of immigrant students and the failure to develop culturally relevant procedures and approaches for engaging this population. A call for attention to such impediments is supported by Lee (2004), who argues that the Board of Education should be better prepared for immigrant students by providing resources and time for them to adapt to a new country, new culture, new educational system, new friends and different language accents. The extent to which schools invest in assessing the needs of these students was clearly an issue for the informants. Many informants highlighted the problem of students who are struggling with social pressures and educational challenges as a result of failure of schools to properly prepare and integrate them into the school community. Informants described the problems in the following ways:

Some West Indian students are really at a loss, and initially find it difficult to identify with the culture around them. They should not be thrown into a foreign classroom. It would be beneficial to spend a week or so in an orientation class to help them learn the new system and way of life.

Another informant described it this way:

These students are in need of social adjustment upon entering this country. They need to have a feeling and experience of welcome and be part of a 'buddy system'. They should receive an orientation when they enter the school... this is vital. These immigrant students should be given more time when they enter the system, many of them seem lost.

In addressing this issue of adequate transition of these students, Mitchell and Bryan, (2007) suggest that school personnel can also be instrumental in working with immigrants' parents and the community to create an environment that is welcoming.

The respondents stated that insufficient consideration has been given to the holistic needs of these children as they attempt to navigate the educational system. Rong and Preissle (1998) point out that education policymakers focus primarily on English language acquisition policy, "although many may agree that educating immigrant children should include a wide range of services" (p. 15). They note further that teachers' classroom practices and school policy toward immigrant students affect their adaptation to the US school system. In support of what can be referred to as an ecological perspective, Bronfenbrenner (2005) noted that children's experiences are not only impacted by their own characteristics, but by elements in their surrounding environment.

Addressing the contentious issue pertaining to the academic placement of immigrant students, informants state the following:

It is unfair to the students because some of them were placed in special Education classes where they do not belong and such placement destroys their self-esteem and develops feelings of hostility. The school system here in New York City is different from the school system in their islands. Most of these children are further ahead than their American counterparts, which I think cause them to be bored which leads to behavioral problems.

A culture-sensitive academic assessment of the immigrant student seems to be essential in determining placement in the appropriate grade level. This view is reflected in the work of Baum and Flores (2011) who urge school administrators in the US to address the obstacles that face immigrant children entering and failing within the system. The immigrant student may or may not perform well in a placement exam, depending on the level of anxiety of being in a different environment or familiarity with the subject matter.

Table 8.2–Challenges in Teaching and Learning

Nature of Challenges	Extent of Challenges	N	%
Preparation For students/Providers	Prepared	7	22
	Somewhat Prepared	6	19
	Unprepared	19	59
	Total	**32**	**100%**
Communication/language	No difficulties	4	12
	Some difficulties	5	16
	Much difficulty	23	72
	Total	**32**	**100%**
Behavioral/disciplinary Problems	No Problems	7	22
	SomeProblems	8	25
	Serious Problems	17	53
	Total	**32**	**100%**
Home/school Interaction	Positive	6	19
	Negative	12	37
	Needs Improvement	14	43
	Total	**32**	**100%**

(SOURCE: MATTHEWS AND MAHONEY, 2005).

Cultural Differences

A number of respondents thought that central to the adjustment problems experienced by Caribbean immigrant students, was the impact of cultural dissonance on their behavior. One respondent reported that fellow teachers complained about poor behavior of some

Caribbean male students, who had difficulties understanding the teachers.

But another observed that they are generally well behaved.

They do not suffer from language problems, it is more culture shock. They have difficulty adjusting to other children, teasing them in the way they talk or their respectful behavior toward teachers. Some of them are withdrawn, stated another Guidance Counselor.

An After-school Coordinator, who worked with adolescents reported:

They are dealing with the culture of this country as it relates to the youth and their development, they are inundated by images created by the media, which they try to live up to in order to be accepted by their American-born peers.

She further observes.

Some of these images are in strict contrast to their own culture and lifestyle that their parents have envisioned for them.

However, a Special Education Teacher remarked that these students, appear to adjust quickly, particularly in terms of dress, speech patterns outside of the home, foods. They learn that such adjustments are necessary for acceptance in peer and community groups.

Similarly, a Social Studies Teacher reported that the students he worked with are, at least second generation Caribbean children and they speak 'Americanized English' while in school.

Communication/Language Difficulties

Many of the disparities in communication between education service providers and immigrant students emerge as a result of differences in expectations, values and socialization relating to teaching and learning. Some students were described by respondents as:

Withdrawn, inattentive and disinterested, demonstrating poor verbal skills and compared to their American counterparts, rarely volunteers for classroom activities, and some appear unmotivated. I wish they would say more in class, and then communication would be better, reported one respondent. While another lamented, I don't know how to interpret their unwillingness to speak up in class, perhaps it has to do with their culture.

Krajewski (2011) notes that a student's pattern of learning is dependent on his or her cultural and educational background and that self-directed learning styles are most welcomed by those learners who are accustomed to having a teacher as a leader of discussions. Furthermore, as Gopal-McNicol (1993) observes, due to the structural arrangements in the Caribbean classroom, and the tendency for the learning experiences of these students to be more auditory than visual/action, as in the United States, the classroom is seen as a place to sit and listen attentively. "When these students are bombarded with visual aids, with little auditory stimulation, they often experience difficulty . . . they may appear to be less academically motivated because of this difference in instructional pattern" (p. 31). Respondents view inadequate communication as emanating from differences in students' accent, as well as in the teaching approach.

One informant puts it this way:

It is clear that this was not a problem of accent, because whenever I teach the students they understand and cooperate. They have difficulty adjusting to the teaching style of teachers. Through dialogue with students, I learned that the teachers spoke too fast so they had problems in understanding what was being said.

Another informant explains:

An immigrant student who has a different accent from the majority should not be perceived as an underachiever or neglected. In extreme situations, a student with a 'foreign' accent may even be asked to speak slowly or repeat what she/he has said, ultimately exposing her/his vulnerability attributed to the accent. This places that student in an uneasy position since the desire to actively participate may be negatively impacted due to fear of being misunderstood or 'exposed'

With regards to any organized strategy to improve communication and helping immigrant students with adjustment, one informant observes,

With the influx of large numbers of immigrants from different parts of the world, the strategy seems to be to encourage foreign students within the public school system to learn by association, whereby they are expected to learn about the school system from their American counterparts. How to address relating to immigrant parents has also become an intended strategy.

Behavioral/Disciplinary Concerns

Respondents identified various behaviors and attitudes that have increased their concern for the academic and social outcomes of these students. Many of these behaviors appear to be consistent with feelings of distrust of service providers; confronting personal experiences related to cultural differences; and conflict arising at the interpersonal and inter-group levels. To illustrate, one respondent observed:

During my teaching experience, teachers complained about the poor behavior of some Caribbean male students. Conflicts can be caused when they are embarrassed to speak, which can lead to truancy and completely withdrawing from school. They are inundated by messages created by the media, which they try to live up to in order to be accepted by their American-born peers. Some of these images are in strict contrast to their own culture and lifestyles that their parents have envisioned for them.

While these behavior patterns were more prevalent among male students, girls also exhibited some of the same behaviors. Informants agreed that expressions of distrust directed at them by some Caribbean immigrant students may be based on students' perception of them as insensitive and/or uncaring. Chavkin and Gonzales (2000) in their study of Mexican youth found that the building of caring relationships, communication of high expectations, positive beliefs and providing of opportunities for participation were important characteristics in supporting productive development of immigrant Mexican youth. This view is consistent with the perception of respondents, who suggested a link between educational performance and service providers' attitude toward them as newcomers to the school system. As stated by one respondent:

These students would be better off if teachers and others would provide an environment in which they adapt well and excel in their work.

Some informants link behavioral and particularly disciplinary problems among some immigrant adolescents, with the dramatic changes that occur in the social environment as a result of their migration. These changes often require students to give up components of their previous identity in order to adjust to their changing life situation. For many Afro-Caribbean students, their school and community reflect the harsh reality of poverty, racism and other forms of oppression. Coupled with the difficulty of adjusting to a new culture, respondents also agree that these experiences within schools and the broader community often result in rebellious and other forms of nonconformist behavior. Respondents expressed their view in the following ways:

Many of these students who display poor behavior in school do so because of their frustration with the school system. They have difficulty understanding the teachers. They have difficulty adjusting to other children teasing them about the way they talk or because of the respectful way that they tend to behave toward teachers. They do not suffer from language problems, it is more from culture shock.

In addition to these personal and institutional challenges, the experiences of these students often result in anger and frustration. Poverty and other pervasive and systemic problems are often rampant in the communities in which they settle, indeed in their schools. In addition, many are relegated to schools that are failing.

Some respondents link disciplinary problems among some Caribbean immigrant students with the differences in disciplinary structure of the schools in the Caribbean and those in the United States. They argue that students from the region often appear to be surprised at the absence of corporal punishment as a disciplinary method in schools (3). Finally, respondents made reference to what they perceive as acting-out behavior by students as a result of family-related conflict, centered on the unresolved feelings of abandonment, loss, grief and guilt which characterizes the separation-reunification syndrome likely to occur as part of the immigration process.

Indo-Caribbean Students: Emerging Issues

Apart from highlighting the experiences of the service providers in working with predominantly Afro-Caribbean students within the public school system, the data from the focus group presented an opportunity to examine the emerging issues among these professionals in their work with East Indian students from the English-speaking Caribbean. The significance of this opportunity is that, unlike students of African heritage, the adjustment of Indo-Caribbean students, whose school enrollment in immigrant communities has increased significantly over the past decade, has not been seriously studied within the context of adaptation and acculturative stress.

Data from this second group (focus interviews) were collected from an elementary public school (the equivalent of a primary government school in the Caribbean) located in the Richmond Hill section of Queens, New York, a community heavily populated by Caribbean East Indian immigrants (primarily from Guyana and Trinidad and Tobago). The cohorts of that school district expressed concerns about their effectiveness in working with the large numbers of East Indian Caribbean students, some of whom were born and raised in the Caribbean and others were American born. The participants were encouraged to share their experiences (stories and observations) in working with this student population. The reported issues and problems faced by these professionals centered on: (a) the lack of knowledge of Caribbean customs, beliefs and practices (b) student behavior and (c) communication between school personnel and parents.

The participants had little or no understanding of English-speaking Caribbean culture. (Only one member of the focused group was of Caribbean background, although she was raised in the United States). This lack of knowledge of the students' heritage, customs and experience as immigrants was viewed by participants as a barrier to providing adequate educational and related services, and they felt that it was imperative that arrangements are made to disseminate information about Caribbean culture among the school teachers and clinicians. In particular, they expressed the need to learn about the history and educational system in the English-speaking Caribbean, the unique cultural practices of East Indians and the ways in which this knowledge could enhance teaching and learning. They also reported that they did not know of any English-speaking Caribbean Community organizations in that school district, but were aware that links with such organizations could provide a vehicle for cultural education.

Several 'stories' were shared in the group. The following two situations are presented to highlight some of the problematic areas. One group member reported that he would invite students to share with the class the things they did over the weekend. Invariably, he said, the East Indian students would have nothing to say about weekend activities, while other children appear anxious to talk about what they had done. He continued, I don't know how to interpret their unwillingness to discuss their weekend experiences, perhaps it has to do with their culture.

In another situation, one teacher stated that although the children are generally attentive, he has had in his class students who appeared inattentive and disinterested. They told the teacher that they did not have to worry about schoolwork because their parents "have shop" (own a business). This was very frustrating to the teacher, who reported that he could not understand their way of thinking and behaving, especially coming from a child. Another teacher reported that on several occasions, a student would fail to complete his/her homework. When asked for an explanation, the student has said, Mommy and Daddy had a fight and I could not do my homework. The teacher wondered about the connection of such a response to the presence of extended kin in the households and the impact on the child's academic progress. One student expressed surprise (with delight), that corporal punishment is not used in the schools as it has been back home.

Discussion

The data provided an understanding of the experiences of teachers and other helping professionals, who work with English-speaking Caribbean students. The study revealed a number of issues and problems that influence the adjustment of Afro and Indo-Caribbean immigrant children to the New York City public school and its environs. Emerging from the sample were clear themes of concerns. In particular, among the principal adjustment factors, is the lack of any orientation/introduction of the students to the new and diverse school setting. The practitioners identified several barriers to the students' adaptation and eventual assimilation into the school system. However, there were no systematic program efforts to alleviate the acculturative stress, often manifested in behavioral problems. Instead, teachers tended to intervene directly with individual students or have a discussion with a parent when a problem arises. Although the School Based Support Team that evaluates students for special education classes was not mentioned as a referral source by the participants, the criteria for assessing immigrant children with behavioral problems need to be re-examined.

Early adaptation of English-speaking Caribbean immigrant students to the new school environment can be enhanced by cultural awareness and culture-specific assessments, as suggested by Humbert, Burket, Deveney and Kennedy (2011) and Gopaul-McNicol (1993), which would complement the needed orientation proposed by the participants of this study. Such an approach will not only be instrumental in alleviating the stress of adjusting to school, but to the larger society. The uncertainty about the new school setting was reported in other studies. For example, Smith (2000) found that students expressed initial confusion and fear of the perceived or anticipated dangers of New York City with the school representing a localized milieu for that fear.

Some students were traumatized by the security searches; others could not differentiate between teachers and students; while some had heard negative accounts about the children in New York City schools. Most of the practitioners had ideas about the importance of orienting the students in a way that would dispel myths, decrease anxiety and offer an informed introduction. Although bothered by these problems, they did not have the skills to implement a program that would offer such a service. For example, only one of them was aware of assessment instruments such as the West Indian Comprehensive Assessment Battery (WICAB), which provides psychosocial and educational assessment of English-speaking Caribbean immigrant students (Gopaul-McNicol, 1993). Furthermore, the New York City Board of Education has not instituted the more generalized adjustment tests, because they were thought to be too intrusive (Smith, personal communication).

At the foundation of effective communication between the immigrant student and service provider is the capacity of each to develop an understanding of the interactive nuances within the teaching/learning continuum. These are manifested in a number of ways, including linguistic and behavioral characteristics, and teaching and learning styles. In order to deal appropriately with such issues, which are highlighted in this study and to ensure effectiveness in the classroom, (London, 1990) stresses the need for training teachers and related service providers to help them comprehend the West Indian cultural heritage and areas of cultural dissonance. In the absence of such training, however, it is significant to note that these professionals demonstrated insight into the dynamics of the students' adjustment and the role of peers and other social forces, such as the media, in that process.

The recent, albeit controversial recruitment drive by the New York City Board of Education, for teachers from the English-speaking Caribbean (Jamaica, Trinidad and Tobago, Barbados and Dominica), points to the currency of the problem of cross-cultural communication in Public Schools. As English (2001) states, "a major reason for the push to bring in Caribbean teachers is a need to bridge a language gap that is viewed as a roadblock to the scholastic achievement of many immigrant Caribbean students" (p. A7). The findings of this study did not indicate any significant differences between Caribbean and non-Caribbean professionals in their interaction with the students. However, those with a Caribbean background tend to identify with aspects of the culture of particular Caribbean nations rather than a broad Caribbean culture per se.

Behavioral issues tended to be more prevalent as a presenting problem than was difficulty with dialect/language between teacher and student. On the one hand, Caribbean students have had a reputation of being disciplined and well-behaved, but behavioral problems emerge, due to factors such as frustration from misplaced grade level and social hurdles within the school environment.

Teachers and related service providers' experience in working with East Indian Caribbean students is a relatively unexplored area of inquiry. The migration of these students and their families to the United States in large measure is a new phenomenon, compared to Caribbean immigrants of African heritage, due to the lack of opportunity or desire to travel abroad prior to the 1970's and a tradition that assumes permanency of settlement. Knowledge of characteristics of Caribbean East Indian culture is essential in assisting educational service providers in responding to the needs of the students. Educational practitioners should know that traditionally, the parents of these children do not customarily depend on experts or outside institutions for childrearing information (Ramadar, 2001).

Many of the Indo-Caribbean immigrants are from rural areas, very community oriented and their families have deep-seated religious beliefs (Hinduism, Muslim, and Christianity). Coming into a more developed society, they may be unprepared for the interpersonal, mental or spiritual adjustments they have to make (Lyall, 2001). Ethnic indoctrination is a central part of childrearing with access to religious training for children among this group, with emphasis on reverence and obedience toward elders. The 'silence' or non-verbal behavior in the classroom observed by respondents may be a reflection of the fact that North American society is generally permissive in the treatment of children and "the right of children to question authority figures goes against the grain of socialization values in the Caribbean" (Roopnarine, 1999, p. 17). Teachers also need to understand that due to structural arrangements in the Caribbean classroom and the tendency for learning experiences of these students to be more auditory than visual/action-oriented as in the U.S., the classroom is seen as a place to sit and listen attentively (Gopaul-McNicol, 1993).

However, in his interaction with East Indian students in the Mandir (a Temple or meeting place for Hindus), Ramadar (2001) found that the children, many of them American born, were verbal and interactive in that venue among peers. The problems experienced in delivering educational and related services in the public school, therefore, may be linked to the difference in setting and other cultural barriers for immigrant students and yet to be determined factors for the American born students of Caribbean parentage. As Gopaul-McNicol (1993) further notes, "when these students are bombarded with visual aids, with little auditory stimulation, they often experience difficulty. West Indian children may appear to be less academically motivated because of this difference in instructional patterns" (p. 31).

Although most of the respondents did not see language/dialect as a problem in working effectively with the students, those who did also recognized that immigrant children had difficulty in understanding school personnel. It is important to note that, although English is their official language, many of the newly arrived students speak Creole and some of the East Indians also speak Hindi. It was recognized by the participants of the study that the stresses experienced by English-speaking Caribbean students are generally related to cultural differences, including speech patterns, and not the ability to learn. However, it is also important to note that the demands on social and cognitive skills may be beyond the age appropriate development of some of the newly arrived students. Invariably, too, because of differences in teaching methods and content of the curriculum (patterned after the British system), "when Caribbean students migrate, they are often 'put back' a year to 'catch up' to American standards of education, despite knowing more or less than their American counterparts" (Yearwood, 2003, p. 8). This may be a consequence of coming from a school system in the Caribbean that has been plagued by a shortage of well-qualified education professionals and other resources, due to emigration and exacerbated by a lack of the American teachers' knowledge of the students' background. Practitioners need to appreciate the educational system in the Caribbean and understand the challenges it faces in its efforts to sustain an effective curriculum, typical of its reputed past.

Finally, concerns expressed by the respondents about possible solutions to the adjustment problems of both Afro-Caribbean and Indo-Caribbean immigrant students, warrant a comparison between the two groups. The basic two-party system in Guyana and Trinidad and Tobago resulted in an increase in ethnic/racial cleavage. Following migration to the United States, there is generally a continuation of Caribbean immigrant residential clusters and recreated cultural communities based on ethnic identity. As a result, there are a number of communities (such as Richmond Hill, Queens) where the student population is primarily East Indian and other communities (such as East Flatbush, Brooklyn) where students of African Caribbean heritage are predominant, reflecting spatial segregation of the two groups. Both communities were represented in this study. It is important that professionals working with these students comprehend the differences in background and customs in order to preclude faulty generalizations. Many East Indian immigrants lived in rural communities, while the Africans generally hailed from urban and coastal areas. Although education is compulsory in the Caribbean and most people place a high premium in it, there is no rigid enforcement, especially in the rural areas.

Among East Indians, virtually every trip between the Caribbean and the U.S. occurs as a family/kinship unit to the extent that this is permitted by immigration policy (Ramadar, 2001). The Principal, who was troubled by the removal of students by parents during the school term, must realize that these parents are struggling with the potential loss of socializing functions to the school. As (Ramadar, 2001) in her discussion of traditional societies notes, "they come from communities where the family is all-important and parental and religious discipline reign supreme" (p. A3). By understanding this and other cultural characteristics, educational practitioners can begin to help parents and students prepare for the changes in the U.S. where there is more stringent legal imposition of social control of behavior. However, it must be made unequivocally clear to the families which decisions and actions would enhance adjustment to school and community, and which could jeopardize the child's education and also get parents in trouble with the law.

Implications for Teaching and Other Interventions

The role of teachers and other service providers in helping to overcome problems of cultural dissonance and acculturative stress among immigrant students become crucial within the context of formal education. A prerequisite for a qualified teacher or other professional in predominant immigrant communities must be characterized by a knowledge base steeped in the customs and migration experience of students and their parents. In order to effectuate their respective professional roles with cultural competence, teachers and other educational personnel, working in Caribbean immigrant communities, "should avoid preconceived notions of students' ability", learn about the student's country of origin and adjustment experience (Yearwood, 2003, p.8; Keengwe, 2010). There appears to be a general urgency to address transnational issues as the diversity of immigrant groups, particularly in urban America, continues to increase. However, this study indicates that there seems to be an absence of the will and resources to institute programs that would respond adequately to the needs of immigrant students. In an appeal to the New York City Board of Education to streamline and diversify teacher training and evaluation, former Colorado teacher, Susan Keyock (2013) calls for improved professional development "to meet new needs and challenges' of a changing student population and transforming classroom environment.

School social workers in particular, need to consider the process of acculturation in their repertoire of intervention skills. In a multicultural education system, they must assist students in cultural transition and empathize with the immigrant community, thus assuming the role of mediator instead of change agent (Roer-Strier and Rosalindnthal 2001). English-speaking Caribbean students are faced with the task of maintaining good academic and social skills in a system that has not adequately responded to their experience as immigrants or children of immigrants, who emphasize ethnic identity and/or national origin. Social Workers are in a position to enhance the students' social functioning in order to facilitate academic progress. To do so, they must ensure that evaluation and placement are not driven by the desire to patronize, placate or accommodate these culturally different students, but instead focus on comprehending their cultural background and areas of cultural conflict that may result in misunderstanding in the classroom.

The Social Worker's contact with the immigrant student usually occurs only if that student is referred to Special Education, a program for those with academic or behavioral problems. Although many Caribbean parents may understand the program's purpose, some families misinterpret it as "extra help". Before a student is placed, the Social Worker completes a social history and is required to make important linkages with parents, explain the meaning of Special Education classes and evaluative tests, listen to their concerns, discuss the role of counseling, and inform them of their rights. As a resource professional connecting the family and school, the Social Worker needs to be sensitive to cultural issues, develop a sound knowledge base of English –speaking Caribbean culture, set the tone for other practitioners, and interpret perceptions and expectations of this student population.

These students are in a bicultural situation and as such, the difficulties resulting from the differences in speech patterns and teaching/learning styles between them and practitioners must be considered by service providers during student evaluations. As Malgady and Zayas (2001) indicated, in assessing "immigrant, ethnoliguistically different clients, the interaction of client and Social Worker in the diagnostic interview and language used by both participants requires attention to arrive at a diagnosis" (p. 45). The intent is not to separate or label students based on cultural differences, which indeed can highlight the 'baggage' of 'minority status', but to prevent misdiagnosis, avoid inappropriate educational placement and ensure crisis-free acculturation for those who experience adjustment problems.

Beyond their responsibilities to the Special Education Program, Social Workers must engage in community outreach with the goal of familiarizing school personnel with the Caribbean immigrant community and its resources, and vice versa. For example, the sponsorship of a Caribbean National Day and forums on issues of community concern, including the participation of the escalating number of immigrants of Caribbean background running for public office, should be encouraged and held in the schools when possible. In order to further effectuate their role as purveyors of a culturally competent system of educational service and to allay the anxieties of immigrant parents, teachers and clinicians must advocate for the implementation of proposed policy changes such as The DREAM Act (The Development Relief and Education for Alien Minors Act of 2003). This bill seeks to grants residency to undocumented immigrant students, who have attended high school in the United States and ensures state tuition benefits for their college attendance (FAIR, 2003).

With the support of the school District Superintendents and Principals, the school service providers could solicit the involvement of religious and social organizations. Some of these organizations, including Hometown Associations (HTAs), have indicated a willingness to help with improving attendance, increase parents' understanding of the requirements of the educational system and the long-term gain for their children, and to contribute to further research on adjustment issues (Matthews, 2012; Ramadar, 2005). Setting up workshops to discuss and inform the community about the school curriculum should be a goal of the school Social Workers, in collaboration with teachers and the school's administration. A critical, related, although difficult topic would be to determine if the presence of extended family members in the household impede or enhance academic progress. The establishment of family support services and explaining to immigrant parents the value of their participation in Parent Teachers' Association will also be instrumental in this process.

CONCLUSION

There are past and emerging problems centered on the effectiveness of teachers and clinical school personnel in providing services to immigrant students. Even though English-speaking Caribbean students have generally done well academically[4], with many advancing to higher education, a number of difficulties have been identified and discussed by researchers and by the practitioners in this study. There is clearly a need for training and holistic educational programming, geared toward helping professionals within New York City Public schools and other school systems predominated by immigrant children, and the development of cultural competence in working with this population and their parents who struggle with adjustment issues.

The view that those human service workers and educators including teachers, who are most informed about the culture of the recipients of services, are likely to be more effective, has been espoused in the literature on multicultural education and training (Carten 2005; Ovando, 1985; Malgady et al., 1987). The findings of this study strongly suggest the need for English-speaking Caribbean students, their families and the school system through its service professionals, to develop an understanding and partnership that would forge a more conducive, learning/teaching environment. As such, the perspectives on students' adaptation, by both parents and school personnel, will inform education policy. A cross-fertilization of ideas and strategies between school and immigrant community is also required. Increased membership of immigrant parents on Community School Boards is one approach, while another is to learn from other immigrant groups, with regards to dealing with some of the problems highlighted in this chapter. The role of parent coordinators is also instrumental in this process.

Although one should not lose sight of the negative impact of the overseas teacher recruitment drive on the education curriculum in the Caribbean, such as "brain drain", with effective orientation and adequate social supports for the new recruits, this policy can contribute to culturally competent intervention in US schools. In the report by English (2001), it was further observed that by recruiting Caribbean teachers "who are most closely connected to the students themselves, the teachers would understand the behaviors of the children, the discipline they were used to, and the language too . . . and it would be easier to get these teachers to engage parents in the system" (p.A7). Along with such teachers, experienced, skilled and professionally sanctioned social workers, counselors and psychologists, schools must begin to provide effective cross-cultural education which has eluded some public school districts in New York and other North American cities with large Caribbean immigrant populations. However, social analysts in Caribbean have expressed concern over the state of education in the Caribbean Educational standards in the region reflected in the high failure rate in basic subjects such as Math and Science. This is likely to affect the academic preparedness of newly arrived immigrant children.

This study has limitations. Generalizations about working with other immigrant groups, particularly those whose native language is not English, cannot be drawn. With a larger sample size, further exploration of similar issues and problems in other school districts with substantive numbers of immigrant and American-born second generation students, would be significant. Such exploration should focus on (1) how the ways in which students identify with other immigrants with other immigrant peers or with their American counterparts affect their adjustment to the school environment (2) how Afro-Caribbean and Indo-Caribbean students identify themselves and the differences or similarities in adjustment patterns and (3) the extent to which students who attend Caribbean-owned private schools or parochial schools, experience acculturative stress. The implementation of programs based on the findings of such investigations would enhance the cultural competence of practitioners in a society whose immigrant population continues to increase in magnitude and diversity in the 21st century.

NOTES

1. Information used in this chapter was drawn from a study conducted by L. Matthews and A. Mahoney, published in The Journal of Ethnic & Cultural Diversity in Social Work: The Haworth Social Work Practice Press (see bibliography).

2. In this chapter, the terms Caribbean immigrants and "West Indians" are used interchangeably and refer to those people who were born in one of the English-Speaking Caribbean countries and subsequently migrated to the United States.

3. Corporal punishment as a standard method of disciplining students in English-Speaking Caribbean Public schools is less prevalent, partly due to more stringent laws regarding child abuse and the continuous debate on the topic among citizens and human rights advocates in the region.

4. Despite the issues of concern addressed in this chapter, data from the US Census Bureau (2010) regarding the educational attainment of foreign-born groups, reveal that in New York City, the high school graduation rate among Jamaican immigrants is 79.8%; Trinidad and Tobagonians–84.6%; and Guyanese–74.7%.

CHAPTER EIGHT
Bibliography

Baptiste, et al. (1997). Clinical Practice with Caribbean Immigrant Families in the United States: The Intersection of Emigration, Immigration, Culture, and Race. In J.L Roopnarine & J. Brown (Eds.), *Caribbean Families: Diversity Among Ethnic Groups* (pp. 275-303), Norwood, NJ: Abex.

Baum, S. and S. M. Flores (2011). "Higher Education and Children in Immigrant Families". The Future of Children. 21 (1), 171-193.

Brendtro, L.K. (2007). "The Vision of Urie Bronfenbrenner: Adults Who are Crazy About Kids". *Reclaiming Children and Youth*: 15(3), pp.162-166.

Bronfenbrenner, U. (2005). *Making Human Beings Human: Bioecological Perspectives on Human Development*. Thousand Oaks, CA: SAGE Publications, Inc.

Bushell, W. (1992). "The Immigrant West Indian Child in School". In Meeting *the Needs of Ethnic Minority Children: A Handbook for Professionals*, (ERIC Document Reproduction Service No. ED406478).

Carten, A., P. Crawford-Brown and A. Goodman (2005). "An Educational Model for Child Welfare Practice with English-Speaking Caribbean Families". *Child Welfare*. Sept-Oct; 84(5): 77-89.

Chavkin, K. and J. Gonzales (2000). "Mexican Immigrant Youth and Resiliency Research and Planning Programs". *ERIC DIGEST*.

Cross, T. (1989). "Toward a Culturally Competent System of Care", Washington, DC. *CASSP* (Georgetown University Child Development Center).

Department of Health and Mental Hygiene, New York City (2009). Population Division - New York City Department of City Planning.

English, M. (2001). "Newest Import: Teachers: Board of Ed. Goes to the Caribbean to Seek Recruits". *Newsday*, Tuesday, May 29.

FAIR (2003). "The Dream Act Hatching Expensive New Amnesty for Illegal Aliens", *Federation for American Immigration Reform, www.fairus.org*.

Foner, N, (2013). One Out of Three: Immigrant New in the 21st Century. NY: Columbia Univ.Press.

Gopaul-McNicol, S. (1993). *Working with West Indian Families*. New York: The Guilford Press.

Hedges, C. (2000). "Translating America for Parents and Family: Children of Immigrants Assume a Difficult Role". *New York Times,* June 19.

Herman, K. (2004). "Developing a Model Intervention to Prevent Abuse in Relationships Among Caribbean and Caribbean American Youth by Partnering with Schools". In A. Mahoney (Ed.) *The Health and Well-Being of Caribbean Immigrants in the United States*. The Haworth Social Work Practice Press, pp 103-116.

Humbert, T. K., A. Burket, R. Deveney and K. Kennedy (2011). "Occupational Therapy Practitioners' Perspectives Regarding International Cross-Cultural Work". Australian Occupational Therapy Journal, 58 (4), 300-309.

Keengwe, J. (2010) Fostering Cross-cultural Competence in Teachers through Multicultural Educational Experience, Journal of Early Childhood Education (3) 197-204.

Keyrock, S. (2013). "Please Help Me be a Better Teacher". *The New York Daily News*. Wednesday, January 2.

Krajewski, S. (2011). "Developing Intercultural Competence in Multilingual

and Multicultural Student Groups". *Journal of Research in International Education*, 10 (2) 137-153.
Lee, H. (2004). *School Restructuring Doesn't Solve Immigrant Parent's Access Problems*. IPA–New York Ethics Press.
London, C. (1981). "Crucibles of Caribbean Conditions: Factors of Understanding for Teaching and Learning with Caribbean Students in American Educational Settings". *Journal of Caribbean Studies*, vol. 2 no. 2-3, Fall-Winter.
———, (1980). "Teaching and learning with Caribbean Students". New York: *ERIC Document Reproduction Service*. No.ED 196 977).
Lyall, S. (2001). "The Immigrant Journey Gets no Easier in Britain". *New York Times*, Friday, July 13.
Malgady, R. et al. (1987). "Ethno Cultural and Linguistic Bias in Mental Health Evaluation of Hispanics". *American Psychologist*, 228-234.
Maldady R. & L.H. Zayas (2001). "Cultural and Linguistic Considerations in Psychodiagnosis with Hispanics: The Need for an Empirically Informed Process Model", Social Work, Vol. 46, No. 1, 39-49.
Matthews, L. (2012). "Back to School: Challenges of English Caribbean Immigrant Students". *Guyana Cultural Association* On-Line Magazine. Volume 8, September.
———, (1994). "Social Worker Knowledge of Client Culture and its Use in Mental Health Care of English-speaking Caribbean Immigrants", *Doctoral Dissertation*, UMI.
Matthews, L. and A. Mahoney(2005). "Facilitating a Smooth Transition for Immigrant Caribbean Children: The Role of Social Workers, Teachers, and Related Professional staff" *Journal of Ethnic and Cultural Diversity in Social Work*. Volume 14, No. 2/3.
McCabe, K. (2011) *Caribbean Immigrants in the US*. Migration policy Institute.
Matute-Bianchi, M.E. (1991). "Situational Ethnicity and Patterns of School Performance among Immigrant and Non-immigrant Mexican-Descent Students". In *Minority Status and Schooling: A Comparative Study of Immigrant and Involuntary Minorities*, ed. By M. Gibson and J.U Ogbu. New York: Garland.
Mitchell, N. A., and J.A. Bryan (2007). "School-Family-Community Partnerships: Strategies for School Counselors Working with Caribbean Immigrant Families". Professional School Counseling, 10 (4), 299-409.
Nwadiora, E. (1995). "*Alienation and Stress Among Black Immigrants: An Exploratory Study*", The Western Journal of Black Studies, Vol. 19, No. 1.
Ovando, C. (1985). *Bilingual and ESL Classroom*, New York; McGraw-Hill.
Patton, M.Q. (1989). *Qualitative Evaluation Methods*, London: Sage Publication.
Ramadar, F. (2001). "Ramadar Talks about Self Development with CEI Youth at SEVA Youth Center", *Caribbean Journal*, July 21.
Rumbaut, R.G. (1995). "The New Californians: Comparative Research on the Educational Progress of Immigrant Children". In *California's Immigrant Children: Theory, Research and Implications for Educational Policy*, (Eds.) R.G Rumbaut and W.A Cornelius. La Jolla, CA: Center for U.S. Mexican Studies, University of California, San Diego.
———, (1977). "Life Events, Change, Migration and Depression". In W.E. Fann & Karachan (eds.), *Phenomenology and Treatment of Depression*, New York: Spectrum.

Roer-Strier & M.K. Rosalindnthal (2001). "Socialization in Changing Cultural Contexts: A Search for Images of the Adaptive Adult", *Social Work,* Vol. 46, No. 3, July, p. 215-228.

Rong, X.L. and J. Preissle (1998). *Educating Immigrant Children.* Thousand Oaks, California: Corwin Press, Inc. Sage Publications.

Roopnaraine, J.L. and M.Shin (1999). *Caribbean Immigrants from English-speaking Countries: Socio-historical Forces, Migratory Patterns, and Psychological Issues in Family Functioning,* New York: Syracuse University.

Rubin, G.E. (1989) Educating the Newest Americans. New York: American Jewish Committee.

Salvo, J. (2011) "Demographic Highlights of a Changing New York". Empire State College. Nov. 10th.

Singleton, S., Pierce, W., Ellis, S. and Munnings, G. (2003). "I'll send you Back Home: Social Work Issues in Working with Caribbean Parents and Children", Paper presented at the 10th Biennial Conference of Caribbean Social Work Educators, Barbados, WI. July 29 - August, 3rd.

Smith, A.R. (2000). *English-speaking Caribbean Adolescents: The Psychosocial and Psychological Effects of Migration and Adolescence and their Impact on Adjustment to New York,* Doctoral Dissertation, UMI Dissertation Services.

Suarez-Orozco, M., and C. Suarez-Orozco (2003). "Rethinking Immigration": *Invited Keynote Address.* Western Illinois University.

Thomas, T. and S. Gopaul-McNicol (1991). *An Immigrant Handbook on Special Education in the United States of America.* New York: Multicultural Educational and Psychological Services.

Waters, M. C. (1996). "Ethnic and Racial Identities of Second-Generation Black Immigrants in New York City". In A. Portes (ed.) *The New Second Generation,* New York: Russell Sage Foundation.

Yearwood, S. (2003). "Calling for More Teacher Sensitivity Toward Caribbean Students by New York Teachers: Lack of Cultural Awareness Nixes Quality Education", *Caribbean Life,* August 5th.

Yedidis, B. and R.W. Weinback (1991). *Research Methods for Social Work.* New York and London: Longman.

Chapter Nine

Indo and Afro-Guyanese Immigrants in New York City: An Analysis of Selected Transnational Experiences

Desmond Roberts

INTRODUCTION

This chapter focuses on immigrants from Guyana, the second largest English speaking Caribbean immigrant group in the U.S. It also attempts to show how the social and political activities of separation in Guyana have been unfortunately replicated among Afro and Indo-Guyanese in the new environment of New York City. In order to contextualize the discussion, the author briefly examines the pre- and post-independence social and political landscapes and how the situation fell neatly into a serendipitous immigration spiral to the developed countries, such as the U.S. and their main cities. As this population moved abroad for betterment and greater social and political predictability, they occupy different living and cultural spaces.

There have been few attempts to bring them together and they continue to reflect the religious and ethnic differences that divided them in Guyana. The history of the struggles of Guyanese living abroad, as well as their connection to the land of their birth, will be explored. Implications for the Wider English speaking immigrant community are noted. There is clearly much more work to be done to present the full picture on both sides of the Diaspora.

Background

Emancipation changed British Guiana from being a black and white (slave and master) to amalgamated plantations marshalling salt and fresh water in empoldered and irrigated estates, using paid labor comprising former slaves and indentured workers from other slave colonies, Europe and mainly India. Former slaves (creoles) bought abandoned estates and created a strong communal village culture while Hindu and Muslim indentured labor was imported heavily from India to break the bargaining power of the skilled creoles. Indians,

Chinese and Portuguese were given credit and cheap land as incentives to create a business class and to discourage no-longer-bound Indians from returning to India. [1]Indentured contracts were for 5 years, with laborers able to return to India if they paid their own passages; after 10 years, their return passages were provided free of cost. The planters offered many incentives to encourage Indians not to return home. Land was bought all along the coast and sold or given (as an incentive to remain in British Guiana) to indentured laborers who had completed their contracts. For remaining on estate land and living in estate 'bound yards' and logies, Indians were also given free medical services. The sirdars or drivers (usually the Brahmin 'retained' caste) were usually given more land and they in turn became rich by leasing or selling land to their fellow Indians. The latter made tremendous sacrifices in order to save and buy or lease land on which the plantation owners allowed them to grow rice, rear cows and manage small businesses. However, the solidarity that grew steadily between working class Indians and Creole Africans up to a decade after the end of World War II was destroyed during the fight for independence (granted in 1966) from Great Britain.[1]

Within another ten years (by 1976), the commanding heights of the economy had been nationalized and Guyana was heading in a socialist and Non-Aligned direction. The oil shocks of 1975, coupled with risky economic investments sent the economy into serious decline.[2] Attempts at self-reliance and south-south solidarity were ineffective as the problems were severe throughout the Third World. As Pelligrino puts it, *"The limits of the economic model of industrialization based on import substitution began to be felt in the 1960s, although it was in the 1970s that they became blatant. Crisis gradually took hold of the region. . . . In the 1980s the debt crisis became widespread, leading to a drop in GDP in much of Latin America, with a decline in the standard of living of the middle class and increased levels of poverty and destitution.[3]"*

The Push and Pull of Migration

Local economic and social hardships and almost total absence of foreign exchange in the late 1970s and early 1980s in Guyana led to ingenious trading and huckstering activity with an appreciation of conditions in regional countries. This in turn led to the pernicious, persistent and endemic drug culture and, eventually, emigration.

Pellegrino sets it out clearly: *"One response to the employment crisis has been the emergence of myriad self employment activities, ranging from highly specialized to unskilled functions. This helped to generate mobility since survival strategies tend to evolve in extended geographical areas, depending on the opportunities offered by the development of communications and access to information."*[4]

After W W II, there was an explosion in population growth among Indians, as a result of the eradication of malaria. However, there was a steep decline in the percentage (49.1% to 8.2%) between 1960 and 1980. For the first time in Guyana's history, there was a decline of approximately 36,000 persons by 1991, a net loss of –4.9 %. The decline in the percentages of females indicated a higher migration rate than for men. There was a reversal of this trend with an increase of 28,000 (3.8%) as of 2002.[5]

Accurate numbers are not immediately available but it is estimated conservatively that there are well over 100,000 Guyanese living in Guyana's neighboring countries of Brazil, Suriname and Venezuela (unusual since Guyana had border issues with the latter two and English was not the spoken language of any of the three); as well as throughout the English speaking Caribbean (especially Trinidad and Tobago, Barbados, Antigua and St. Lucia). Not surprisingly, the Guyana Bureau of Statistics lists Surinamese (27.6%), Brazilian (12.6%) and Venezuelan (12.4%) as the top three of the tiny but influential (1.3%) foreign-born population. The upcoming census in Guyana might produce better answers but an examination of the male to female ratios suggest that Brazilian miners might account for the significant growth in their numbers (as does the sudden growth in Chinese migrants) while other foreign-born border groups (as well as those from the Caribbean and the USA and Canada) might reflect remigration or other shorter term patterns of *Guyanese* families returning from living abroad.[6]

Migration patterns can be ad hoc or well orchestrated. However, immigration patterns after World War II were well organized by the developed countries to meet shortages of manpower or skills. As Saskia Sassen points out: "... the large migrations of the post-war era capture the ongoing weight of colonialism and postcolonial forms of empire on major processes of globalization today, and, specifically those processes binding countries of emigration and immigration. Although the specific genesis and contents of their responsibility will vary from case to case and period to period, none of the major immigration countries are passive bystanders in their immigration histories."[7]

The devastation of the economy and the loss of British youth as a result of WW II created the need for immigrants for the rebuilding effort. This social and economic reality was reaffirmed in the British 1948 Nationality Act that allowed citizens of the Commonwealth the right to enter Britain freely. The 1950s saw many Guyanese travel to the 'Mother Country' to enjoy the 'better life'—to study or work. Mary Waters highlights interestingly that America had allowed unlimited immigration from the Western Hemisphere and Caribbean people, with their higher literacy rates and over representation in the professions, had used their colonial status to utilize Britain's quota. Between 1900-1930, some 85,000 West Indians immigrated to the USA, settling mainly in New York—Harlem and Central Brooklyn. The Depression created anti-immigrant feelings and some West Indian immigrants actually returned home. Finally, the McCarran-Walter Act of 1952 reduced the colonies to 100 persons per annum, shifting the volume of immigration to Britain itself.[8]

By the early 1960s, however, despite black immigrants making up only 0.5% of the population (with unemployment below 3%) the backlash against the "blacks" (from the Caribbean, India and Pakistan) resulted in the requirement in the 1962 Act for work vouchers before entering Britain, with exemptions for dependents' families and students. The Labour Party, which came into power in 1965, promising to repeal the 1962 Act, instead reduced the number of work vouchers.[9]

Canada also began welcoming migrants. See Figure 9.1 for the movement of Guyanese immigrants into Canada. The permanent migration to Canada was the first to reflect the fears of socialist self government: it was the business classes—Chinese and Portuguese who favored Canada—who were first moving and venturing abroad. Over the 30-year period (1961-1991), Guyana lost over *88,000* of its more qualified, entrepreneurial and educated citizens and their families to Canada.[10] The data on the categories of migrants will be analyzed at another time.

Immigration Statistics

The Migration and Remittances Factbook 2011 suggests a stock of Guyanese emigrants (as of 2010) at almost 433,000 in the wider Diaspora. This total emigrant stock is 56.9% of the population, far higher than other regional emigrant communities (Antigua and Barbuda—48.3%; Barbados—41%; Jamaica—36.1%). Pellegrino, in her Figure 9.2 chart below, shows Guyana with easily the highest percentage (over 25%) of emigrants to the overall population among 13 other Latin American countries.[11] Compounding the problem, the Migration and Remittances Handbook 2011 shows that in 2000, Guyana had the outlandishly highest emigration rate in the world of its tertiary educated population at 89%.[12] [ii]Even more disconcerting, the UN World Population Prospects Demographic Profiles report projects that Guyana will be among the few countries in the world with a rapidly diminishing population, creating doubts about its ability to sustain itself as a viable state. Much like the 5.7% reduction in overall population in Guyana between the difficult 1980 and 2000 period, Guyana will see a 12.4% decrease in its population between 2040 and the end of the century. The Guyana population will be lower in 2100 than it was in 1970. Migration is seen as the main cause of this destabilizing phenomenon and deserves special attention.

FIGURE 9.1 Guyanese Emigration to Canada 1966 - 1996

	Year	Immigrants
	1966	628
	1967	736
2,187	1968	823
	1969	1,869
	1970	2,090
	1971	2,384
8,319	1972	1,976
	1973	4,808
	1974	4,030
	1975	4,394
16,662	1976	3,430
	1977	2,567
	1978	2,253
	1979	2,473
	1980	2,279
12,410	1981	2,838
	1982	3,438
	1983	2,606
	1984	1,896
10,241	1985	2,301
	1986	3,905
	1987	6,073
	1988	2,875
16,229	1989	3,376
	1990	2,714
	1991	3,180
8,762	1992	2,888
	1993	3,304
	1994	4,122
	1995	3,884
13,596	1996	2,286
TOTAL		**88405**

Source: Compiled from Department of Manpower and Immigration, Canada Immigration Division, Ottawa, Immigration Statistics

FIGURE 9.2: Percentage of Migration from Latin America and the Caribbean

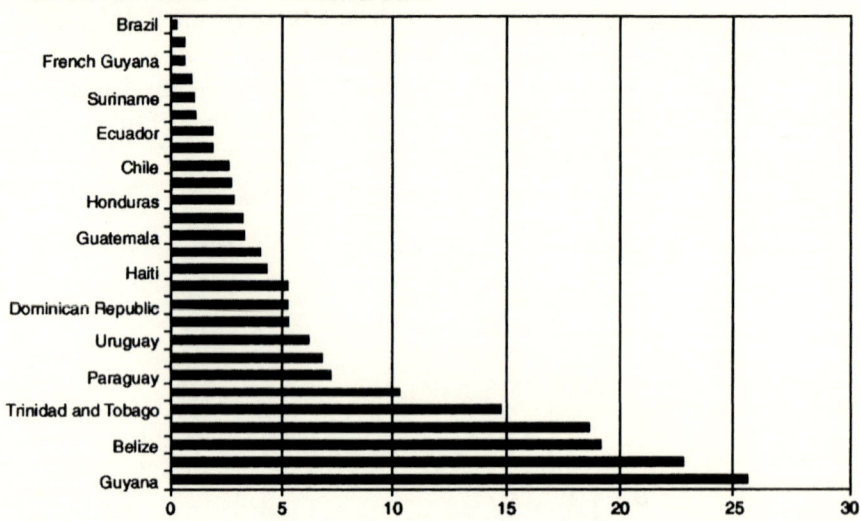

Country	Percentage
Brazil	~0.5
French Guyana	~1
Suriname	~1.5
Ecuador	~2
Chile	~3
Honduras	~3
Guatemala	~4
Haiti	~5
Dominican Republic	~5
Uruguay	~6
Paraguay	~7
Trinidad and Tobago	~10
Belize	~15
Guyana	~19

Source: Trends in International Migration in Latin America and the Caribbean: UNESCO 2000.

Although the United States of America was proud of its reputation of being a "nation of immigrants," much of the earlier 1920s legislation had been designed to use 'foreign' workers for temporary gain only and to keep the nation one in which mainly Northern and Western Europeans would be encouraged to migrate and settle. But as the 1960s civil rights era ushered in fundamental changes in the American society, some of the more odious aspects of immigration policy were also changed. As Roy Bryce-Laporte states the case formally, "Distinct from the much more exclusionary, selective and racist character of legislation from 1882 to 1962, the Immigration and Nationality Act of 1965 replaced the national quota system with hemispheric ceilings."[13] There was a resultant steep increase in immigrants to the United States between the late 1970s to the present time.[14] Unfortunately, there have been very high and increasing levels of unemployment from 2007 to the present time, creating difficult arrival conditions for immigrants, notwithstanding the slightly lower number of arriving immigrants.[15]

The 1965 Act provided another serendipitous moment for a change in migratory direction. Britain had begun closing its doors to unlimited access, Canadian immigration policy was still developing[16] and the US had begun to exert noticeable influence in the economic and political affairs of Guyana. The emphasis on occupations required in America[17] meant that skilled workers were being recruited. However, the main movement of Guyanese was to the United States of America. African-Guyanese who traveled to the USA came as skilled tradesmen after their Panama Canal sojourn[18] but the numbers of Guyanese entering the US were low for the first half of the 20th century.

Table 9.1: Guyanese Arrivals in the United States

Pre 1980 Arrivals US:	1980-1989	1990-1999	2000-2010	Total
39,931	81,879	66,597	66,696	266,103

Source: center for Immigration Studies: Immigrants in the US 2010

These numbers include undocumented immigrants and students. As shown, there was a very heavy, steady increase in migration to the United States after 1980, especially during the difficult economic years (the late 1970s and early 1980s). Catering for attrition from deaths and other movement, there were officially **211,189** Guyanese-born residents in the United States in 2000.[20]

Guyanese in New York City

Even though they live in several states in America, Guyanese continue to choose New York City as their favorite US location for settlement. As pointed out in the 1990 Census, Guyanese show the highest proclivity of all immigrant groups to make New York City their home. Ten years later, Guyanese still love New York: Six of ten Guyanese settle in New York City (Dominicans, the next highest group, are at 40%). The Guyanese population in New York City increased by 300% from 31,690 in 1980 to 130, 647 in 2001.[21] In 2011, there were 139,947 Guyanese-born residents in New York City, an increase of 9,300. [22]

While both African and Indian Guyanese have migrated to the United States, with most remaining in New York City, they have found separate boroughs of the city to congregate, live and solidify social and cultural ties. Table 9.1a (see addendum) shows the top 5 areas in each borough of New York City where Guyanese live. The Borough of Queens holds the majority of the 130,647 Guyanese (66,918 or 51%) in New York State and celebrate Helen Marshall (of Guyanese parentage) as the borough president; Brooklyn (Kings County) has approximately 46,425 foreign born Guyanese or 36% and can boast of John Sampson, a Guyanese, as Head of the Democratic Party caucus in the New York State delegation. However, there are also significant numbers of Guyanese in bordering New Jersey, with influential pockets in Long Island and Connecticut.[23]

A more detailed study of the current housing, education, employment and household data will be done separately to highlight the comparisons between Guyanese in their boroughs and other Caribbean and ethnic groups in New York City. Using the 2000 Census data for New York City, education levels (high school dropouts and college grads) for the Guyanese are below the city average but they are likely to change with more tertiary educated Guyanese arriving in heavy numbers.[24] Guyanese are above the NYC median for household income and below the percentage under the poverty level.[25]

The consolidated Table 9.3 shows the breakdown of Guyanese average earnings in the five boroughs of NYC in 2010. As can be seen from the ACS derived numbers, Guyanese in Manhattan occupied the lower ends of the quantity and percentage of those at the lower end of the household incomes in Brooklyn and Manhattan respectively. Queens occupied most of the higher numbers at the high end of the Guyanese household income numbers (though Guyanese in Manhattan had the highest percentage of the highest incomes - $200,000 and above), while Brooklyn dominated the household incomes between $35-45,000).[26] Queens had higher numbers in the average household than the other boroughs.

In 2000, Guyanese women —61%—(and other Caribbean women too) were among the highest for female labor force participation rates in NYC, with a high percentage (17%) of them being government workers. Several were in the service and sales industries and earned less than their more professional Filipino and Indian counterparts. Although far less than Dominican, Honduran, Jamaican and Trinidadian women, 21.9% of Guyanese women were heads of household, at far higher rates than Asians.[27]

In 2000, Guyanese males also had very high labor force participation rates (70%), higher than Jamaicans and Trinidadians and much higher than Europeans. Guyanese were far more likely to be married (55.5%) than their Caribbean counterparts and only 6.2% men were single heads of household. This high labor force participation (see Table 9.4) allowed Guyanese male to have household incomes above the city median.[28]

The numbers can be disaggregated and are skewed when it is considered that the two main groups of Guyanese arrived at different times, under different conditions and occupy different physical and sociological spaces. As pointed out earlier, literacy rates were much higher among African-Guyanese than among Indian-Guyanese in the first half of the 20th century, which would suggest that Guyanese migration to the United States before Guyana's independence would have been mainly African-Guyanese going to the urban centers and mainly New York City. Further investigation of movement out of Harlem and into the other boroughs and other cities is needed.

Table 9.2: Top 5 Guyanese populations in NYC boroughs and neighboring New Jersey counties

Guyanese overall population in New York City was 130,647

BOROUGH						Total of 5 areas	# in Boro as % of Guyanese in NYC
BRONX 14,868	Southview-Classon 2,023	Wakefield 1,669	Parkchester-Van Neet 1,349	Norwood-Williamsburg 1,325	Tremont 1,040	7,406	11.40%
BROOKLYN 46,425	East Flatbush 5,796	Cypress Hill 5,669	Flatbush 5,508	Flatlands-Canarsie 4,995	Crown Heights 4,769	26,737	35.50%
NEW YORK 1,727	East Harlem 253	Washington Heights 242	Hamilton Heights 206	Central Harlem 187	Lower East Side - East Village 152	1,040	1.30%
QUEENS 66,918	Richmond Hill 17,555	South Ozone Park 8,552	Woodhaven-Ozone Park 7,167	Northern Queens Village 4,552	Jamaica-Hillcrest 4,454	42,280	51.20%
STATEN ISLAND 709	Stapleton-Todt Hill 296	Castleton Corners-New Springville 104	Totenville 55	Mariners Harbor-Port Ivory 55	Rosebank - Old Town 51	561	5%
Total Guyanese in Essex County 7,827	Stapleton-Todt Hill, Hudson County 2,732	Newark, Essex County 1,964	East Orange, Essex County 1,658	Irvington, Essex County 1,468	Orange, Essex County 939	Total of 5 Areas 8,761	% of Top 4 in Essex County 77%

Source: Compiled from "The Newest New Yorkers 2000: Immigrant New York in the New Millennium" New York City Department of City Planning, Population Division

Table 9.3: Household income of Guyanese in New York City based on American Community Survey Data 2006-2010
(Averages And Estimates) for past 12 months 2010
Citywide Median Income is $50,285 in 2010
Inflation Adjusted Dollars

33,975 Households		BRONX		BROOKLYN (Kings)		MANHATTAN (New York)		QUEENS		STATEN ISLAND (Richmond)	
Income Category	TOTAL	3,618	% of total	14,290	% of total	768	% of total	14,960	% of total	339	% of total
Less than $10,000	2,563	235	6.50%	1,429	10.00%	132	17.19%	747	4.99%	20	5.90%
$10,000-14,999	1,226	188	5.20%	570	3.99%	89	11.59%	349	2.33%	30	8.85%
$15,000-19,999	1,740	295	8.15%	1,018	7.12%	27	3.52%	400	2.67%	0	0.00%
$20,000-24,999	1,826	312	8.62%	742	5.19%	11	1.43%	747	4.99%	14	4.13%
$25,000-29,999	1,595	84	2.32%	700	4.90%	94	12.24%	685	4.58%	32	9.44%
$30,000-99,999	4,260	246	6.83%	1,828	5.63%	30	3.60%	2,794	15.29%	50	0.08%
$35,000-39,999	2,870	400	21.54%	986	6.83%	50	6.99	1,593	3.64%	55	13.62%
$40,000-44,999	1,686	185	2.33%	764	5.35%	26	3.38	873	5.84%	0	0.00%
$45,000-49,999	1,833	169	3.62%	601	3.09%	18	1.09	836	4.92%	0	0.00%
$50,000-59,999	2,806	428	0.17.4%	992	8.98	66	7.87	1,436	8.98%	44	12.13%
$60,000-74,999	3,297.5	3658	15.37%	1,429	10.67%	768	5.99%	2,058	13.76%	369	20.35%
$75,000 and above	48,78	1,256	7.08	6,842	12.7	308	4.69	8,84	16.9	232	15.3
Median	4	7						1			
% above city median	55.14%	52.99%		47.88%		39.32%		63.11%		68.44%	

Source: *Compiled from American Community Survey (ACS), Selected Population Tables, 2001 – 2006 US Census, Fact Finder*

Table 9.4: Labor force Participation and Class of Worker for Males by Country of Birth, New York City 2000

	TOTAL	IN THE LABOR FORCE	LABOR FORCE PARTICIPATION RATE	TOTAL EMPLOYED
TOTAL, New York City	2,901,795	1,871,013	64.5	1,699,811
Native-born	1,634,401	1,023,094	62.6	917,307
Foreign-born	1,267,394	847,919	66.9	782,504
Dominican Republic	148,145	89,746	60.6	78,036
China	120,160	79,255	66.0	74,113
Jamaica	66,576	46,593	70.0	42,205
Guyana	55,755	40,666	72.9	37,600
Mexico	68,131	49,169	72.2	45,344
Ecuador	55,544	38,344	69.0	35,212
Haiti	39,420	25,487	64.7	22,661
Trinidad and Tobago	34,802	24,741	71.1	22,452
Colombia	32,945	21,953	66.6	20,288
Russia	33,978	20,389	60.0	18,948
Italy	35,334	18,219	51.6	17,460
Korea	31,461	21,643	68.9	20,570
Ukraine	28,870	16,150	55.9	14,964
India	35,212	26,818	76.2	25,829
Poland	28,765	17,277	60.1	16,150
Philippines	18,522	13,657	73.7	12,738
Bangladesh	20,770	15,321	73.8	14,261
Pakistan	20,943	15,100	72.1	14,325
Honduras	13,194	8,836	67.0	8,017
Greece	15,314	9,469	61.8	9,046

Source: American Survey of Selected Population Tables - 2006-2010

African Guyanese in New York City

As with emancipation, there were advantages in being first in America for African Guyanese. Arriving in significant numbers as they did immediately after the civil rights struggles, several opportunities presented themselves for upward mobility. As has been suggested, "While the segmented assimilation model sees assimilation into native minority status as a path toward downward mobility, our study reveals that being classified as a native minority can also provide access to institutional supports that promote success. The civil rights movement, along with the minority advancement in mainstream institutions, has created a legacy of opportunity for new members of old minority groups."[29]

Several African Guyanese have benefited from opportunities to advance educationally, in government and in the business sector. There is more research needed to pinpoint the numbers and the skills that left the Brooklyn 'enclave' after their initial success to live in the 'outer boroughs' and in the wider metropolitan areas of New Jersey and Connecticut.[30]

Guyanese have, without much effort, tried to live in certain communities they consider healthy environments for their families. However, they often find themselves in the dilemma of being 'black in America since many of the earlier African Guyanese migrants were from the 'middle class', they often sought out areas where there was low crime, better schools and generally safer streets. Mary Waters, in some of her interviews with Guyanese and West Indian parents, highlights the problem of first generation residents moving to 'better' areas, only to find whites leaving and their less well behaved compatriots "following them" and bringing the neighborhood down with loud music and 'hanging out'. Crown Heights (where there is a concentration of Guyanese), she said, was one of few successful anomalous situations by sheer unintended consequences; despite some of the troubles between Hasidic Jews and Blacks remaining or re-entering Crown Heights, there is greater safety in this now integrated neighborhood.[31]

One of these neighborhoods where upwardly mobile African Guyanese (and Jamaicans) in Brooklyn moved was Flatlands-Canarsie, which saw a tripling of the Guyanese population between 1990 and 2000.[32] Several of the more successful moved out of Brooklyn altogether to even more expensive areas in Queens, such as Cambria Heights-St.Albans-Rochdale and Springfield Gardens-Laurelton-Rosedale. [33]

Both white Americans and African West Indians and Guyanese feel that African Americans are less ambitious and more sensitive to racism than they are. African Guyanese generally feel, like other

West Indians, more confidence in their capabilities and abilities to resist racism than those born into the African American experience. Waters quotes C L R James as explaining why he was a successful person: *"It was because I was from the Caribbean (where) we blacks form a majority. So that our attitude is that things can happen if we will only do it. That's why we are able to go abroad and take part; we have a feeling that we are not defeated in any way."*[34] Whether numerically superior or not, the experience of running one's own affairs, or seeing all levels of achievement in your own society by people looking like you, is a confidence booster.[35] In a society where racism against American Blacks has "changed from a caste system to a subtle intersection of past discrimination, class and race interactions",[36] West Indian and Guyanese Blacks find that "remaining an immigrant means higher status because becoming American for West Indians entails becoming black American—something that they perceive as downward mobility."[37]

African Guyanese, however, generally live in areas that are predominantly Black. Black is used generically to embrace other non-Hispanic Caribbean ethnicities as well as African Americans. While there are cultural advantages of 'identity' in living deeply 'within the culture', surrounded by one's food, music and 'language', there is the reality of racism in America, directly affecting all Blacks, based solely on their color. From the 'Stop and Frisk' practice that targets Blacks and Hispanics disproportionately[38] to the constant scrutiny while shopping in non-black areas, to on-the job, face to face racism, Guyanese Blacks are forced to distance themselves from the negative (and often unfair) stereotypes associated with Black Americans; and to create and confirm their own stereotypes of hard work, saving, owning property and being ambitious.[39] Especially because the new Caribbean immigrant who takes a low paying service job has a good chance of being a female head of household or a less well credentialed man, they have formed coping mechanisms to deal with prejudice from Black Americans as well as whites.[40] Remarkably, in a conversation with two friends—a Grenadian and a Guyanese—about ignoring interpersonal racism in the workplace and focusing on their mission of self-improvement—they both gave almost verbatim answers and attitudes to both whites and African Americans respectively, as did several of Mary Water's respondents.[41]

But it is with their children that first generation immigrants have difficulties. Whether still here as illegal immigrants, having legal status or recently naturalized, Guyanese face the problem of how to 'hold on to their children' in a society where parental control is limited by long working hours, lack of community oversight, weak disciplinary systems and not having caretaker services in the home or neighborhood.[42] Family reunification has accounted for significant enough numbers of older males and females in the Guyanese population to see a possible amelioration of this problem.[43]

The difficulty, though, is with sending children to schools with poor disciplinary systems and different standards than those in the Caribbean for teacher respect and attendance. First generation immigrants see education as the means to positively change one's intergenerational status and, therefore, take schooling seriously. Guyanese established two highly regarded private schools—in Brooklyn and in Newark, New Jersey - utilizing several experienced or/and retired teachers from Guyana. There was competition to gain entry because of their strict discipline and high academic standards. However, both failed for assorted reasons.[44]

The 2000 Census shows that first generation West Indians, including Guyanese, are the most highly segregated geographically.[45] This first generation "endows their children with differing amounts of cultural and social capital (ethnic networks and values) and different opportunity structures, resulting in several distinct paths toward incorporation."[46] The choices for the second generation who live among American Blacks (or Latinos) and accept these 'gifts' follow either the "linear ethnicity" of assimilation into a native white ethnic category, or "segmented assimilation" into a retained immigrant identity that distinguishes them from American Blacks or Latinos." Those who choose to "become American" and embrace the values of their local ghettos will suffer discrimination, limited opportunities; and will develop *oppositional* identities becoming rebellious or questioning the value of education.[47] Those who choose segmented assimilation tend to do better because they can take advantage of networks and follow positive community role models.[48]

One of the racist traps into which African Guyanese can fall involuntarily is becoming entangled in the law enforcement, incarceration boondoggle. Table 9.5 below is a list of Guyanese deported from the United States from 2001 to 2010. Apart from the pervasive and pernicious 'stop and frisk' policy that not only demeans youths, there are other ready means of propelling youths into some aspect of the juvenile, probationary or prison system in this country. As Michelle Alexander so persuasively argues, the incarceration of blacks in particular and then denying them many of their citizenship rights – voting, jury, educational loans, housing as well as insidious job denials – has created and perpetuates an underclass that is structured and racist.[49]

TABLE 9.5 Deportation of Guyanese from the United States: 2001-2010

Category	2001	2002	2003	2004
Total Deportations	134	321	356	388
Criminal	43	237	182	230
Non-Criminal	91	84	174	158
Percentage Criminal	32.09%	73.83%	51.12%	59.28%

Category	2005	2006	2007	2008
Total Deportations	396	289	293	284
Criminal	255	174	191	188
Non-Criminal	141	115	102	96
Percentage Criminal	64.39%	60.21%	65.19%	66.20%

TABLE 9.5
Deportation of Guyanese from the United States: 2001-2010

Category	2009	2010	Total
Total Deportations	305	219	2985
Criminal	216	166	1882
Non-Criminal	89	53	1103
Percentage Criminal	70.82%	75.80%	63.05%

Source: Compiled from 2010 Yearbook of Immigration Statistics; Office of Immigration Statistics; Homeland Security

Indo-Guyanese in New York City

By and large, for Indo-Guyanese, the reality is not the same as Afro-Guyanese for the first generation immigrants, but the outcomes are not too dissimilar for the second generation. Much like the inducements after the expiration of indentured contracts in British Guiana, there was much serendipity associated with the influx of Indo-Guyanese into New York City, and mainly into Queens, particularly into Southwest Queens, and even more specifically, into the Richmond Hill, South Ozone Park and Woodhaven-Ozone Park neighborhoods.[50] Although this area requires further detailed research, it was the parlous state of the sugar industry that prompted the first major venturing out of Guyana for Indian Guyanese. Labor unrest and lack of capitalization in the 1980s had driven mainly Indian Guyanese cane cutters to the Caribbean islands where pay and opportunities were higher.[iii] Another push factor was the projected ending of the European Union (EU) Generalized System of Preferences (GSP). Even though there would be a flurry of production utilizing the period of higher prices and preferences (using EU-affiliated countries in the region, mainly Aruba and Suriname), it was clear that from 1997, the banana, sugar and rice industries in the Caribbean would not be able to export to the EU competitively in an open market.[iv] Many small islands in the Caribbean were forced out of sugar and banana exports immediately. Guyana's sugar and rice industries are still struggling to find the right production and marketing mix but many of the workers and small farmers might have joined the heavy migration exodus into Queens, New York City.

Interestingly, most of the Guyanese living directly across Guyana's eastern and western borders are Indians. Indian farmers are major contributors to the rice industry in the Nickerie region of Surinam, Guyana's eastern neighbor; similarly, the Indian population on the Esssequibo Coast of Guyana provided the sometimes itinerant settlements of Guyanese in the border towns of Puerto Ordaz and San Felix in Venezuela. The accelerating forces of rapid and lower costs of communication and transportation along with the easily disseminated information on opportunities for work and freedom, have created *"incentives for migration that have been spurred by the buildup of population pressure in agricultural regions with only limited capacity for additional labor absorption."*[51]

New York City suffered devastating depopulation in the 1970s (over 800,000) and 1980s (NYC government had taken ownership of over 60,000 vacant buildings and 40,000 units in occupied and semi-occupied apartment buildings) due to suburbanization, high taxes, reduced subsidies and rampant crime. One of these depressed areas was the Irish-Italian Richmond Hill in Southwest Queens which saw a massive influx of Indian Guyanese who were able to capitalize on an eclectic mix of the 100 programs of Mayor Koch's 1985 inspired loan facilitation, property tax abatements and other incentives for rehabilitating and renewing the housing stock of the city.[52]

A thriving enclave of Indian Guyanese, with some Indo-Trinidadian and other East Asian migrants, made the Richmond Hill-Ozone Park area one of new businesses that soon attracted Guyanese to its streets of Asian and Guyanese food smells, music and nostalgia. There have been several articles written in the New York Times on the benefits and the cultural developments in the enclave.[53] There have also been features on local as well as citywide radio [54] But the tensions of identity in the new mix of Indianness have also been highlighted in the New York Times.[55]

While African Guyanese face identity issues over color racism and trying to separate themselves from the African-American stigmatization and discrimination, Indian Guyanese face discrimination and ethnic distancing from East Asian groups. In the aftermath of the destruction of the World Trade Center buildings in September 2001, Muslims and East Asians in general were treated with suspicion and faced discrimination and even violence. Many darker skinned Guyanese Indians shaved their heads and began wearing 'hoodies' and caps in order to pass as blacks. However, when Guyanese with Muslim names made the headlines with a concocted alleged attempt to bomb facilities at JFK International Airport,[56] Indian Guyanese were quick to point out that those arrested were African and not Indian Guyanese, so as to stave off unwanted negative attention to their group. The lack of education on ethnicity and cultures among the general American public make incidents involving Sikhs, Afghans, Bangladeshis, Indians, Muslims and any Asian looking persons, an attack on all members of all groups. There was also the recent scandal that showed unwarranted surveillance of Muslims in New York and Newark, New Jersey.[57]

However, within the enclave itself, there has been the struggle for an Indian Guyanese ethnic identity. Solidly sub-continent Indian in their cultural and religious orientation in Guyana, notwithstanding the different philosophical and ritual emphases within Hindu and Muslim practices, there has been an attempt to recreate that unifying theme in Richmond Hill. As Frankie Ramadar points out, *"Their religious affiliations were primarily Hinduism and Islam, and Christianity to a lesser extent. In Queens, they have literally re-established the East Indian sub-culture. They are busy setting up temples, mandirs, mosques and Christian churches."*[58]

East Asians find similarities and purpose in the religious celebrations of Phagwah and Deepavali that Guyanese Indians perform but there is no affinity in execution as the East Asians consider the Guyanese rituals obsolete and quaint. With few Guyanese Indians having any ability to speak any of the Indian languages, this cultural identifier of indentureship serves to further segregate Indian Guyanese from their East Asian counterparts.[59] Though they listen and dance to Indian music and wear Indian dress on occasion, these trappings are also sources of tension between enclave groups and generations. Narmala Halstead has a very interesting piece on contradictions and assimilative difficulties that challenge the dominance of men and the hold of tradition on women and youth in the enclave. He also highlights the role of the holy men and men who do not 'behave properly'[60] Lear Matthews has hinted at mental health problems among Guyanese Indians and David A Baptiste has written on the delicacy of treatment modalities among East Asians.[61]

There is still that feeling of not quite fitting in. The strain of wanting to be so many things is expressed poignantly by Arnold Itwaru, *"We cannot go with the flow in these domains within the Diaspora, though many of us seek this impossibility. In a way this consuming desire is understandable, for we exist in a double outsidership. We do not belong here, and we do not belong there in the region of our birth. There, emotively referred to as "home" is a nostalgic hankering, a need for rootedness in an uprooted reality, a place we were born in, even grew up in, but to which we have now become strangers. We visit there. We return here where we do not and cannot belong, where despite the speeches, the victims never change..."*[62]

This need to not become part of the Creole culture of the Caribbean (and by extension African) culture was well expressed by the learned and respected Swami Aksharananda in a newspaper interview, when asked a question on the dangers (raised by a minister of government in Trinidad and Tobago) of the "rum and chutney culture"[63] to Hinduism and Indians in Guyana: *"We have to appreciate that Indian and Hindu culture has to survive in a wider "Guyanese" culture. Until recently, the official, approved culture of our national institutions has excluded Indian forms."* He went on to compare the annual Guyanese Mashramani celebrations as wholesale copy of the Trinidad Carnival, which was all about "wining down, jamming and drinking" he claimed.[64] He might have been more charitable to earlier attempts by the "approved culture" to incorporate Indian holy days into the national holiday calendar and have all other members attempt to join in expressing solidarity during these celebrations.

This is the conundrum of identity faced by Indian Guyanese in the New York area. For though outsiders see a monolithic Indian culture in the Caribbean, that is not the case, based on the disparate cultural origins and religions (among Hindus, Muslims and Christians). There are even differences between Guyanese and Trinidadian Indians and especially between Indian Indians and Caribbean

Indians. Halstead also deals with the question of assimilation into the local American culture and the difficulty of retaining 'authentic' home grown cultural standards, for the children and the women.[65]

As Roopram Ramharack says feelingly, *"Let me tell you who I am. I am an Indo-Guyanese – plain and simple. Always was and always will be. It says everything about me: it announces my culture, my ancestry and my country, which, of course, are the most definitive descriptors about me. I cannot call myself just Guyanese because there are many kinds of Guyanese. I cannot call myself Indian because there are many kinds of these too. Indo-Guyanese says it all. . . The slogan "One People, One Nation, One Destiny" had the effect of marginalizing and DeIndianizing us. Now, some of our friends and detractors are trying to dump us in another pool – the IndoCaribbean pool. . . again, we will be diluted and lost. . . I cannot understand how we can become citizens of the United States, live here permanently and still be content with being second class, in the periphery, in the margin. I demand to be treated as a first class citizen at school, at work, in the subway or in the park."*[66]

Clearly, there is much more work to be done in establishing movement into and out of the enclave, the stresses of living within the group, educational difficulties, and social and racial coping mechanisms. Attempts are being made to reconcile differences among the different East Asian communities for communal good – commerce, census and political benefits and making the best of their immigrant status in the United States.[67] The Richmond Hill community is raising awareness to demand changes to the Census to allow for choices that will bring resources and political clout to the representative ethnic groups.[68]

While the natural tendency is for immigrant groups to move away from the initial enclave as their educational levels and earning power increase, long periods of slow economic growth can lead to a piling up of second generation in the enclave. While this can assist with transmitting and retaining cultural differences, it also benefits political networks of patronage and redistribution.[69] Enclaves also become easy prey for unscrupulous exploitation, especially in the political and real estate fields. Hundreds of Guyanese in the Queens area were victims of a $50 million mortgage fraud perpetrated by Edul Ahmad, a fellow Guyanese broker.[70] And Albert Baldeo, a Guyanese attorney and political prospect, who had stepped down in 2008 [71] to facilitate another Democratic candidate's City Council election (to whom he had narrowly lost previously) was indicted on corruption charges in October 2012.[72]

Manifestations of Transnationalism in the Guyanese Community

In an excellent summary of the theoretical discussions of migration and an appeal for a recognition of transmigration as a different conception of migration, Hirschman et al explore not only the facility of movement and communication but places status in the home country as against discrimination and loss of identity in the receiving country, among the reasons why this new trend is in need of more scholarly research.[73] Transnational migrants extend networks across international borders, with migrants moving into new physical space but maintaining ties with their countries of birth through remittances in cash and kind, frequent conversations, business arrangements and travel home for various periods of time for vacations or longer periods with friends and relatives.[74]

Several countries are reaping optimum benefits from their Diasporal communities. In 2010, $325 Billion were remitted to developing countries, more than 10% of their overall GDP and more than aid flows.[75] The World Bank report estimates that Guyana received $253 million in remittances in 2009 (in 2010, it was estimated at $280 million), some 17% of GDP.[76] However, Clive Thomas argues that the annual 40% increase in remittances from 2000 is not reflected in the weak economic performances of the sending economies and suggests criminal transferences.[77] This inference is reasonable since there are daily reports of drugs (and recently precious minerals—gold) being found at ports in Guyana or sourced from Guyana.[78]

The importance of these remittances to political parties and to charitable ventures in Guyana has not been overlooked by the political parties and the government. Aubrey Bonnet has some interesting views on the several uses that organized remittances might have on the Guyanese economy.[79] Each of the political parties in Guyana has offered suggestions ranging from representation in the parliament to special investment schemes. More recently, the Government of Guyana held a preliminary, co-sponsored launch of a registration exercise for Diaspora skills.[80] There is widespread agreement that the value of remittances is much higher, especially as it is well known that other unofficial means are used to deliver goods and services to relatives, organizations and friends. The percentage of contribution to GDP might also, therefore, be much higher.

Some of the persons to whom remittances might be sent are deportees, whose presence became a source of concern since their numbers (especially those with criminal convictions) increased significantly over the years. Over the period 2001-2010, there were 2,985 Guyanese deportees, of whom 1,882 (or 63%) were criminal deportations.[81]

Almost mirroring the great efforts to buy and build their villages after emancipation, African Guyanese in New York belong to a plethora of Hometown Associations (HTAs) which serve several purposes that include: maintaining identity with the village; providing financial support for needy children and the elderly; and supplying infrastructural support, especially for schools and recreation centers. Many other Guyanese HTAs also reflect a close affinity to and provide assistance for their churches, former places of work and their schools.[82] Manuel Orozoco has done substantial work on Caribbean HTAs, including Guyanese HTAs. There is useful information on remittance sending outlets and telephone calls but there is also a need for a more comprehensive study on HTAs, who they represent, their annual transfers and the causes to which they donate.[83] It would be useful to compare HTAs in the Indian and African Guyanese communities based on a hypothesis that Africans focus on villages and places of earlier employment wile Indians focus on religious institutions and religion-based schools.

CONCLUSION

Kirschman et al have argued for greater emphasis on long-term outcomes of the international migration on both the receiving societies and on the immigrants and their descendants. Longer time horizons of 50 years assess the adjustments and impacts of the immigration process rather than the policy issues and social problems after a shorter period of say five years.[84] Bryce-Laporte also calls for in-depth probing of Caribbean immigrants and the stories they have to tell of the immigration journey.[85]

Similarly, there is a need to institute the initiative between Caribbean governments and International Migration Organizations to register skills and initiate research to answer the larger emigration and Diasporal questions: What are the migration push/pull factors; what forces influence emigration; what are the conditions under which Guyanese and other Caribbean immigrants live abroad and how have they fared; what is the level of involvement in the cultural and political life of their adopted and home countries; the amount, frequency and recipients of remittances; what conditions would facilitate remigration or investment; what should be the political involvement in the adopted and home countries; how often and for how long do they visit the home country.

If the potentially disastrous outflow of immigration is to be staunched, as well as an attempt to attract especially talented Guyanese back home, there must be appeals to national unity and the adoption of a culture of good governance. More research is needed to quantify all relevant data on Guyanese in New York City and elsewhere in

North America. A separate exercise needs to be undertaken in the Caribbean and countries neighboring Guyana. This scholarly effort needs official support. Projections of loss of talent and youth and women from Guyana have political consequences as well as potentially dire economic and security impacts. Only with a joint effort to encourage positive ethnic and political discourse will Guyanese, at home and in the Diaspora, be able to exploit the bounties of a country rich in every aspect.

Guyanese have gained a reputation for hard work and entrepreneurship. Guyanese are above the average New York City household income, above its labor participation rate and many of its nationals have done well in academia, politics, business and public service. There was a well-publicized story of over 2,000 Guyanese Indians being targeted and specially recruited by the Mayor of Schenectady 10 years ago to save his 'failed city' that had lost its industrial base and was losing its population rapidly. In a reprise of land for retention after indentureship in Guyana, houses in the city were sold by Guyanese real estate agents at subsidized prices (for as little as one dollar), much to the irritation of the locals. There is a need to follow up.[86]

A partnership involving government, academic and non-governmental funding can launch a comprehensive exploratory effort to investigate the condition of the Guyanese Diaspora with a view to making sensible policy at both sides of the transnational divide.

Acknowledgments

I would like to acknowledge the assistance provided by Dr. Joe Salvo; Ms. Gaskin of the US Census Bureau Office, New York City; the Newark Public Library for research material; June Persaud for printing and acquiring research material and Dr. Lear Matthews for his supply of research materials, understanding and his endless patience. I also thank all my children for heightening my interest in the transnational experience, and particularly my teenage son for keeping me energized with his easy but questioning grasp of the transnational idea; they are each in different stages of the process.

NOTES

i. See Mangru, ibid and Rodney, P 86; 110-112; 155. Mangru, Basdeo, "Indians in Guyana," Self Published, March 1999.

ii. United Nations Department of Economic and Social Affairs/Population Division. World Population Prospects: The 2010, Volume II: Demographic Profiles

iii. Ferguson, ibid p 346

iv. See www. Eclac.org/portofspain/noticias/paginas/2/9792/ECLAC IB6

1. Rodney, Walter. "*A History of the Guyanese Working People, 1881-1905.*" The Johns Hopkins University Press, 1981, see Chapter 1 and p 189 and Conclusion.

2. Ferguson, Tyrone. "To Survive Sensibly or to Court Heroic Death: Management of Guyana's Political Economy 1965-1985." Public Affairs Consulting Enterprise, Georgetown 1999. Ch.7.

3. Pellegrino, Adela. "*Trends in International Migration in Latin America and the Caribbean.*" UNESCO 2000, Blackwell Publishers, p 404.

4. Pellegrino, p 404.

5. Guyana Bureau of Statistics, 2012. Population and Housing Census, Chapter 1, National Population Trends.

6. Guyana Bureau of Statistics, ibid Table 1.5.

7. Sassen, Saskia, *Whose City is It? Globalization and the Formation of the New Claims; Lechner and Boli, ed., The Globalization Reader,* p 74: Blackwell Publishers, Massachusetts, 2000.

8. Waters, Mary. "*Black Identities: West Indian Immigrant Dreams and American Realities.*" Harvard University Press, 1999.

9. Karapin, Roger. "The Politics of Immigration Control in Britain and Germany: Subnational Politicians and Social Movements." Comparative Politics, Vol 31, No.4 (July 1999), pp 423-444; Published by Ph.D. Program in Political Science of the City University of New York, p428.

10. Department of Manpower and Immigration, Canada, Immigration Division, Ottawa. Citizen and Immigration Statistics from 1966-1996, Minister of Public Works and Government, Canada 1999.

11. Pellegrino, ibid Figure 2 p 404.

12. Ratha, Dilip et al. The Migration and Remittances Handbook 2011, p 9.

13. Bryce-Laporte, Roy Simon. "Introduction: New York City and the New Caribbean Immigration: A Contextual Statement." International Migration Review, Vol.13. No.2. Special Issue: International Migration in Latin America (Summer, 1979) pp.214-234. See p 215. The legislation (called the Hart-Celler Act, named for the sponsor Senator Phillip

Hart and the proposer Rep Emanuel Celler) was passed as result of the Civil Rights upheaval in the USA and President Johnson signed the bill at the foot of the Statue of Liberty in a symbolic gesture.

14. Camarota, Steven A. Center for Immigration Studies, Immigrants in the United States, 2010, A Profile of America's Foreign-Born Population.
15. Camarota, Steven. Ibid. See Table 3
16. Canada had made special agreements with Jamaica, Trinidad and Tobago and Guyana to send temporary workers. See Pellegrino, ibid p 6.
17. New York City Department of City Planning. "The Newest New Yorkers 2000, Immigrant New York in the New Millennium."
18. Thomas, Kevin, ibid.
19. Camarota, Steven A. Center for Immigration Studies, Immigrants in the United States, 2010, A Profile of America's Foreign-Born Population.
20. New York City Department of City Planning, *"The Newest New Yorkers 2000, Immigrant New York in the New Millennium."* P 11.
21. New York City Department of City Planning, *"The Newest New Yorkers 2000, Immigrant New York in the New Millennium."* P 13, See Table 2-3.
22. Information kindly provided by Joe Salvo of the Department of City Planning, NYC.
23. NYC Dept of Planning ibid, Appendix 5 Table 9.
24. The Newest New Yorkers, 2000, ibid. Unless equivalency is established several Guyanese are required to pass the GED to show high school level training. See also The Migration and Remittances Handbook, 2011."
25. The Newest New Yorkers, 2000, ibid.
26. See Table ...consolidated from US Census Bureau, Fact Finder, 2006-2010. American Community Survey Selected Population Tables.
27. Newest New Yorkers, p 152; pp 166-168.
28. Ibid.
29. Kasinitz, Phillip; Mollenkopf, John; Waters, Mary C." *Becoming American/Becoming New Yorkers: Immigrant Incorporation in a Majority Minority City."* The International Migration Review, Winter 2002, p 1032. See also Douthat, Ross, *"A Little Bit Indian."* Op Ed. NYT Sunday Review, May 19, 2012.
30. A study of New Jersey in particular is indicated. Anecdotally, several Guyanese in the professional fields still speak nostalgically of the "days in Brooklyn." However, there is a new wave of out-migration of lower educational and economic 'classes' who seem to be coming to New Jersey to acquire lower cost housing.

31. Waters, Mary C. Ibid, p251.
32. Newest New Yorkers ,2000, p 96.
33. Ibid, p 80. See also Table 9.
34. Waters. Ibid, p 100.
35. Conversation(s) with Herman Ferguson, who lived in Guyana as an 'exile'. He was fascinated, notwithstanding his militant black nationalist posture in New York, to see black people totally in charge of all aspects of a society. See his book, *An Unlikely Warrior* (in Collaboration with his wife Iyaluua), Black Classic Press 2011.
36. Waters. Ibid, p 42.
37. Ibid. p 12.
38. Grynbaum, Michael M and Connelly, Marjorie. New York Times, "Majority in City See Police Dept. As favoring Whites, a Poll Finds." August 21, 2012, Pages A1, 16 and 17.
39. Waters. Ibid, pp 118-139.
40. Waters. ibid, Ch. 5
41. Waters, Ibid, Ch 5.
42. Waters. Ibid, pp. 203-210.
43. 2006-2010 ACS Selected Population Tables – Sex by Age by Employment Status for the Population 16 Years and Over.
44. The two schools were The People's Cathedral School of Brooklyn, New York and Chad Academy in Newark, Essex County, New Jersey.
45. Kasinitz, Mollenkopf and Waters. Ibid, p 1027.
46. Ibid, p 1030.
47. Ibid, p 1031. Waters (1999) explains Ogbu's term *'oppositional identities'* as involuntary minorities come largely to define themselves in their core identities in terms of their opposition to the dominant group. For blacks it means not being 'white'. p 142.
48. Kasinitz et al, ibid. And Waters (1999) p 196.
49. Alexander, Michelle. *"The New Jim Crow: Mass Incarceration in the Age of Colorblindness."* New Press, New York, 2010.
50. Newest New Yorkers 2000, ibid, Executive Summary, p xiii.
51. Hirschman, Charles; Kasinitz, Philip and DeWind, Josh. "The Handbook of International Migration: The American Experience." Russell Sage Foundation, New York. p 8.
52. Furman Center for Real Estate and Urban Policy, New York University. *"Housing Policy in New York City: A Brief History, Working Paper 06-01"*.
53. Kilgannon, Corey. *"India in Queens, With a Caribbean Accent."* The New York Times, May 24, 2009.

CHAPTER NINE

54. The Brian Lehrer Show: *"The New Littles: Guyanans, Italians and a Map."* September 16, 2011. Despite the title, the residents were referred to as Guyanese.
55. See NYT articles Chan, Eric. *"NEIGHBORHOOD REPORT: RICHMOND HILL; For Indians Born Far Apart, Bridges of Sing and Sugar Cane"*, December 5, 2004 and Berger, Joseph. *"Indian, Twice removed; Guyanese Immigrants Cautious About Being Labeled."* December 17, 2004.
56. Sulzberger, A.G. "2 Men Convicted in Kennedy Airport Plot." NYT, August 2, 2010.
57. Human Rights Watch, News Release March 20, 2012.
58. Ramadar, Frankie B. First Generation Caribbean East Indian Americans and Voluntary Community Participation, pp 140-141; Tilokie, Depoo, ed. *"The East Indian Diaspora: 150 years of Survival, Contributions and Achievements"*; Asian American Center, 1993.
59. Baksh-Riches, Sabrina. Ibid, pp 66-68.
60. Halstead, Narmala. (2012) *"East Indians as Familiars and Partial Others in New York."* History and Anthropology, 23:1, 149:169.
61. See Matthews, Lear. "Mental Health Problems among Caribbean Immigrants in New York: Implications for Intervention among East Indians." Pp 129-135 Tilokie, Dipoo op cit 1993. Also Baptiste, David A. *"Family Therapy with East Indian Families Raising Children in the United States: Parental Concerns, Therapeutic Issues and Recommendations."* Contemporary Family Therapy 27 (3) September 2006.
62. Itwaru, Arnold H. *Self as Other in the Diaspora,* pp 145–149. Tilokie, Depoo, ed, ibid.
63. Rum is the alcoholic beverage produced from sugar cane and widely consumed in the Caribbean. Chutney is the name given to the 'fusion' of Indian and Soca music that is the syncretic expression of the Indian coming to terms with his twin identity of being Indian in a Caribbean where African rhythms dominate. Originally sung by Indians in both Indian and English versions, it incorporates a Soca calypso beat and lyrics with Indian movie song and movements (some say lewd gyrations). Much like the Bangladeshi *bhangra*, it has become so popular that separate annual competitions are held.
64. Guyana Times International Interview (conclusion) with Swami Aksharananda, Week Ending November 25, 2012.
65. Halstead. Ibid p 151.
66. Ramharack, Roopram, *"A Guyana Perspective":* Cedar Publishing, 1998.
67. Baksh-Riches. Ibid, pp 79-82. See also Chan, NYT ibid above.
68. Koplowitz, Howard. *"Richmond Hill Readies for Census."* New York Post. February 11, 2010.

69. Hirschman et al. Ibid, p 132.
70. Ellick, Adam E., *"Queens Broker is Accused of Bringing Immigrants' Ruin."* NYT January 8, 2012
71. Hicks, Jonathan P., *"Democrat Withdraws From Race in Queens."* NYT August 23, 2008.
72. See all the NYC dailies of October 24, 2012.
73. Hirschman et al. *"Theories and Concepts of International Migration."* The Handbook of International Migration: The American Experience. Ibid, p 15 .
74. Ibid.
75. Dilip, Ratha, The Remittances Handbook 2011, ibid.
76. Ibid. Pp 14 and 132.
77. Thomas, Clive Y. "Guyana: Economic Performance and Outlook (The Recent Scramble for Resources) April 2012 Paper". Excerpted from articles written in 2011.
75. Stabroek News Newspaper - Headline Stories, December 4, 2012.
79. Bonnet, Aubrey. *"The West Indian Diaspora to the USA: Remittances and Development of the Homeland."* The Forum on Public Policy. 2006
80. Launch of the Diaspora Project, with the International Organization for Migration, organized by the Consulate of Guyana, held at the Manhattan Marriot Hotel on September 26, 2012. The main speaker was the President of Guyana.
81. Compiled from the 2010 Yearbook of Immigration Statistics, Office of Immigration Statistics, Homeland Security.
82. Bonnett, op cit p 11.
83. Orozco, Manuel. *"Remitting Back Home and Supporting the Homeland: The Guyanese Community in the US."* Inter-American Dialogue; Working Paper Commissioned for USAID GEO Project, January 2003.
84. Hirschman, Charles et al. Introduction p 8.
85. Bryce-Laporte, Roy, op cit, p 230.
86. Kershaw, Sarah. "For Schenectady, A Guyanese Strategy; Mayor Goes All Out to Encourage a Wave of Hardworking Immigrants." New York Times, July 26, 2002.

CHAPTER NINE
List of Figures and Tables

Figure 9.1: Compiled from Canadian Manpower and Immigration Statistics Annual Report data 1966-1996

Figure 9.2: Trends in International Migration in Latin America and the Caribbean. UNESCO 2000.

Table 9.1: Guyanese Arrivals in the United States. The Center for Immigration Studies.

Table 9.2: Dispersion of Guyanese in New York City by Borough. Compiled from The newest New Yorkers, 2000. New York City Department of city Planning. population Division.

Table 9.3: Levels of Guyanese Household Earnings: New York city 2000. US Census Bureau, Fact Finder, 2001- 2010.

Table 9.4: Labor Force Participation. New York City Department of City Planning. Population Division.

Table 9.5: Guyanese deportees from the United States: 2000--2010. Yearbook of International Statistics. Office of Homeland Security.

Bibliography

American Community Survey (ACS); Selected Population Tables, 2001-2006. US Census, Fact Finder.

Alexander, Michelle. *The New Jim Crow: Mass Incarceration in the Age of Colorblindness.* New Press, New York, 2010.

Alleyne, Frederick, "*Barbadian Migration to British Guiana, 1840-1960; The Search for El Dorado.*"

Baksh-Riches, "A History of Indo-Guyanese Identity from India to Guyana to Richmond Hill, New York." *MA Thesis*. Department of History, University of Utah. May 2011.

Baptiste, David A. "Family Therapy with East Indian Families Raising Children in the United States: Parental Concerns, Therapeutic Issues and Recommendations." *Contemporary Family Therapy* 27 (3) September 2006.

Birbalsingh, Frank. *From Pillar to Post.* Tsar Publications 1997.

Bonnett, Aubrey. "The West Indian Diaspora to the USA: Remittances and Development of the Homeland." *The Forum on Public Policy.* 2006.

Bryce-Laporte, Roy Simon, "Introduction: New York City and the New Caribbean Immigration: A Contextual Statement," *International Migration Review, Vol.13. No.2.* Special Issue: International Migration in Latin America (Summer, 1979).

Camarota, Steven A, "Immigrants in the United States, 2010, A Profile of America's Foreign-Born Population". *Center for Immigration Studies.*

Department of Manpower and Immigration, Canada, Immigration Division, Ottawa, Citizen and Immigration Statistics from 1966-1996.

Dev, Ravi, Guest Editorial, *Caribbean New Yorker;* May 3, 2002, p 3.

Eclac.org/portofspain/noticias/paginas/2/9792/ECLAC IB6.

Ellick, Adam E "Queens Broker is Accused of Bringing Immigrants Ruin." *NYT* January 8, 2012.

Ferguson, Tyrone, "To Survive Sensibly or to Court Heroic Death: Management of Guyana's Political Economy 1965-1985." *Public Affairs Consulting Enterprise, Georgetown 1999.*

Granger, David A, "National Defence: A Brief History of the Guyana Defence Force 1965-2005." *Free Press,* Georgetown, 2005.

Grynbaum, Michael M. and Connelly, Marjorie, "Majority in City See Police Dept. as favoring Whites, a Poll Finds." *The New York Times.* August 21, 2012.

Guyana Bureau of Statistics, 2012 Population and Housing Census.

Guyana Times International Interview (conclusion) with Swami Aksharananda, Week Ending November 25, 2012.

Halstead, Narmala. (2012) "East Indians as Familiars and Partial Others in New York," *History and Anthropology,* 23:1.

Harper, Elsa and Matthews, Paula. "When We Grew Up in the Land of the Mighty Roraima." *Xlibris Corp* 2007.

Hicks, Jonathan P., *"Democrat Withdraws From Race in Queens."* NYT August 23, 2008.

Hirschman, Charles; Kasinitz, Philip and DeWind, Josh. *The Handbook of International Migration: The American Experience.* Russell Sage Foundation, New York.

Itwaru, Arnold H. (1993). "Self as Other in the Diaspora". *D. Tilokie (Ed.) The East Indian Diaspora: 150 Years of Survival, Contributions and Achievements. Asian American Center, pp 145-149.*

Jagan, Cheddi. (1993). Keynote Address. *D. Tilokie (Ed.) The East Indian Diaspora: 150 Years of Survival, Contributions and Achievements. Asian American Center, pp 13-31.*

Karapin, Roger, "The Politics of Immigration Control in Britain and Germany: Subnational Politicians and Social Movements." *Comparative Politics,* Vol 31, No.4 (July 1999), pp 423-444; Published by Ph.D. Program in Political Science of the City University of New York.

Kasinitz, Phillip; Mollenkopf, John; Waters, Mary C. "Becoming American/Becoming New Yorkers: Immigrant Incorporation in a Majority Minority City." *The International Migration Review,* Winter 2002.

Kershaw, Sarah. "For Schenectady, A Guyanese Strategy; Mayor Goes All Out to Encourage a Wave of Hardworking Immigrants." *New York Times,* July 26, 2002.

Kilgannon, Corey, "India in Queens, With a Caribbean Accent." *The New York Times,* May 24, 2009.

Koplowitz, Howard. "Richmond Hill Readies for Census." *The New York Post.* February 11, 2010.

Majeed, Halim. *Forbes Burnham: National Reconciliation and National Unity 1984-1985.* Global Communications Publishing. New York 2005.

Mangru, Basdeo (1993). "Severing the Bond: The Migration of Indian Indentured Labor Overseas". *D. Tilokie (Ed.) The East Indian Diaspora: 150 Years of Survival, Contributions and Achievements. Asian American Center, pp 43-61.*

Mangru, Basdeo, "Indians in Guyana," Self Published, March 1999.

Matthews, Lear (1993). "Mental Health Problems Among Caribbean Immigrants in New York: Implications for Intervention with East Indians". *D. Tilokie (Ed.) The East Indian Diaspora: 150 Years of Survival, Contributions and Achievements. Asian American Center, pp*

129-135.

New York City Department of City Planning, "The Newest New Yorkers 2000, Immigrant New York in the New Millennium."

Office of Immigration Statistics, Homeland Security, 2010 Yearbook of Immigration Statistics.

Orozco, Manuel. "Remitting Back Home and Supporting the Homeland: The Guyanese Community in the US." Inter-American Dialogue; Working Paper Commissioned for US AID GEO Project. January 2003.

Pellegrino, Adela, "Trends in International Migration in Latin America and the Caribbean" *UNESCO* 2000. Blackwell Publishers.

Perreira, Joseph. "Living My Dreams." With Katherine Atkinson, Self Published 2010.

Ramadar, Frankie B. (1993). "First Generation Caribbean East Indian Americans and Voluntary Community Participation". *D. Tilokie (Ed.) The East Indian Diaspora: 150 Years of Survival, Contributions and Achievements. Asian American Center, pp 105-141.*

Ramharack, Roopram, *A Guyana Perspective.* Cedar Publishing, 1998.

Ratha, Dilip; Mohapatra, Sanket and Silwal, Ani compiled "The Migration and Remittances Handbook 2011", Second Edition. *Migration and Remittances Unit*, World Bank.

Rodney, Walter *A History of the Guyanese Working people, 1881-1905.* The Johns Hopkins University Press, 1981.

Sassen, Saskia, "Whose City is It? Globalization and the Formation of *the New* Claims"; *Lechner and Boli, ed., The Globalization Reader:* Blackwell Publishers, Massachusetts, 2000.

Seecharan, Clem, *Sweetening Bitter Sugar: Jock Campbell, the Booker Reformer in British Guiana. 1934-1966.* Ian Randle Publishers, Kingston 2005.

Sulzberger, A.G, "2 Men Convicted in Kennedy Airport Plot." *The New York Times,* August 2, 2010.

Thomas, Clive Y. "Guyana: Economic Performance and Outlook: The Recent Scramble for Resources" April 2012 Paper. Excerpted from articles written in 2011.

Thomas, Kevin J. A. "A Demographic Profile of Black Caribbean Immigrants in the United States." *Migration Policy Institute/National Center on Immigration Integration Policy.* April 2012.

Tilokie, Depoo,(ed.) *The East Indian Diaspora: 150 years of Survival, Contributions and Achievements. City University of New York, Asian American Center,* 1993

Waters, Mary. *Black Identities: West Indian Immigrant Dreams and American Realities.* Harvard University Press, 1999.

Yergin, Daniel and Stanislaw, Joseph, *"The Commanding Heights: The Battle Between Government and the Marketplace that is Remaking the Modern World"*, Lechner and Boli, ed., *The Globalization Reader:* Blackwell Publishers, Massachusetts, pp 212-220: 2001.

About the Editor

Lear Matthews, DSW, is Professor in the department of Community and Human Services, State University of New York, Empire State College. A former lecturer at the University of Guyana, Faculty of Social Science, he is a member of the Editorial Board of the Caribbean Journal of Social Work. He is a certified clinical social worker and Chair of the Advisory Board of the Caribbean-American Social Workers Association. He served as Clinic Director of the Bedford Stuyvesant Community Mental Health Center in Brooklyn, New York for over ten years. A Guyanese by birth, Dr. Matthews earned a BA in Sociology at Inter American University of Puerto Rico, an MA in Sociology at Ohio University and his doctorate in Social Welfare at the Hunter Graduate School of Social Work. He has written extensively on the adaptation of immigrants in North America, cultural retentions and coping with the trauma of natural disasters. His published research is included in college curricula across the United States and the Caribbean and used in the training of human services practitioners working with immigrants. He has published in Journals such as Caribbean Journal of Social Work and Journal of Ethnic and Cultural Diversity. Dr. Matthews is noted for his ability to link scholarship and community service. He is the recipient of numerous awards including the 2009 Distinguished Caribbean Social Work Educators Award and the prestigious SUNY Jane Altes Prize for exemplary community service.

Contributors

Christiana Best-Cummings, LMSW, Ph.D., has over 25 years of experience in class and spatial inequalities public and private child welfare in which she has served as an administrator, staff developer, field instructor, supervisor, clinician and child protective worker. She is an Adjunct Lecturer and has taught courses on the Immigrant Experience at the Silberman School of Social Work, at New York University focusing on the impact of economy, race, and gender. As an immigrant in the United States, Dr. Best-Cummings has always had a special connection to the trials and tribulations experienced by her fellow immigrants. Her book entitled "The Long Goodbye: Challenges of Transnational Parenting", is a qualitative study based on the immigration and resettlement experiences of African Caribbean women and their children from the English-Speaking Caribbean. This book delineates the difficulties involved in transnational parenting and the impact of the separation on both the mothers and the children.

Desmond Roberts won a Mayor of New York Scholarship and graduated from the Milano School (Urban Policy and Management) at the New School University where he developed a strong interest in Transnational Studies. He also has a Finance degree from the University of Maryland at College Park. Roberts has held several management positions in youth and mental health organizations with the City of New York; in finance in Virginia and Maryland as well as managing agriculture and hydropower projects in the hinterland of Guyana, his native country. He has published numerous articles in the Army newspaper and the Scarlet Beret magazine, the official organs of the Guyana Defense Force, where he served for many years as a senior officer. His management of sports organizations has taken him to the Olympics (Seoul 1988) as well as across the Caribbean. Roberts has traveled widely in Brazil, Tanzania and Zambia and has lived in Nigeria and China for year-long periods.

Beverley Russell, Ph.D., MPH, RN is a public health nurse with broad experiences in the areas of international and minority health, community-based participatory research, program planning and evaluation, and health disparities. Dr. Russell has special research interests in maternal and child health, transnational migration and aging minority populations, particularly Caribbean elders and their quality of life and chronic diseases. She has expertise in quantitative and qualitative research methods, particularly focus groups and interviews, having developed and implemented focus groups with community residents, academic researchers and health center providers on such topics as lupus, asthma, hypertension and diabetes. She has served as an investigator on grants from the NHLBI, HRSA and CDC.

Annette Mahoney, DSW, is an Assistant Professor at Hunter College School of Social Work, City University of New York. She teaches graduate courses in Social Policy, Human Behavior and Social Work Practice with substance abusers and with victims of violence. She served as co-coordinator of the part-time MSW program at Hunter College from 2001-2003. Dr Mahoney has published articles in scholarly journals on issues related to the Caribbean immigrant population, crime and violence, and trauma and recovery. She has been active in community agencies focused on issues impacting immigrant populations and incarcerated women and adolescents. Additionally, she has had a long working history with the New York-based Caribbean Women's Health Association where she serves as a member of the Board of Directors. Her published book, The Health and Well-Being of Caribbean Immigrants in the United States, addresses a cross-section of critical issues relating to the health and welfare of Caribbean immigrants and offers a culturally specific prescriptive intervention model. She has presented scholarly papers at various national and international conferences.

Joyce Hamilton Henry, Ph.D., M.S.W. is known nationally and internationally for her contributions to the field of social work. Her areas of expertise include U.S. Immigration policy, race and ethnic relations, and the Caribbean family. She has taught for over 20 years at the University of Hartford in African American Studies and in the Departments of Sociology and Psychology. She is the author of No One Asked Us: The Under-representation of African Americans and Latinos on Local Boards and Commissions. She has presented scholarly papers at national and international forums including the Caribbean Social Work Educators Triennial Conference.

Rosalind October-Edun is a doctoral student in the General Advanced Studies in Human Behavior Program at Capella University. In addition to serving as a faculty member at Empire State College, State University of New York, where she teaches social service-related studies, she is a private clinical practitioner. She serves as a board member of Guyana Cultural Association, an organization that is centered in promoting Caribbean culture, and a member of the Caribbean American Social Workers Association. Since completing her Master of Social Work degree in 1997 at Fordham University, Ms. October-Edun has held leadership positions at agencies specializing in substance abuse and related services, as she is licensed as a social worker, and certified as an alcohol and substance abuse counselor. During those experiences, she has worked with diverse populations that include individuals who abuse substances, involved with the criminal justice system and Administration of Childrens Services.

Mary Spooner Ph.D. received her Masters of Science degree in Social Policy and Planning in Developing Countries from the London School of Economics and Political Science and her doctorate in Public Policy from the University of Massachusetts Boston. Dr. Spooner is a Research Assistant Professor at Northwestern University's Feinberg School of Medicine. Her research interests are in the fields of gender and development, family violence, community mental health, quality assurance and outcomes management. She has worked in a managerial capacity in the field of development banking and micro enterprise development. Most recently her work has focused on evaluation of programs in mental health with particular emphasis on quality assurance and outcomes management. Dr. Spooner is a Caribbean national and a founding director of the Change Centre, a non-profit organization in the Federation of St. Kitts and Nevis, that supports disadvantaged families and advocates for the improvement in the overall wellbeing of women and their families in Caribbean States. She teaches a course in U.S. Mental Health Policy, has published and made presentations at the national level on topics related to family violence and children's mental health. Dr. Spooner is a member of several professional associations and the editorial board of the Journal of Family Violence.

Index

Access to Resources, 82
Acculturated, 35
    Acculturative stress, 49
Acculturation process, 55-56, 69, 141-142
Acculturative stress, 138
Adaptation, xiii-xviii, 8
    Adaptation process, xiii-xviii
Adaptation and acculturative stress, 153
Afro-Caribbean immigrant, 97-98
Aggressive compensatory behavior, 38
Aging population, 76, 77, 78, 79, 82, 87, 90
Altered socio-economic status, xv-xviii
American Community Survey (ACS), 195
    See also ACS
American stratification system, 11
Anglophone Caribbean, xiv-xviii, 17
Assimilation model, 35
Assimilative difficulties, 184

Barrel children, 24
Bi-cultural existence, 14
Bi-national families, 96
Bicultural experience, xii-xviii
Brief Solution-Focused Therapy, 70
British 1948 Nationality Act, 169-170

Caribbean women, 17, 18-19, 20-21, 22-23, 24-25, 25-26, 27, 28-29, 30, 31, 32, 74, 92
Cerebrovascular diseases, 77
Child Fostering, 56
Chronic obstructive pulmonary, 77
Chronic obstructive pulmonary disease, 77
Class and spatial inequalities, 23

Collateral impact of family remittances, 118
Collective groupings, 56
Collective remittances, xii-xviii
Communication, 146, 149, 150, 151, 152, 153, 155-156
Connectedness, 9
Connections, 1, 5, 6, 9, 11
Contemporary transnational linkage, 132-133
Countries of settlement, 5
Credentialing system, 130
Crisis, 168-169
Crisis of loss, 38-39, 141-142
Cross-continental linkage, 117
Cross-continental operational, 133
Cross-continental operational discrepancies, 133
Cross-cultural, 138-139, 142-143, 156, 162, 164
Cross-national collaboration, 87-88
    Cultural awareness, 140, 155, 166
    Cultural competence, 139, 142-143, 161, 162
    Cultural Diversity, 162
    Cultural capital, 39
    Cultural differences, 41, 42
    Cultural dissonance, 36, 42
Cultural advantages, 179
Cultural advantages of 'identity, 179
Cultural and ethnic heterogeneity, 3
Cultural cohesion, 118
Cultural competence, 133
Cultural diffusion, 5
Cultural dissonance, 8
Cultural incompatibility, 13
Cultural orientation, 140
    Cultural sensitivity training, 145
    Cultural dissonance, 141, 149-

150, 156, 159
Cultural transition, 159
Cultural spaces, 167
Culturally competent intervention, 116
Culturally competent services, 137
Culturally-consonant communities, 96
Culture, 2, 4, 6, 10, 12, 138-139, 141, 147, 148-149, 150, 152, 153-154, 155, 156, 160, 161, 164, 165

Deferred Action for Childhood Arrivals, 12
Dependency theorists, 23
Dependency theory, 118
Development activity, 113
Diabetes mellitus, 77
Diaspora, 2, 113, 114, 117, 118-119, 120, 122, 126, 130, 131, 132-133, 134, 135, 136
Diaspora activities, xii-xviii
Diaspora Development Projects, xvi-xviii
Differentials in migration patterns, 18
Discrimination, 179, 180, 183, 186
    Discrimination and loss of identity in the receiving country, 186
Discrimination and loss of, 186
Disjuncture with communities of origin, 10
Displacement, 2, 61
Domestic immigrant integration, 122
Drugs for the elderly program, 79, 94

Economic dependency, 61
Education, 18, 19, 22, 24-25, 29, 30
Emancipation, 187
Emotional connectedness, 6
Enclave, 178, 183, 184, 185
Engagement barriers, xvi-xviii
Ephemeral interface, 117
Ethnic networks, 35, 180
Ethnicity and cultures, 183
European colonialism, 3
Exigent health needs, 74-75
Existential duality, xvi-xviii

Exploratory study, 121

Facility of movement, 186
Facility of movement and communication, 186
Faith-based organizations, 78-79
Family links, 116
Family network, 139
    Family networks, 96, 103
    Family remittances, 118
    Family reunification, xii-xviii
    Family reunification, 180
    Family-sponsoring system, xii-xviii
Fusion, 7

'give-back' philanthropic organizations, 10
Global capitalism, 2, 104
Global nursing home, 77
Globalization, xi-xviii, 103, 110, 112
Guyana Diaspora Project, 111
GUYD Project, 8
Guyanese Diaspora, 188

Hart Celler Act of 1965, 4
Hart-Cellar Immigration Act of 1965, 19
Hart-Celler Act of 1965, 54
Helping professions, 113, 114, 123
Homelands, 1
Hometown Associations, 113, 118-119, 120, 134, 136
Hometown Associations (HTAs), xvi-xviii, 187
Host society accommodation, 38-39
Households, 57
Human capital, xii-xviii, 1, 35, 50
Hybridity, 2
    Hybridization, 7
Hyper segregation, 100-101

Identity formation, xvi-xviii
    see Identity formation and adaptation to the new social environment, 106
Illegal Immigration Reform and Immigrant Responsibility Act, xiii-xviii, 101
Immigrant, 1, 2, 4, 5, 6, 7, 10, 12, 13, 14, 15, 16

Index

Immigrant incorporation, 2
Immigrant integration, 1
Immigration, vii-xviii
Immigration and Nationality Act of 1965, 172
Immigration Reform and Control, xii
Incorporation, 2
Indentured contracts, 182
Indigenous, 25
Indo-Caribbean, xiii
Indo-Caribbean immigrant, 97, 154-155, 158
Indo-Caribbean immigrants,, 107
Indo-Guyanese, 167, 182, 185, 195
Institutional knowledge, 25
Institutionalized transactions, 117
Integration, 1, 10
Inter-territorial proximity, 9
Inter-territorial variations, 95
Interactional forces, 132
Intergenerational status, 180
International migration, 1, 35, 50, 51, 52
Interpersonal and social adaptation, xiii
Intervention strategies, 14
Involuntary transformation of vocation, 33
Ischemic heart disease, 77
Isolation, 83, 84, 85

Jamaica, xvi, 5

Kinship networks, 95, 97, 101-102, 103-104, 107

Labor, 167-168, 174, 182, 188, 196
Labor Force Participation Rate, 97
Labor force participation rates in NYC, 174
Leadership, 143
Linkages, 9
Long-distance migration stream, 3

Mandirs, 183
Marginalization, 1, 13
Marginalized, 96, 99
McCarran-Walter Act of 1952, 170
Membership, 10
Migrant generated remittances, 114

Migration, 54, 55, 56-57, 58, 59, 62, 63, 68, 71-72, 138, 152, 156, 158, 159, 165, 166
migration to the United States, 158
Migration and Remittances, 170-171, 189, 190, 197
Migration and Remittances Handbook 2011, 170-171
Migration models, 23
Migration Process, 23, 32
Migratory sacrifices, 49
Migratory trend, 169
Ministry of Health (MOH)., 79-80
Modernity, xii, xiv
Modernity, 71
Mothering from a distance, 53-54, 72

National Council for Senior Citizens, 80, 93
Nativism, 37, 52
Natural helping networks, 104
Neo-classical, 23
Neo-classical Marxists, 23
Networks, 180, 185, 186
Non-probability (snowball) sample, 58
Non-residential parenting, 96-97

Occupational change, 33, 34-35, 39-40, 41-42, 43, 44, 47, 48, 49, 50, 51, 52
Occupational compromises, 49
Occupational displacement, 48
Occupational dissonance of foreign professionals, 35
Opportunity structures, 180
Outmigration, 78
Outmigration, 19-20

Pan Caribbean communities, 132
Parenting, 53-54, 56, 57, 58, 59, 60-61, 63, 64-65, 67-68, 69-70, 71
Parenting from a distance, 53-54, 64, 67-68, 98-99
Paternalistic orientation, 11
Paths toward incorporation, 180
Phagwah and Deepavali, 183-184
Phenotypic similarity, 37

Philanthropic organizations, 4
Philanthropy, 114, 116, 117, 133, 136
Pluralism, 35
Political connections, 134
Political networks of patronage and redistribution, 185
Post-migration, 14
Post-migration transnational connections and identity, xi
Post-migratory childrearing methods, 105
Pre-migratory ethnic relations, 11
Professional identity, 49, 50, 133
Project replicability, 131
Psychological barriers, 34-35
Psychosocial functioning, 106, 138
Psychosocial needs of seniors, 87
Psychosocial problems, 142
Psychosocial stressor, 40
Purveyors of connectedness, xv

Racialized identity, 100
Racialized social structures, 25-26
Rational economic choice, 43-44
Re-acculturation, 76
Receiving countries, 132-133
Receiving society, 36
Reciprocal transnational ties, 1
Relationships, ix-xviii
Remittance sending outlets, 187
Remittances, 6, 113-114, 116, 118, 119, 120, 122, 131, 133-134, 135, 136
    Sending society, 115
    Snowball approach, 121
    transformative practice environment, 114
    Transnational activities, 125, 128, 132, 134
    transnational connections, 115, 117, 120, 123, 136
    unilateral flow of remittances, 118
Remittances, 61, 68, 72
Repatriation incentives, 8
Resource identification, 46
Retained immigrant identity, 180
Return migrants, 75-76, 92
Reunification, 18, 62, 66, 68, 69, 96, 108-109
    Family reunification, 18

Role conflicts, 39
Role diminishment, 48
Rubric of globalization, 103

Secure Communities Programs, xiii
Segmented assimilation, 178, 180
Segregation indices, 100-101
Self-actualization, 44
Self-actualizing abilities, 39
Self-fulfillment from vocational competence, 39
Sending countries, 24
Sending country, 7
Sending economies, 186
    Sending children, 180
Sending societies, vii
Separation-reunification syndrome, 153
Serial immigration, 96-97
Serial Migration, 56, 57, 59, 72
Shared identities, 95, 97, 104
Social adaptation, 45-46, 49, 50
Social Adjustment, 33, 52
Social capital, 7, 16, 39, 51, 108-109, 112, 180
    Social identity, 107
    Social integration, 100
Social fields, 99
Social identity, 39, 47
Social intervention, 139
Social networking, xii
Social networking, 61-62
Social Networking, 28
Social/ethnic categorization, 37
Socialization, 62
Socialization agents, xv-xviii
Socio-cultural adaptation, xi-xviii
Socio-cultural issues, 12
Socio-cultural ties, xi
Socio-demographic characteristics, 21
Socio-political circumstances, xii
Socioeconomic characteristics, 38
Socioeconomic progress, xi
Sociological adaptations, xvi
Sociopolitical climate, 76
Solution-Focused Therapy, 70
Spatial arrangement of family/household constellations, 48
Spatial segregation, 158
Status in the home country, 186
Sstrength perspective, 143

Index

Structural acculturation patterns, 106
Structural and human interactional forces, 132
structural barriers, 13, 49, 106
structural obstacles, 34-35
structural pluralism, 35
structural restrictions, 59, 60
symbolic collaboration, 12

Tertiary educated Guyanese, 174
Ties, 1, 2, 3, 5, 6, 7, 10
Traditionalism, 38-39
Trans-context lifestyle, 9, 96-97
Transmigration, xiv-xviii, 186
Transmitting remittances, 18
Transnational, 9, 53-54, 56, 57, 58, 59, 60, 62, 63, 64, 67, 69, 71, 72, 95-96, 96-97, 98-99, 99-100, 102, 103-104, 107, 108-109, 110, 111-112
    Transnational activities, 99-100, 103-104
    Transnational Communities, 95, 97, 103-104
    Transnational connections., 99-100
Transnational context, 75, 78, 88
    Practice and Policy, 87
Transnational divide, 188
Transnational experiences, xiv
    Transnational identity, xiv
    Transnational links, 95-96, 109
    Transnational family, 97
    Transnational Motherhood,, 103
Transnational migration, xv 73, 75, 87, 93, 94
    Immigration, xvi
Transnational practices, xiv
Transnational process, xiii
Transnational ties, xiii, 34-35
    See Transnationalism
Transnationalism, 58, 71, 72, 75, 94
Trust networks, 3

Uniform assimilation process, 10
Unilinear assimilationist, 2

Voluntary migration, 3, 54

Xenophobic stereotyping, 13

Addendum For Chapter Two
Table 1. Caribbean Populations Migrating Overseas from Selected Countries by Gender

	2000		2005		2010	
	Estimated number of female migrants at mid-year	Estimated number of male migrants at mid-year	Estimated number of female migrants at mid-year	Estimated number of male migrants at mid-year	Estimated number of female migrants at mid-year	Estimated number of male migrants at mid-year
Anguilla	2,153	1,910	2,750	2,346	3,336	2,734
Antigua and Barbuda	8,574	7,292	10,039	8,183	11,754	9,174
Barbados	14,558	9,951	1,5755	10,479	17,050	11,030
Dominica	17,43	1,980	2,093	2,433	2,511	2,990
Grenada	4,161	3,782	5,779	5,064	6,831	5,766
Guyana	3,703	4,270	4,638	5,346	5,389	6,210
Jamaica	12,344	12,308	13,438	13,740	14,815	15,147
Montserrat	85	97	51	59	50	58
Saint Kitts and Nevis	1,902	2,145	2,092	2,427	2,336	2,710
Saint Lucia	3,797	3,603	4,453	4,226	5,223	4,957
St Vincent and the Grenadines	3,296	3,084	3,837	3,575	4,466	4,145
Trinidad and Tobago	22,411	19,239	20,397	17,426	18,565	15,783

Source: United Nations, Department of Economic and Social Affairs, Population Division (2009). *Trends in International Migrant Stock: The 2008 Revision* (United Nations database, POP/DB/MIG/Stock/Rev.2008).